The Oera Linda book

From a manuscript of the
thirteenth century

William R. Sandbach,

C. Over de Linden

Alpha Editions

This edition published in 2019

ISBN : 9789353866334

Design and Setting By
Alpha Editions
email - alphaedis@gmail.com

THE

OERA LINDA BOOK

FROM

A Manuscript of the Thirteenth Century

WITH THE PERMISSION OF THE PROPRIETOR

C. OVER DE LINDEN, OF THE HELDER

The Original Frisian Text

AS VERIFIED BY DR J. O. OTTEMA

ACCOMPANIED BY AN

ENGLISH VERSION OF DR OTTEMA'S DUTCH TRANSLATION

BY

WILLIAM R. SANDBACH

LONDON
TRÜBNER & CO., LUDGATE HILL
1876

became a lawgiver at Athens, than that a goddess sprang, full grown and armed, from the cleft skull of Jupiter?

There is nothing in the narratives of this book inconsistent with probability, however they may vary from some of our preconceived ideas; but whether it is really what it pretends to be—a very ancient manuscript, or a more modern fiction—it is not the less a most curious and interesting work, and as such I offer it to the British public.

In order to give an idea of the manuscript, I have procured photographs of two of its pages, which are bound with this volume.

I have also followed Dr Ottema's plan of printing the original Frisian opposite to the translation, so that any reader possessing a knowledge of the language may verify the correctness of the translation.

In addition to the Preface which I have translated, Dr Ottema has written two pamphlets on the subject of the Oera Linda Book (1. Historical Notes and Explanations; 2. The Royal Academy and Het Oera Linda Bok), both of which would be very valuable to any one who wished to study the controversy respecting the authenticity of the work, but which I have not thought it necessary to translate for the present publication.

There has also appeared in the "Deventer Courant" a series of twelve letters on the same subject. Though written anonymously, I believe they are from the pen of Professor Vitringa. They have been translated into German by Mr Otto.

The writer evidently entered upon his task of criticism with a feeling of disbelief in the authenticity of the book; but in his last letter he admits that, after a minute examination, he is unable to pronounce a positive conviction either for or against it.

His concluding remarks are to the following effect :—

" If the book is a romance, then I must admit that it has been written with a good object, and by a clever man, because the sentiments expressed in it are of a highly moral tendency; and the facts related, so far as they can be controlled by regular history, are not untruthful ; and where they deal with events of which we have no historical records, they do not offend our ideas of possibility or even probability."

WM. R. SANDBACH.

INTRODUCTION.

C. OVER DE LINDEN, Chief Superintendent of the Royal Dockyard at the Helder, possesses a very ancient manuscript, which has been inherited and preserved in his family from time immemorial, without any one knowing whence it came or what it contained, owing to both the language and the writing being unknown.

All that was known was that a tradition contained in it had from generation to generation been recommended to careful preservation. It appeared that the tradition rests upon the contents of two letters, with which the manuscript begins, from Hiddo oera Linda, anno 1256, and from Liko oera Linda, anno 803. It came to C. over de Linden by the directions of his grandfather, Den Heer Andries over de Linden, who lived at Enkhuizen, and died there on the 15th of April 1820, aged sixty-one. As the grandson was at that time barely ten years old, the manuscript was taken care of for him by his aunt, Aafje Meylhoff, born Over de Linden, living at Enkhuizen, who in August 1848 delivered it to the present possessor.

Dr E. Verwijs having heard of this, requested permission to examine the manuscript, and immediately recognised it as very ancient Fries. He obtained at the same time permission to make a copy of it for the benefit of the Friesland Society, and was of opinion that it might be of great importance, provided it was not supposititious, and invented for some deceptive object, which he feared. The manu-

B

script being placed in my hands, I also felt very doubtful, though I could not understand what object any one could have in inventing a false composition only to keep it a secret. This doubt remained until I had examined carefully-executed facsimiles of two fragments, and afterwards of the whole manuscript—the first sight of which convinced me of the great age of the document.

Immediately occurred to me Cæsar's remark upon the writing of the Gauls and the Helvetians in his "Bello Gallico" (i. 29, and vi. 14), "Græcis utuntur literis," though it appears in v. 48 that they were not entirely Greek letters. Cæsar thus points out only a resemblance —and a very true one—as the writing, which does not altogether correspond with any known form of letters, resembles the most, on a cursory view, the Greek writing, such as is found on monuments and the oldest manuscripts, and belongs to the form which is called lapidary. Besides, I formed the opinion afterwards that the writer of the latter part of the book had been a contemporary of Cæsar.

The form and the origin of the writing is so minutely and fully described in the first part of the book, as it could not be in any other language. It is very complete, and consists of thirty-four letters, among which are three separate forms of *a* and *u*, and two of *e, i, y,* and *o*, besides four pairs of double consonants—*ng, th, ks,* and *gs*. The *ng*, which as a nasal sound has no particular mark in any other Western language, is an indivisible conjunction; the *th* is soft, as in English, and is sometimes replaced by *d;* the *gs* is seldom met with—I believe only in the word *segse*, to say, in modern Fries *sidse*, pronounced *sisze.*

The paper, of large quarto size, is made of cotton, not very thick, without water-mark or maker's mark, made upon a frame or wire-web, with not very broad perpendicular lines.

An introductory letter gives the year 1256 as that

in which this manuscript was written by Hiddo overa Linda on foreign paper. Consequently it must have come from Spain, where the Arabs brought into the market paper manufactured from cotton.

On this subject, W. Wattenbach writes in his "Das Schriftwesen im Mittelalter" (Leipzig, 1871), s. 93:—

"The manufacture of paper from cotton must have been in use among the Chinese from very remote times, and must have become known to the Arabs by the conquest of Samarcand about the year 704. In Damascus this manufacture was an important branch of industry, for which reason it was called *Charta Damascena*. By the Arabians this art was brought to the Greeks. It is asserted that Greek manuscripts of the tenth century written upon cotton paper exist, and that in the thirteenth century it was much more used than parchment. To distinguish it from Egyptian paper it was called *Charta bombicina, gossypina, cuttunea, xylina*. A distinction from linen paper was not yet necessary. In the manufacture of the cotton paper raw cotton was originally used. We first find paper from rags mentioned by Petrus Clusiacensis (1122–50).

"The Spaniards and the Italians learned the manufacture of this paper from the Arabians. The most celebrated factories were at Jativa, Valencia, Toledo, besides Fabriano in the March of Ancona."[*]

In Germany the use of this material did not become very extended, whether it came from Italy or Spain. Therefore the further this preparation spread from the East and the adjoining countries, the more necessity there was that linen should take the place of cotton. A document of Kaufbeuren on linen paper of the year 1318 is of very doubtful genuineness. Bodman considers the oldest pure

---

[*] Compare G. Meerman, Admonitio de Chartæ nostralis origine. Vad. Letteroef. 1762. P. 630.

J. H. de Stoppelaar, Paper in the Netherlands. Middelburg, 1869. P. 4.

linen paper to be of the year 1324, but up to 1350 much mixed paper was used. All carefully-written manuscripts of great antiquity show by the regularity of their lines that they must have been ruled, even though no traces of the ruled lines can be distinguished. To make the lines they used a thin piece of lead, a ruler, and a pair of compasses to mark the distances.

In old writings the ink is very black or brown; but while there has been more writing since the thirteenth century, the colour of the ink is often grey or yellowish, and sometimes quite pale, showing that it contains iron. All this affords convincing proof that the manuscript before us belongs to the middle of the thirteenth century, written with clear black letters between fine lines carefully traced with lead. The colour of the ink shows decidedly that it does not contain iron. By these evidences the date given, 1256, is satisfactorily proved, and it is impossible to assign any later date. Therefore all suspicion of modern deception vanishes.

The language is very old Fries, still older and purer than the Fries Rjuchtboek or old Fries laws, differing from that both in form and spelling, so that it appears to be an entirely distinct dialect, and shows that the locality of the language must have been (as it was spoken) between the Vlie and the Scheldt.

The style is extremely simple, concise, and unembarrassed, resembling that of ordinary conversation, and free in the choice of the words. The spelling is also simple and easy, so that the reading of it does not involve the least difficulty, and yet with all its regularity, so unrestricted, that each of the separate writers who have worked at the book has his own peculiarities, arising from the changes in pronunciation in a long course of years, which naturally must have happened, as the last part of the work is written five centuries after the first.

As a specimen of antiquity in language and writing, I believe I may venture to say that this book is unique of its kind.

The writing suggests an observation which may be of great importance.

The Greeks know and acknowledge that their writing was not their own invention. They attribute the introduction of it to Kadmus, a Phenician. The names of their oldest letters, from Alpha to Tau, agree so exactly with the names of the letters in the Hebrew alphabet, with which the Phenician will have been nearly connected, that we cannot doubt that the Hebrew was the origin of the Phenician. But the form of their letters differs so entirely from that of the Phenician and Hebrew writing, that in that particular no connection can be thought of between them. Whence, then, have the Greeks derived the form of their letters?

From " thet bok thêra Adela folstar " ("The Book of Adela's Followers") we learn that in the time when Kadmus is said to have lived, about sixteen centuries before Christ, a brisk trade existed between the Frisians and the Phenicians, whom they named Kadhemar, or dwellers on the coast.

The name Kadmus comes too near the word Kadhemar for us not to believe that Kadmus simply meant a Phenician.

Further on we learn that about the same time a priestess of the castle in the island of Walcheren, Min-erva, also called Nyhellenia, had settled in Attica at the head of a Frisian colony, and had founded a castle at Athens. Also, from the accounts written on the walls of Waraburch, that the Finns likewise had a writing of their own —a very troublesome and difficult one to read—and that, therefore, the Tyrians and the Greeks had learned the writing of Frya. By this representation the whole thing explains itself, and it becomes clear whence comes the ex-

terior resemblance between the Greek and the old Fries
writing, which Cæsar also remarked among the Gauls; as
likewise in what manner the Greeks acquired and retained
the names of the *Phenician* and the forms of the Fries writing.

Equally remarkable are the forms of their figures. We
usually call our figures Arabian, although they have not
the least resemblance to those used by the Arabs. The
Arabians did not bring their ciphers from the East, because the Semitic nations used the whole alphabet in writing numbers. The manner of expressing all numbers by
ten signs the Arabs learned in the West, though the form
was in some measure corresponding with their writing, and
was written from left to right, after the Western fashion.
Our ciphers seem here to have sprung from the Fries
ciphers (*siffar*), which form had the same origin as the
handwriting, and is derived from the lines of the Juul?

The book as it lies before us consists of two parts, differing widely from each other, and of dates very far apart.
The writer of the first part calls herself Adela, wife of
Apol, chief man of the Linda country. This is continued
by her son Adelbrost, and her daughter Apollonia. The
first book, running from page 1 to 88, is written by Adela. -
The following part, from 88 to 94, is begun by Adelbrost
and continued by Apollonia. The second book, running
from page 94 to 114, is written by Apollonia. Much later,
perhaps two hundred and fifty years, a third book is
written, from page 114 to 134, by Frethorik; then follows from page 134 to 143, written by his widow, Wiljow; after that from page 144 to 169 by their son, Kone-
reed; and then from page 169 to 192 by their grandson,
Beeden. Pages 193 and 194, with which the last part
must have begun, are wanting, therefore the writer is
unknown. He may probably have been a son of Beeden.

On page 134, Wiljow makes mention of another writing
of Adela. These she names " thet bok thêra sanga (thet

boek), thêra tellinga," and "thet Hellênia bok;" and afterwards "tha skrifta fon Adela jeftha Hellênia."

To fix the date we must start from the year 1256 of our era, when Hiddo overa Linda made the copy, in which he says that it was 3449 years after Atland was sunk. This disappearance of the old land (*âldland, âtland*) was known by the Greeks, for Plato mentions in his " Timæus," 24, the disappearance of Atlantis, the position of which was only known as somewhere far beyond the Pillars of Hercules. From this writing it appears that it was land stretching far out to the west of Jutland, of which Heligoland and the islands of North Friesland are the last barren remnants. This event, which occasioned a great dispersion of the Frisian race, became the commencement of a chronological reckoning corresponding with 2193 before Christ, and is known by geologists as the Cimbrian flood.

On page 80 begins an account in the year 1602, after the disappearance of Atland, and thus in the year 591 before Christ; and on page 82 is the account of the murder of Frâna, "Eeremoeder," of Texland two years later—that is, in 589. When, therefore, Adela commences her writing with her own coming forward in an assembly of the people thirty years after the murder of the Eeremoeder, that must have been in the year 559 before Christ. In the part written by her daughter Apollonia, we find that fifteen months after the assembly Adela was killed by the Finns in an attack by surprise of Texland. This must accordingly have happened 557 years before Christ. Hence it follows that the first book, written by Adela, was of the year 558 before Christ. The second book, by Apollonia, we may assign to about the year 530 before Christ. The latter part contains the history of the known kings of Friesland, Friso, Adel (Ubbo), and Aséga Askar, called Black Adel. Of the third king, Ubbo, nothing is said, or rather that part is lost, as the pages 169 to 188 are missing. Frethorik, the first writer, who appears now, was a contemporary of the occurrences which he relates, namely, the arrival of Friso. He was a friend of Liudgert den Geertman, who, as rear-admiral of the fleet of Wich-hirte, the sea-king, had come with Friso in the year 303 before Christ, 1890 years after the disappearance of Atland. He has borrowed most of his information from the log-book of Liudgert.

The last writer gives himself out most clearly as a con-temporary of Black Adel or Askar, about the middle of his reign, which Furmerius states to have been from 70 before Christ to 11 after the birth of Christ, the same period as Julius Cæsar and Augustus. He therefore wrote in the middle of the last century before Christ, and knew of the conquest of Gaul by the Romans. It is thus evident that there elapsed fully two centuries between the two parts of the work.

Of the Gauls we read on page 84 that they were called the "Missionaries of Sydon." And on page 124 "that the Gauls are Druids." The Gauls, then, were Druids, and the name Galli, used for the whole nation, was really only the name of an order of priesthood brought from the East, just as among the Romans the Galli were priests of Cybele.

The whole contents of the book are in all respects new. That is to say, there is nothing in it that we were ac-quainted with before. What we here read of Friso, Adel, and Askar differs entirely from what is related by our own chroniclers, or rather presents it in quite another light. For instance, they all relate that Friso came from India, and that thus the Frisians were of Indian descent; and yet they add that Friso was a German, and belonged to a Persian race which Herodotus called Germans (Γερμάνιοι). According to the statement in this book, Friso did come from India, and with the fleet of Nearchus; but he is not therefore an Indian. He is of Frisian origin, of Frya's people. He belongs, in fact, to a Frisian colony which after the death of Nijhellênia, fifteen and a half centuries before Christ, under thè guidance of a priestess Geert, settled in the Punjab, and took the name of Geertmen. The Geertmen were known by only one of the Greek writers, Strabo, who mentions them as Γερμᾶνες, differing totally and entirely from the Βραχμᾶνες in manners, language, and religion.

The historians of Alexander's expeditions do not speak of Frisians or Geertmen, though they mention Indo-scythians, thereby describing a people whò live in India, but whose origin is in the distant, unknown North.

In the accounts of Liudgert no names are given of places where the Frieslanders lived in India. We only know that they first established themselves to the east of the Punjab, and afterwards moved to the west of those rivers. It is mentioned, moreover, as a striking fact, that in the summer the sun at midday was straight above their heads. They therefore lived within the tropics. We find in Ptolemy (see the map of Kiepert), exactly 24° N. on the west side of the Indus, the name Minnagara; and about six degrees east of that, in 22° N., another Minnagara. This name is pure Fries, the same as Walhallagara, Folsgara, and comes from Minna, the name of an Eeremoeder, in whose time the voyages of Teunis and his nephew Inca took place.

The coincidence is too remarkable to be accidental, and not to prove that Minnagara was the headquarters of the Frisian colony. The establishment of the colonists in the Punjab in 1551 before Christ, and their journey thither, we find fully described in Adela's book; and with the mention of one most remarkable circumstance, namely, that the Frisian mariners sailed through the strait which in those times still ran into the Red Sea.

In Strabo, book i. pages 38 and 50, it appears that Eratosthenes was acquainted with the existence of the strait, of which the later geographers make no mention. It existed still in the time of Moses (Exodus xiv. 2), for he encamped at Pi-ha-chiroht, the "mouth of the strait." Moreover, Strabo mentions that Sesostris made an attempt to cut through the isthmus, but that he was not able to, accomplish it. That in very remote times the sea really did flow through is proved by the result of the geological investigations on the isthmus made by the Suez Canal Commission, of which M. Renaud presented a report to the Academy of Sciences on the 19th June 1856. In that report, among other things, appears the following: "Une question fort controversée est celle de savoir, si à l'époque où les Hebreux fuyaient de l'Egypte sous la conduite de Moïse, les lacs amers faisaient encore partie de la mer rouge. Cette dernière hypothèse s'accorderait mieux que l'hypothèse contraire avec le texte des livres sacrés, mais alors il faudrait admettre que depuis l'époque de Moïse le seuil de Suez serait sorti des eaux."

With regard to this question, it is certainly of importance to fall in with an account in this Frisian manuscript, from which it seems that in the sixteenth century before Christ the connection between the Bitter Lakes and the Red Sea still existed, and that the strait was still navigable. The manuscript further states that soon after the passage of the Geertmen there was an earthquake ; that the land rose so high that all the water ran out, and all the shallows and alluvial lands rose up like a wall. This must have happened after the time of Moses, so that at the date of the Exodus (1564 B.C.) the track between Suez and the Bitter Lakes was still navigable, but could be forded dry-foot at low water.

This point, then, is the commencement of the isth-

mus, after the forming of which, the northern inlet was
certainly soon filled up as far as the Gulf of Pelusium.

The map by Louis Figuier, in the "Année scientifique
et industrielle" (première année), Paris, Hachette, 1857,
gives a distinct illustration of the formation of this land.

Another statement, which occurs only in Strabo, finds
also here a confirmation. Strabo alone of all the Greek
writers relates that Nearchus, after he had landed his
troops in the Persian Gulf, at the mouth of the Pasitigris,
sailed out of the Persian Gulf by Alexander's command,
and steered round Arabia through the Arabian Gulf. As the
account stands, it is not clear what Nearchus had to do
there, and what the object of the further voyage was. If,
as Strabo seems to think, it was only for geographical
discovery, he need not have taken the whole fleet. One
or two ships would have sufficed. We do not read that he
returned. Where, then, did he remain with that fleet?

The answer to this question is to be found in the
Frisian version of the story. Alexander had bought the
ships on the Indus, or had had them built by the descendants of the Frisians who settled there—the Geertmen—
and had taken into his service sailors from among them,
and at the head of them was Friso. Alexander having
accomplished his voyage and the transport of his troops,
had no further use for the ships in the Persian Gulf,
but wished to employ them in the Mediterranean. He had
taken that idea into his head, and it must be carried into
effect. He wished to do what no one had done before him.
For this purpose Nearchus was to sail up the Red Sea,
and on his arrival at Suez was to find 200 elephants, 1000
camels, workmen and materials, timber and ropes, &c., in
order to haul the ships by land over the isthmus. This
work was carried on and accomplished with so much zeal
and energy that after three months' labour the fleet was
launched in the Mediterranean. That the fleet really

came to the Mediterranean appears in Plutarch's "Life of Alexander;" but he makes Nearchus bring the fleet round Africa, and sail through the Pillars of Hercules.

After the defeat at Actium, Cleopatra, in imitation of this example, tried to take her fleet over the isthmus in order to escape to India, but was prevented by the inhabitants of Arabia Petræa, who burnt her ships. (See Plutarch's "Life of Antony.") When Alexander shortly afterwards died, Friso remained in the service of Antigonus and Demetrius, until, having been grievously insulted by the latter, he resolved to seek out with his sailors their fatherland, Friesland. To India he could not, indeed, return.

Thus these accounts chime in with and clear up each other, and in that way afford a mutual confirmation of the events.

Such simple narratives and surprising results led me to conclude that we had to do here with more than mere Saga and Legends.

Since the last twenty years attention has been directed to the remains of the dwellings on piles, first observed in the Swiss lakes, and afterwards in other parts of Europe. (See Dr E. Rückert, "Die Pfahlbauten;" Wurzburg, 1869. Dr T. C. Winkler, in the "Volksalmanak," t. N. v. A. 1867.) When they were found, endeavours were made to discover, by the existing fragments of arms, tools, and household articles, by whom and when these dwellings had been inhabited. There are no accounts of them in historical writers, beyond what Herodotus writes in book v. chapter 16, of the "Paeonen." The only trace that has been found is in one of the panels of Trajan's Pillar, in which the destruction of a pile village in Dacia is represented.

Doubly important, therefore, is it to learn from the writing of Apollonia that she, as "Burgtmaagd" (chief of the virgins), about 540 years before Christ, made a journey up the Rhine to Switzerland, and there became acquainted with the Lake Dwellers (Marsaten). She describes their dwellings built upon piles—the people themselves—their manners and customs. She relates that they lived by fishing and hunting, and that they prepared the skins of the animals with the bark of the birch-tree in order to sell the furs to the Rhine boatmen, who brought them into commerce. This account of the pile dwellings in the Swiss lakes can only have been written in the time when these dwellings still existed and were lived in. In the second part of the writing, Konerèd oera Linda relates that Adel, the son of Friso (± 250 years before Christ), visited the pile dwellings in Switzerland with his wife Ifkja.

Later than this account there is no mention by any writer whatever of the pile dwellings, and the subject has remained for twenty centuries utterly unknown until 1853, when an extraordinary low state of the water led to the discovery of these dwellings. Therefore no one could have invented this account in the intervening period. Although a great portion of the first part of the work—the book of Adela—belongs to the mythological period before the Trojan war, there is a striking difference between it and the Greek myths. The Myths have no dates, much less any chronology, nor any internal coherence of successive events. The untrammelled fancy develops itself in every poem separately and independently. The mythological stories contradict each other on every point. " Les Mythes ne se tiennent pas," is the only key to the Greek Mythology.

Here, on the contrary, we meet with a regular succession of dates starting from a fixed period—the destruction of Atland, 2193 before Christ. The accounts are natural and simple, often naïve, never contradict each other, and are always consistent with each other in time and place. As, for instance, the arrival and sojourn of Ulysses with the

Burgtmaagd Kalip at Walhallagara (Walcheren), which is the most mythical portion of all, is here said to be 1005 years after the disappearance of Atland, which coincides with 1188 years before Christ, and thus agrees very nearly with the time at which the Greeks say the Trojan war took place. The story of Ulysses was not brought here for the first time by the Romans. Tacitus found it already in Lower Germany (see "Germania," cap. 3), and says that at Asciburgium there was an altar on which the names of Ulysses and his father Laërtes were inscribed.

Another remarkable difference consists in this, that the Myths know no origin, do not name either writers or relaters of their stories, and therefore never can bring forward any authority. Whereas in Adela's book, for every statement is given a notice where it was found or whence it was taken. For instance, "This comes from Minno's writings—this is written on the walls of Waraburch—this in the town of Frya—this at Stavia—this at Walhallagara."

There is also this further. Laws, regular legislative enactments, such as are found in great numbers in Adela's book, are utterly unknown in Mythology, and indeed are irreconcilable with its existence. Even when the Myth attributes to Minos the introduction of lawgiving in Crete, it does not give the least account of what the legislation consisted in. Also among the Gods of Mythology there existed no system of laws. The only law was unchangable Destiny and the will of the supreme Zeus.

With regard to Mythology, this writing, which bears no mythical character, is not less remarkable than with regard to history. Notwithstanding the frequent and various relations with Denmark, Sweden, and Norway, we do not find any traces of acquaintance with the Northern or Scandinavian Mythology. Only Wodin appears in the person of Wodan, a chief of the Frisians, who became the son-in-law of one Magy, King of the Finns, and after his death was deified. - *He was the first Odin, there were* —

The Frisian religion is extremely simple, and pure Monotheism. Wr-alda or Wr-alda's spirit is the only eternal, unchangeable, perfect, and almighty being. Wr-alda has created everything. Out of him proceeds everything—first the beginning, then time, and afterwards Irtha, the Earth. Irtha bore three daughters—Lyda, Finda, and Frya—the mothers of the three distinct races, black, yellow, and white—Africa, Asia, and Europe. As such, Frya is the mother of Frya's people, the Frieslanders. She is the representative of Wr-alda, and is reverenced accordingly. Frya has established her "Tex," the first law, and has established the religion of the eternal light. The worship consists in the maintenance of a perpetually-burning lamp, *foddik*, by priestesses, virgins. At the head of the virgins in every town was a Burgtmaagd, and the chief of the Burgtmaagden was the Eeremoeder of the Fryasburgt of Texland. The Eeremoeder governs the whole country. The kings can do nothing, nor can anything happen without her advice and approval. The first Eeremoeder was appointed by Frya herself, and was called Fâsta. In fact, we find here the prototype of the Roman Vestal Virgins.

We are reminded here of Velleda (Welda) and Aurinia in Tacitus ("Germania," 8. Hist., iv. 61, 65; v. 22, 24. "Annals," i. 54), and of Gauna, the successor of Velleda, in Dio Cassius (Fragments, 49). Tacitus speaks of the town of Velleda as "edita turris," page 146. It was the town Mannagarda forda (Munster).

In the county of the Marsians he speaks of the temple Tanfane (Tanfanc), so called from the sign of the Juul. (See plate I.)

The last of these towns was Fâstaburgt in Ameland, temple Foste, destroyed, according to Occa Scarlensis, in 806.

If we find among the Frisians a belief in a Godhead

and ideas of religion entirely different from the Mythology of other nations, we are the more surprised to find in some points the closest connection with the Greek and Roman Mythology, and even with the origin of two deities of the highest rank, Min-erva and Neptune. Minerva (Athéné) was originally a Burgtmaagd, priestess of Frya, at the town Walhallagara, Middelburg, or Domburg, in Walcheren. And this Min-erva is at the same time the mysterious enigmatical goddess of whose worship scarcely any traces remain beyond the votive stones at Domburg, in Walcheren, Nehallenia, of whom no mythology knows anything more than the name, which etymology has used for all sorts of fantastical derivations.*

The other, Neptune, called by the Etrurians Nethunus, the God of the Mediterranean Sea, appears here to have been, when living, a Friesland Viking, or sea-king, whose home was Alderga (Ouddorp, not far from Alkmaar). His name was Teunis, called familiarly by his followers Neef Teunis, or Cousin Teunis, who had chosen the Mediterranean as the destination of his expeditions, and must have been deified by the Tyrians at the time when the Phenician navigators began to extend their voyages so remarkably, sailing to Friesland in order to obtain British tin, northern iron, and amber from the Baltic, about 2000 years before Christ.

Besides these two we meet with a third mythological person—Minos, the lawgiver of Crete, who likewise appears to have been a Friesland sea-king, Minno, born at Lindaoord, between Wieringen and Kreyl, who imparted to the Cretans an "Asagaboek." He is that Minos who, with his brother Rhadamanthus and Æacus, presided as

---

* Min-erva was called Nyhellenia because her counsels were *ny* and *hel*, that is, new and clear.   In Paul's epitome of S. Pomponius Festus, *de verborum* Significatione, we find "Min-erva dicta quod bene moneat."   See Preller, Roman Mythology, p. 258.

judges over the fates of the ghosts in Hades, and must not be confounded with the later Minos, the contemporary of Ægeus and Theseus, who appears in the Athenian fables.

The reader may perhaps be inclined to laugh at these statements, and apply to me the words that I myself have lately used, fantastic and improbable. Indeed at first I could not believe my own eyes, and yet after further consideration I arrived at the discovery of extraordinary conformities which render the case much less improbable than the birth of Min-erva from the head of Jupiter by a blow from the axe of Hephæstus, for instance.

In the Greek Mythology all the gods and goddesses have a youthful period. Pallas alone has no youth. She is not otherwise known than adult. Min-erva appears in Attica as high priestess from a foreign country, a country unknown to the Greeks. Pallas is a virgin goddess, Min-erva is a Burgtmaagd. The fair, blue-eyed Pallas, differing thus in type from the rest of the gods and goddesses, evidently belonged to Frya's people. The character for wisdom and the emblematical attributes, especially the owl, are the same for both. Pallas gives to the new town her own name, Athènai, which has no meaning in Greek. Min-erva gives to the town built by her the name Athene, which has an important meaning in Fries, namely, that they came there as friends—" Âthen."

Min-erva came to Attica about 1600 years before Christ, the period at which the Grecian Mythology was beginning to be formed. Min-erva landed with the fleet of Jon at the head of a colony in Attica. In later times we find her on the Roman votive stones in Walcheren, under the name of Nehallenia, worshipped as a goddess of navigation; and Pallas is worshipped by the Athenians as the protecting goddess of shipbuilding and navigation.

Time is the carrier who must eternally turn the "Jol" (wheel) and carry the sun along his course through the

c

firmament from winter to winter, thus forming the year, every turn of the wheel being a day. In midwinter the "Jolfeest" is celebrated on Frya's Day. Then cakes are baked in the form of the sun's wheel, because with the Jol Frya formed the letters when she wrote her "Tex." The Jolfeest is therefore also in honour of Frya as inventor of writing.

Just as this Jolfeest has been changed by Christianity into Christmas throughout Denmark and Germany, and into St Nicholas' Day in Holland ; so, certainly, our St Nicholas' dolls—the lover and his sweetheart—are a memorial of Frya, and the St Nicholas letters a memorial of Frya's invention of letters formed from the wheel.

I cannot analyse the whole contents of this writing, and must content myself with the remarks that I have made. They will give an idea of the richness and importance of the contents. If some of it is fabulous, even as fabulous it must have an interest for us, since so little of the traditions of our forefathers remains to us.

An internal evidence of the antiquity of these writings may be found in the fact that the name Batavians had not yet been used. The inhabitants of the whole country as far as the Scheldt are Frya's people—Frieslanders. The Batavians are not a separate people. The name Batavi is of Roman origin. The Romans gave it to the inhabitants of the banks of the Waal, which river bears the name Patabus in the "Tabula Pentingeriana." The name Batavi does not appear earlier than Tacitus and Pliny, and is interpolated in Cæsar's " Bello Gallico," iv. 10. (See my treatise on the course of the rivers through the countries of the Frisians and Batavians, p. 49, in " De Vrije Fries," 4th vol. 1st part, 1845.)

I will conclude with one more remark regarding the language. Those who have been able to take only a superficial view of the manuscript have been struck by the polish of the language, and its conformity with the present Friesland language and Dutch. In this they seem to find grounds for doubting the antiquity of the manuscript.

But, I ask, is, then, the language of Homer much less polished than that of Plato or Demosthenes? And does not the greatest portion of Homer's vocabulary exist in the Greek of our day?

It is true that language alters with time, and is continually subject to slight variations, owing to which language is found to be different at different epochs. This change in the language in this manuscript accordingly gives ground for important observations to philologists. It is not only that of the eight writers who have successively worked at the book, each is recognisable by slight peculiarities in style, language, and spelling; but more particularly between the two parts of the book, between which an interval of more than two centuries occurs, a striking difference of the language is visible, which shows what a slowly progressive regulation it has undergone in that period of time. As the result of these considerations, I arrive at the conclusion that I cannot find any reason to doubt the authenticity of these writings. They cannot be forgeries. In the first place, the copy of 1256 cannot be. Who could at that time have forged anything of that kind? Certainly no one. Still less any one at an earlier date. At a later date a forgery is equally impossible, for the simple reason that no one was acquainted with the language. Except Grimm, Richthofen, and Hettema, no one can be named sufficiently versed in that branch of philology, or who had studied the language so as to be able to write in it. And if any one could have done so, there would have been no more extensive vocabulary at his service than that which the East Frisian laws afford. Therefore, in the centuries lately elapsed, the preparation

of this writing was quite impossible. Whoever doubts
this let him begin by showing where, when, by whom,
and with what object such a forgery could be committed,
and let him show in modern times the fellow of this
paper, this writing, and this language.

Moreover, that the manuscript of 1256 is not original,
but is a copy, is proved by the numerous faults in the
writing, as well as by some explanations of words which
already in the time of the copyist had become obsolete
and little known, as, for instance, in page 82 (114), " to
thêra flête jefta bedrum ;" page 151 (204), "bargum jefta
tonnum fon tha besta bjar."

A still stronger proof is that between pages 157 and
158 one or more pages are missing, which cannot have been
lost out of this manuscript, because the pages 157 and 158
are on the front and the back of the same leaf.

Page 157 finishes thus : " Three months afterwards Adel
sent messengers to all the friends that he had gained, and
requested them to send him intelligent people in the
month of May." When we turn over the leaf, the other
side begins, " his wife, he said, who had been Maid of Texland," had got a copy of it.

There is no connection between these two. There is
wanting, at least, the arrival of the invited, and an account
of what passed at their meeting. It is clear, therefore,
that the copyist must have turned over two pages of the
original instead of one. There certainly existed then an
earlier manuscript, and that was doubtless written by Liko
oera Linda in the year 803.

We may thus accept that we possess in this manuscript,
of which the first part was composed in the sixth century
before our era, the oldest production, after Homer and
Hesiod, of European literature. And here we find in our
fatherland a very ancient people in possession of develop-
ment, civilisation, industry, navigation, commerce, litera-

ture, and pure elevated ideas of religion, whose existence we had never even conjectured. Hitherto we have believed that the historical records of our people reach no farther back than the arrival of Friso the presumptive founder of the Frisians, whereas here we become aware that these records mount up to more than 2000 years before Christ, surpassing the antiquity of Hellas and equalling that of Israel.

This paper was read at a meeting of the Frisian Society, February 1871.

VERGELIJKENDE

VAN DE OUD FRIESCHE WETTEN,

Dyo forme need is : hweerso en kynd jongh is finsen ende fitered noerd wr hef, jefta (sud) wr birgh. Soe moet die moder her kindes eerwe setta ende sella ende her kynd lesa ende des lives bihelpa.

Dioe oder need is : jef da jere diore wirdat, ende di heta honger wr dat land faert, ende dat kynd honger stere wil, so moet dio moder her kindes eerwe setta ende sella ende capia her bern ky ende ey ende coern deerma da kinde des lives mede helpe.

Dyo tredde need is : Als dat kind is al stocnaken, jefta huus laes, ende dan di tiuestera nevil ende calde winter oen comt sa faert allermanick oen syn hof ende oen sin huis ende an waranne gaten, ende da wiilda dier seket diin holla baem ende der birgha hlii, aldeer hit siin liif oen bihalda mey. Soe weinet ende scryt dat onieriga kind ende wyst dan syn nakena lyae ende syn huuslaes, ende syn fader deer him reda schuld, to ienst dyn honger ende winter nevil cald, dat hi so diepe ende dimme mitta fiower neylen is onder eke ende onder da eerda bisloten ende bitacht, so moet dio moder her kindes eerwe setta ende sella omdat hio da bihield habbe ende biwaer also lang so hit onierich is, dat hit oen forste ner oen honger naet forfare.

Anjumer druk. e.i.i.

(1466.)

TAALPROEVE

EN DE TAAL VAN HET HANDSCHRIFT.

Thju forma nêd is : Sâhwersa en bârn jvng is fensen ånd fêterad northward vr-et hef jeftha sûdward vr tha berga, sa åch thju måm hjara bârns erva to settande ånd to seljande ånd hjra bârn to lêsane ånd thes lives to bihelpane.

Thju ôthera nêd is : jef tha jêra djura wårthat ånd thi hête hvnger wr thet lånd fårth ånd thåt bârn stjera wil, sa mot thju måm hjara bârns erva setta ånd selja ånd kåpja hiri bårne ky ånd skêp ånd kêreu thêr mitha mån thet bârn thes lives bihelpe.

Thju tredde nêd is : sâhwersa thåt bârn is stoknåked jefta hûslås ånd then thi tjustera nêvil ånd kalda winter ankvmth, sa fårth allera månnalik an sin hof ånd an sin hus ånd an wårande gåta, ånd thet wilde kwik sykath thene hola båm ånd thêre berga hly thêr-it sin lif an bihalda mêi, sa wênath ånd krytath thåt vnjêrich bârn ånd wyst then sin nåkeda litha ånd sin hûslås-så ånd sin tåt thêr him hrêda skolde tojenst tha hvnger ånd tha kalda winter nêvil, that hi sa djap ånd dimme mith fjuwer nêilum vndera êke ånd vnder tha irtha bisletten ånd bidobben is, sa mot thju måm hjara bârns erva setta and selja vmbe that hju tha bihield håve ånd tha wåringa al sa long sa hit vnjêrich sy, til thju-t hor an frost ner an hvnger navt vmkvma ne mêi.

Vertaald door J. G. O.

ADELA.

2

Okke min Svn—

Thissa boka mot i mith lif ånd sêle wârja. Se vmbi-
fattath thju skêdnise fon vs êle folk åk fon vsa êthlum.
Vrlêden jêr håb ik tham ut-er flod hred tolik mith thi ånd
thinra moder. Tha hja wêron wet wrden; thêr thrvch
gvngon hja åfternei vrdarva. Vmbe hja navt to vrlysa
håb ik-ra vp wrlandisk pampyer wrskrêven. Sa hwersa
thu se erve, mot thu se åk wrskryva. Thin bårn alsa til
thju hja nimmerthe wêi navt ne kvma.
Skrêven to Ljuwert. Nêi åtland svnken is* thåt thria
thû sond fjvwer hvndred ånd njugon ånd fjvwertigoste jêr,
thåt is nei kersten rêknong that tvelfhvndred sex ånd fifti-
goste jêr. Hidde tobinomath oera Linda.—Wåk.

Ljawa ervnôma. Vmb vsa ljawa êthlas wille ånd vmb
vsa ljawa fridoms wille, thusånd wåra så bidd-ik to jo.
Och ljawa ne lêt tha ågon ênis påpekappe tach nimmerthe
over thissa skrifta ne wêja. Hja sprêkath swêta wirda :
men hja tornath vnmårksêm an alles hwat fon vs fryas
trefth. Vmbe rika prebende to winnande så hêlath hja
mith tha poppa kêninggar. Thissa wêtath that wi hjara
gråteste fianda send. thrvchdam wi hjara liuda to sprêke
thvra vr frijdom, rjucht ånd forstne plicht. Thervmbe
lêtath hja alles vrdiligja, hwat fon vsa êthlum kvmt ånd
hwat thêr jeta rest fon vsa alda sêdum. Och ljawa ik håv
by tham et hove wêst. Wil Wr.alda-t thjelda ånd willath
wi vs navt sterik ne måkja hja skilun vs algådur vrdiligja.
Skrêven to Ljudwerd. Acht hondred ånd thrju jêr nei
kersten bigrip. Liko tonômath ovira Linda.

---

* 3449-1256 = 2193 voor Chr.

OKKE MY SON —

You must preserve these books with body and soul. They contain the history of all our people, as well as of our forefathers. Last year I saved them in the flood, as well as you and your mother; but they got wet, and therefore began to perish. In order not to lose them, I copied them on foreign paper.

In case you inherit them, you must copy them likewise, and your children must do so too, so that they may never be lost.

Written at Liuwert, in the three thousand four hundred and forty-ninth year after Atland was submerged—that is, according to the Christian reckoning, the year 1256. Hiddo, surnamed Over de Linda.—Watch.

Beloved successors, for the sake of our dear forefathers, and of our dear liberty, I entreat you a thousand times never let the eye of a monk look on these writings. They are very insinuating, but they destroy in an underhand manner all that relates to us Frisians. In order to gain rich benefices, they conspire with foreign kings, who know that we are their greatest enemies, because we dare to speak to their people of liberty, rights, and the duties of princes. Therefore they seek to destroy all that we derive from our forefathers, and all that is left of our old customs.

Ah, my beloved ones! I have visited their courts! If Wr-alda permits it, and we do not shew ourselves strong to resist, they will altogether exterminate us.

LIKO, *surnamed* OVER DE LINDA.

Written at Liudwert,
Anno Domini 803.

---

* 3449-1256 is 2193 before Christ.

4

THET BOK THÊRA ADELA FOLSTAR.

THRITTICH jêr åftere dêi that thju folksmoder wmbrocht was thrvch thêne vreste Mågy stand et er årg vm to. Alle ståta thêr-er lidsa anda ôre syde thêre Wrsara, wêron fon vs ofkêrth ånd vnder-et weld thes Magy kêmen, ånd-et stand to frêsane, that er weldig skolde wertha vr-et êlle lånd. Vmbe thât vnluk to wêrane hêde mån êne mêna åcht bilidsen, hwêr gådurath wêron ållera månnelik, thêr ann-en gode hrop stande by tha fåmna. Tha néi thât-er mår vrlåpen wêron as thrjv etmelda, was al go-rêd anda tys ånd al-ên sa by hjara kvmste. Thå to tha lesta frêge Adela thåt wird, ånde kêth. J alle wêt-et that ik thrjv jêr burchfåm wêsen sy. Ak wêt j that ik kêren sy to moder, ånd åk, that ik nên moder nêsa* navt nilde,* thrvch-dam ik Apol to min êngå jêrde. Thach hwat j navt nête,* thåt is, that ik alle bêrtnisa nêigvngen håw, êvin as ik en wrentlike folksmoder wêsen wêre. Ik håv al-an fon ånd witherfåren to sjande hwåt-er bêrde. Thêr thrvch send my fêlo sêka bår wrden, thêr ôra navt nête. J håweth jester sêith, thåt vsa sibba an tha ôra syd thêre Wrsara njvt ånd låf wêre. Thå ik mêi sedsa to jv, thåt-er Mågy† se nên yne gå of wnnen heth thrvch thåt weld synra wêpne, men blåt thrvch årgelestige renka, ånd jeta mår thrvch thåt gyrich sa thêra hyrtogum ånd thêra êthelinga. Frya heth sêit wi ne skoldon nên vnfrya ljvd by vs tolêta, thå hwat håvon hja dên? hja håvon vsa fjand nêi folged : hwand an stêd fon hjara fensenum to dêiande, jeftha fry to lêtane, håvon hja Fryas rêd minacht ånd se to hjara slåfonum måked. Thrvchdam hja sok dêdon, macht Frya navt longer wåka ovir hjam : hja håvon ynes ôtheris fry-dom binimen, ånd thåt is êrsêke, thåt hja hjara

---

* nêsa = ne wêsa. nilde = ne wilde. nête = ne wête.
† Magy, Koning der Magyaren en Finnen.

THE BOOK OF ADELA'S FOLLOWERS.

THIRTY years after the day on which the Volksmoeder was murdered by the commander Magy, was a time of great distress. All the states that lie on the other side of the Weser had been wrested from us, and had fallen under the power of Magy, and it looked as if his power was to become supreme over the whole land. To avert this misfortune a general assembly of the people was summoned, which was attended by all the men who stood in good repute with the Maagden (priestesses). Then at the end of three days the whole council was in confusion, and in the same position as when they came together. Thereupon Adela demanded to be heard, and said :—

You all know that I was three years Burgtmaagd. You know also that I was chosen for Volksmoeder, and that I refused to be Volksmoeder because I wished to marry Apol; but what you do not know is, that I have watched everything that has happened, as if I had really been your Volksmoeder. I have constantly travelled about, observing what was going on. By that means I have become acquainted with many things that others do not know. You said yesterday that our relatives on the other side of the Weser were dull and cowardly; but I may tell you that the Magy has not won a single village from them by force of arms; but only by detestable deceit, and still more by the rapacity of their dukes and nobles.

Frya has said we must not admit amongst us any but free people ; but what have they done? They have imitated our enemies, and instead of killing their prisoners, or letting them go free, they have despised the counsel of Frya, and have made slaves of them.

Because they have acted thus, Frya cared no longer to watch over them. They robbed others of their freedom, and therefore lost their own.

---

* *Nêsa*, contraction for *ne wêsa*, *nilde* for *ne wilde*, *nête* for *ne wête*.
† Magy, King of the Magyars or Finns.

håwe. Thach thât ella is jo selva åken. Men ik wil sedsa
to jo, ho hja nêi grådum så lêg vrsylth send. Thêra fin-
num hjara wiva krêjon bårn. Thissa waxton vppa mith
vsa frya bårn. Altomet tvildon ånd joldon hja to samne
vppa hêm, jeftha hja wêron mith ekkorum by thêre hêrd.
Thêr hêrdon hja mith lustum nêi tha vrdwålska finna
sågum, thrvchdam hja thjvd ånd nêi wêron. Så send hja
vntfryast vnthônkes thene wald hjarar aldrum. As tha
bårn gråt wrdon ånd sagon thât tha finna-ra bårn nên
wêpne hantêra machte, ånd blåt wårka moste, thå krêjon
hja anneth wårka en gryns ånd wrdon hårde håchfårande.
Tha båsa ånd hjara storsta svnum krupton by tha lodderiga
finna mangêrtum ; ånd hjara åjne toghatera thrvch thât
vvle fårbild fon-a wêi brocht, lêton hjara selva bigorda
thrvch tha skênesta finna knåpa, hjara vvle aldrum to spot.
Tha thêne Magy thât anda nôs kryg, tha nam-er tha skênesta sinar Finna ånd Magyara vrlovende rå ky mith golden
horna, sa hja ra thrvch vs folk fata dêdon, åfterdam sina
lêr vtbrêda. Men sin ljuda dêdon mår : bern wrdon to
sok makad, nei vpsalåndum wêibrocht, ånd såhwersa hja
vpbrocht wêron an sina vvla lêr, thån wrdon hja to bek
sendon. Thå tha skinslåvona vsa tål måchtich wêron,
thå klivadon hja tha hêrtoga ånd êthelinga an bord, ånd
kêthon, hja moston thene Magy hêroch wertha, sa kvndon
hjara svnum vpfolgja tham, oni* thrvch-et folk kêron
to wrdane. Thêra thêr vmbe goda dêdum en fårdêl to-ra
hus kryen hêde-vrlovadon hja fon sinant wêgum. jeta-n
åfter-dêl bij ; hoka tham en får ånd åfter-dêl kryen hêde
sêidon hja en rond-dêl to, ånd tham en rond-dêl hêde en
êlle ståt. Wêron tha êthla to hårde fryas, thå wendon hja
tha stêwen ånd hildon vppar vrbastera svnum an. Jester-
dêi wêron-er mong† jo tham allet folk to håpa hropa wilde

---

* Oni, oud Holl. ane, Duitsch ohne = zonder.
† Mong, among, emong = onder.

This is well known to you, but I will tell you how they came to sink so low. The Finn women had children. These grew up with our free children. They played and gamboled together in the fields, and were also together by the hearth.

There they learned with pleasure the loose ways of the Finns, because they were bad and new; and thus they became denationalised in spite of the efforts of their parents. When the children grew up, and saw that the children of the Finns handled no weapons, and scarcely worked, they took a distaste for work, and became proud.

The principal men and their cleverest sons made up to the wanton daughters of the Finns; and their own daughters, led astray by this bad example, allowed themselves to be beguiled by the handsome young Finns in derision of their depraved fathers. When the Magy found this out, he took the handsomest of his Finns and Magyars, and promised them "red cows with golden horns" to let themselves be taken prisoners by our people in order to spread his doctrines. His people did even more. Children disappeared, were taken away to the uplands, and after they had been brought up in his pernicious doctrines, were sent back.

When these pretended prisoners had learned our language, they persuaded the dukes and nobles that they should become subject to the Magy—that then their sons would succeed to them without having to be elected. Those who by their good deeds had gained a piece of land in front of their house, they promised on their side should receive in addition a piece behind; those who had got a piece before and behind, should have a rondeel (complete circuit); and those who had a rondeel should have a whole freehold. If the seniors were true to Frya, then they changed their course, and turned to the degenerate sons. Yesterday there were among you those who would have called the whole people together,

---

* *Oni*, in Old Dutch, is *one ;* in German, *ohne* or *zonder*.

† *Mong*, among, or *emong*, is, in Dutch, *onder ;* in English, *among*.

vmb tha åstlike stâta wither to hjara plyga to tvangande.
Thach nêi min ynfalda myning skolde thât falikant* utkvm-
ma. Thånk ynes thêr was wêsen en hårde lvngsyakte
among-eth fja, ånd thât-er thêr jeta årg vvde, skolde j-eth
thån wel wågja vmbe jvw hêlena fja to fårande among hjara
syaka fja? åmmer nå. Såhwersa allra månnelik nw biåma
ånd bijechta mot, thât-eth thêr mitha stapel årg of kvma
skolde, hwa skohle thån alsa dryst wêsa vmbe sina bårn to wa-
gande among en folk thât êlle ånd al vrdêren is. Macht ik
jo rêd jêva, ik skolde sedsa to jo, j moste bifara alle dingum
jo en nêie folksmoder kyasa. Ik wêt wel thât j thêrmitha
anda brvd sitte, vt hawede thât-er fon tha thredtine burchfâmna than wi jeta ower håve wel achte send thêr nêi thêre
êra dinge, men thât skold ik navt ne melda. Tüntja thêr
fâm is et-er burch Mêdêasblik het er nåmmer nêi tålth; tach
is hja fol witskip ånd klarsyan, ånd wel sa hårde vppir folk
ånd usa plyga stålth as all ôthera etsamne. Forth skold-
ik rêda j moste nêi tha burgum gå, ånd thêr vpskrywa
alle êwa fryas tex, bijvnka alle skydnisa, jå ella thât er to
finda sy vppa wågum, til thju ella navt vrlêren ni gå, ånd
mitha burgum alsa vrdên navt ne werth. Thêr stât ask-
riwen: thiu moder ånd jahwelik burchfâm skil håva buta
helpar ånd senda bodon, yn and twintich fâmna ånd sjugon
lêrfâmkis. Macht ik thêr hwat to dvande, thå skol-ik
skrywa, ånd alsa fêlo êrsêma toghatera vmbe to lêrane, sa
thêr vppa burgum wêsa müge; hwand ik seg an trowe
ånd tîd skil-eth jechta, såhwersa j åfta Fryas bårn wille
nåmmer to winnande, hor thrvch lesta ner thvch wêpne,
sa hagath j to nvdande thât jvwe toghatera åfta frya
wiva wrde. Bårn mot mån lêre, ho grât vs lånd êr
wêsen sy, hokke gråte månniska vsa ethla wêron, ho
grât wi jeta send, sa wi vs dål ledsath bij ôra, mån

---

* Falikant, få likande = weinig gelijkende, niet conform.

to compel the eastern states to return to their duty. According to my humble opinion, they would have made a great mistake. Suppose that there was a very serious epidemic among the cattle, would you run the risk of sending your own healthy cattle among the sick ones? Certainly not. Every one must see that doing that would turn out very badly for the whole of the cattle. Who, then, would be so imprudent as to send their children among a people wholly depraved? If I were to give you any advice, it would be to choose a new Volksmoeder. I know that you are in a difficulty about it, because out of the thirteen Burgtmaagden that we still have remaining, eight are candidates for the dignity; but I should pay no attention to that.

Teuntia, the Burgtmaagd of Medeasblik, who is not a candidate, is a person of knowledge and sound sense, and quite as attached to our people and our customs as all the rest together. I should farther recommend that you should visit all the citadels, and write down all the laws of Frya's Tex, as well as all the histories, and all that is written on the walls, in order that it may not be destroyed with the citadels.

It stands written that every Volksmoeder and every Burgtmaagd shall have assistants and messengers—twenty-one maidens and seven apprentices.

If I might add more, I would recommend that all the respectable girls in the towns should be taught; for I say positively, and time will show it, that if you wish to remain true children of Frya, never to be vanquished by fraud or arms, you must take care to bring up your daughters as true Frya's daughters.

You must teach the children how great our country has been, what great men our forefathers were, how great we still are, if we compare ourselves to others.

---

* *Falikant,* or *fâ likande,* is very improbable or unlikely.

mot tâla hjam fon tha wicharda ånd fon hjara wichand-
lika dêdum, åk wra fâra sêtochta. Al thissa tållinga
hagath dên to werthande bij thêre hêrd, vppa hêm ånd
hwêr-et wêsa mêi, så bij blyskip as bij târum. Men skil-
et standfåst kvma an dat bryn ånd andåt hirta, thån
moton alle lêringa overa wêra jvwera wiva ånd toghatera
thêr-in strâma. Adelas rêd is vpfolgath.

Thit send tha nâma thêra grêvetmanna, vnder hwam-
mis wald thit bok awrochten is. Apol, Adelas man, Thria
is-er sêkening wêsen, nw is-er grêvetman over Ast-flylånd
ånd ovir-a Linda-wrda. Tha bvrga Ljvdgârda, Lindahêm,
ånd Stâvja send vnder sin hod.

Ther Saxman Storo, Sytjas man, grêvetman ovir-a hâga
feuna ånd walda. Njvgun wâra is-er to hêrtoga, thåt is
to hyrman, kêren. Tha burga Bvda ånd Manna-gârda-
forda send vnder sin hod.

Abêlo, Jaltjas man, grêvetman ovir tha Sudar Flylånda.
Fjvwers is-er hyrman wêsen. Tha burga Aken, Ljvdburch
ånd Kâtsburch send vnder sin hod.

Enoch Dywek his man, grêvetman ovir West-flylånd
ånd Texland. Njvgun mel is-er to sêkening kêren. Thiu
Wâraburch, Mêdêasblik, Forâna ånd ald Fryasburch send
vnder sin hod.

Foppa, man fon Dunrôs, grêvetman ovir tha Sjvgon
êlânda. Fîf mel is-er sêkening wêsen. Thju burch Walhallagâra is vnder sin hod.

Thit stand vppa tha wâgum et Fryasburch to Texland
askrywen, thåt stêt åk to Stâvia ånd to Mêdêas blik.

Thåt was Frya his dêi ånd to thêre stonde was et vrlêden
sjvgun wâra sjvgun jêr, thåt Fâsta was anståld as folksmoder nêi Fryas jêrta. Thju burch Mêdêasblik was rêd ånd
en fâm was kêren. Nw skoldè Fâsta thju nêja foddik vp-
stêka, ånd thå thåt dên was an åjnwarda fon thåt folk,

You must tell them of the sea-heroes, of their mighty deeds and distant voyages. All these stories must be told by the fireside and in the field, wherever it may be, in times of joy or sorrow ; and if you wish to impress it on the brains and the hearts of your sons, you must let it flow through the lips of your wives and your daughters.

Adela's advice was followed.

These are the Grevetmen under whose direction this book is composed :—

Apol, Adela's husband; three times a sea - king; Grevetman of Ostflyland and Lindaoorden. The towns Liudgarda, Lindahem, and Stavia are under his care.

The Saxman Storo, Sytia's husband ; Grevetman over the Hoogefennen and Wouden. Nine times he was chosen as duke or heerman (commander). The towns Buda and Manna-garda-forda are under his care.

Abêlo, Jaltia's husband; Grevetman over the Zuiderflylanden. He was three times heerman. The towns Aken, Liudburg, and Katsburg are under his care.

Enoch, Dywcke's husband ; Grevetman over Westflyland and Texel. He was chosen nine times for sea - king. Waraburg, Medeasblik, Forana, and Fryasburg are under his care.

Foppe, Dunroo's husband; Grevetman over the seven islands. He was five times sea-king. The town Walhallagara is under his care.

This was inscribed upon the walls of Fryasburg in Texland, as well as at Stavia and Medeasblik.

It was Frya's day, and seven times seven years had elapsed since Festa was appointed Volksmoeder by the desire of Frya. The citadel of Medeasblik was ready, and a Burgtmaagd was chosen. Festa was about to light her new lamp, and when she had done so in the presence

thâ hrop Frya fon hira wâkstâre, sâ thât allera mânnalik
thât hêra machte : Fâsta nim thinra stifte ånd writ tha
thinga thêr ik êr navt sedsa ne machte. Fâsta dêde alsa
hja boden wårth. Sâ send wy Fryas bårn an vsa forma
skêdnise kêmen.

Thât is vsa forma skêdnise.

Wr. alda* tham allêna god ånd êvg is, måkade t. anfang,
dana kêm tid, tid wrochte alle thinga åk jrtha. Jrtha bårde
alle gårsa, krûdon ånd boma, allet djara kwik ånd allet
årge kwik. Alhwat god ånd djar is, brocht hju by dêgum
ånd alhwat kwâd ånd årg is, brocht hju thes nachtis forth.
After-et twilifte jol-fêrste bårde hja thrja mangêrta.

Lyda wårth ut glyande,
Finda wårth ut hêta ånd
Frya ut warme stof.

Thâ hja blât kêmon spisde Wr.alda hjam mith sina
âdama ; til thju tha månneska an him skolde bvnden wêsa.
Ring as hja rip wêron krêjon hja früchda ånd nochta anda
drâma Wr.aldas. Od† tråd to-ra binna : ånd nw bårdon
ek twilif svna ånd twilif togathera ek joltid twêu. Thêrof
send alle månneska kêmen.

Lyda was swart, krolhêred alsa tha lômera : lik ståra
blonken hjra ôgon ; ja thes gyrfügels blikkar wêron vnmo-
dich by hjras.

Skårpe Lyda. Annen sanåka kvn hju kruppa hêra, ånd
hwersa thêr fiska invr wêter wêre n-vntgong thât hira
nostera navt.

Rådbvwde Lyda. En store bâm kvn hju bûgja ånd
sahwersa hja run ne bråk nêne blomstâl vnder hjara fyt.

Weldige Lyda. Hård was hjra steme ånd krêt hju ut
grimme sâ run ek flux wêi.

---

* Wr.alda. Altijd geschreven als zamengesteld woord beteekent: de over-
oude, het oudste wezen.

† Od, wortel van het Lat. odi, ik haat.

of all the people, Frya called from her watch-star, so that every one could hear it : " Festa, take your style and write the things, that I may not speak." Festa did as she was bid, and thus we became Frya's children, and our earliest history began.

This is our earliest history.

Wr-alda, who alone is eternal and good, made the beginning. Then commenced time. Time wrought all things, even the earth. The earth bore grass, herbs, and trees, all useful and all noxious animals. All that is good and useful she brought forth by day, and all that is bad and injurious by night.

After the twelfth Juulfeest she brought forth three maidens :—

Lyda out of fierce heat.

Finda out of strong heat.

Frya out of moderate heat.

When the last came into existence, Wr-alda breathed his spirit upon her in order that men might be bound to him. As soon as they were full grown they took pleasure and delight in the visions of Wr-alda.

Hatred found its way among them.

They each bore twelve sons and twelve daughters—at every Juul-time a couple. Thence come all mankind.

Lyda was black, with hair curled like a lamb's ; her eyes shone like stars, and shot out glances like those of a bird of prey.

Lyda was acute. She could hear a snake glide, and could smell a fish in the water.

Lyda was strong and nimble. She could bend a large tree, yet when she walked she did not bruise a flower-stalk.

Lyda was violent. Her voice was loud, and when she screamed in anger every creature quailed.

---

* *Wr-alda*, always written as a compound word, meaning the *Old Ancient*, or the *Oldest Being*.

† *Od*, the root of the Latin *odi*, I hate.

Wonderfvlle Lyda. Fon êwa nilde hju navt nêta: hjra dêda wrdon thrvch hjra tochta stjvrat. Vmbe tha têdra to helpâne, dâde hju tha stôra ånd hwersa hju-t dên hêde grâjde hju by-t lik.

Arme Lyda. Hju wårth gris fon-t vnwisse bihjelda ånd vpp-it ende sturf hja fon hirtsêr vmbe tha bårn-ra kwâd.

Vnwisa bårn. Hja tichtegadon ekkorum, fen måm-ra dåd, hja gråjadon lik wolva, fjvchtadou alsa ånd dahwile hja that dêdon êton tha fügelon thåt lik. Hwâ mêi sin tåra hwither to haldane.

Finda. Was gêl ånd hjr hêr så tha måna êner hors: êne thrê ne kv hja navt ni bûgja; men hwêr Lyda annen lavwa macht to dêjande, thêr dåde hja wel tjån.

Vrlêdalike Finda. Svet was hjra stemme ånd nannen fügel kvn sjonga lik hju. Hjra êgon lokton ånd lordon, men thêrer ansach wårth slåf.

Vnrêdalika Finda. Hju skrêf thûsande êwa, tha hju ne folgde nên er fon vp. Hja vrfyade tha goda vmbe hjara frymod, thå an slikmåmkes jêf hju hjr selva hast wêi.

That was hir vnluk. Hjra håved was to fvl: tha hjr hirte to ydel; hju ne minde nimmån sa hja selva ånd hju wilde thåt ek hja lyaf håwe skolde.

Falske Finda. Hüning swet wêron hjra wirda, thâ hok tham hja trjvwade wêre vnluk nêi by.

Selvsjochta Finda. Ovir ella wilde hju welda, ånd hjra svnum wêron lik hju; fon hjara susterum lêton hja ra thjanja ånd ekkorum slogon hja vmb-et måsterskip dåd.

Dubbelhirta Finda. Vmbe skotse wirda wårth hju yre, ånd tha årgste dêda ne rorde hja navt. Sach hju eu nyndask en spinne vrslynna, thån wårth hju omm-et hirte sa ys; men sach hju hjra bårn en fryas vrmorde så swol hjra bosm fon nocht.

Wonderful Lyda! She had no regard for laws; her actions were governed by her passions. To help the weak she would kill the strong, and when she had done it she would weep by their bodies.

Poor Lyda! She turned grey by her mad behaviour, and at last she died heart-broken by the wickedness of her children. Foolish children! They accused each other of their mother's death. They howled and fought like wolves, and while they did this the birds devoured the corpse. Who can refrain from tears at such a recital?

Finda was yellow, and her hair was like the mane of a horse. She could not bend a tree, but where Lyda killed one lion she killed ten.

Finda was seductive. Her voice was sweeter than any bird's. Her eyes were alluring and enticing, but whoever looked upon them became her slave.

Finda was unreasonable. She wrote thousands of laws, but she never obeyed one. She despised the frankness of the good, and gave herself up to flatterers.

That was her misfortune. Her head was too full, but her heart was too vain. She loved nobody but herself, and she wished that all should love her.

False Finda! Honey-sweet were her words, but those who trusted them found sorrow at hand.

Selfish Finda! She wished to rule everybody, and her sons were like her. They made their sisters serve them, and they slew each other for the mastery.

Treacherous Finda! One wrong word would irritate her, and the cruellest deeds did not affect her. If she saw a lizard swallow a spider, she shuddered; but if she saw her children kill a Frisian, her bosom swelled with pleasure.

Vnluke Finda. Hju sturf anda blomtid fon hjra lêva, ånd-t is jeta tjvester ho hju fallen sy.

Skinhêliga bårn. Vnder kestlike stêna lêidon hja hjra lik dêl, mit kwabbjana skriftum smukton hja tham vppa, togråjande vmbe hêrath to wårthande men an stilnise ne wênadon hja nênen ênge tår.

Vrijfalik folk. Thi tex thêr Finda nêi lêt was in golden blêder wryt : thach tha besta hwêr-far i måkad was, wêr i nåmmer to not. Tha goda êwa wrdon utfågad ånd selfv sjocht wryte thêr kwåda far in.

O Finda. Tha wårth jrtha fvl blod, ånd tha håveda thêr månneska måjadon thin bårn lik gårs hålma of. Ja Finda thåt send tha früchda thinera ydlenise. Sjan dål fon thinre wåkstår ånd wên.

Frya. Was wit lik snêi bij-t môrneråd ånd thåt blåw hjrar ôgnum wn-et jeta thêre rêinbôge of.

Skêne Frya: Lik strêlon thêre middêi svnne blikadon hjra hêron, thêr sa fin wêron as rach.

Abela Frya. Vntlvkton hjra wêra, thån swêgon tha fügelon ånd ne rordon tha blêdar navt mar.

Weldige Frya. Thrvch thêne kråft hjrar blikkar strêk thene låwa to fara hjara fyt dål ånd held thene addur sin gif tobåk.

Rêne Frya. Hjra yta was hüning ånd hjra drank was dåwa, gådvrad anda bôsma thêra blommur.

Lichte Frya. Thåt forma hwat hju hjra bårn lerde was selv-twang, thåt ôthera was lyafte to düged, ånd thå hja jêroch wrdon, thå lêrde hju hjam thju wêrtha fon tha frij- dom kånna : hwand sêide hju svnder frijdom send alle ôthera dügedon allêna god vmbe jo to slåvona to måk- jande, jvwe ofkvmste to êvge skantha.

Milde Frya. Nåmmer lyt hju mêtal ut jrtha dålva vmb åjnbåt, men såhwersa hja-t dêde wêr-et to jahwelikis not.

Unfortunate Finda! She died in the bloom of her age, and the mode of her death is unknown.

Hypocritical children! Her corpse was buried under a costly stone, pompous inscriptions were written on it, and loud lamentations were heard at it, but in private not a tear was shed.

Despicable people! The laws that Finda established were written on golden tables, but the object for which they were made was never attained. The good laws were abolished, and selfishness instituted bad ones in their place. O Finda! then the earth overflowed with blood, and your children were mown down like grass. Yes, Finda! those were the fruits of your vanity. Look down from your watch-star and weep.

Frya was white like the snow at sunrise, and the blue of her eyes vied with the rainbow.

Beautiful Frya! Like the rays of the sun shone the locks of her hair, which were as fine as spiders' webs.

Clever Frya! When she opened her lips the birds ceased to sing and the leaves to quiver.

Powerful Frya! At the glance of her eye the lion lay down at her feet and the adder withheld his poison.

Pure Frya! Her food was honey, and her beverage was dew gathered from the cups of the flowers.

Sensible Frya! The first lesson that she taught her children was self-control, and the second was the love of virtue; and when they were grown she taught them the value of liberty; for she said, "Without liberty all other virtues serve to make you slaves, and to disgrace your origin."

Generous Frya! She never allowed metal to be dug from the earth for her own benefit, but when she did it it was for the general use.

Lukigoste Frya. Alsa tha stâra om jrtha omswyrmia swirmadon hjara bârn om hja.

Wise Frya. Thâ hju hjra bârn vpbrocht hêde alto thêre sjugonde kny, thâ hrop hju-ra alle a Flylând to sâmne. Thêr jêf se hjam hjra tex, ånd sêide, lêt tham jvwe wêiwisar wêsa, thâ ne skil thåt jo nå navt kwalik ni gå.

Utforkêrena Frya. Thâ hju-t sêid hêde, bêvade jrtha lîk Wr.aldas sê, Flylândis bodem svnk an grâda vnder hjara fyt dål. Thju loft wârt swart ånd nylof* fon târa to stirtane ånd thâ hja nêi moder omsâgon, was hju al lang vppira wâkstår. Thâ to tha lesta språk tongar ut-a wolka ånd blixen schrêf an thåt loftrvm, wâk.

Farsjanda Frya. Thåt lând fon hwêr hju was vpfaren was nw en strâm ånd buta hira tex was thêr in ella bidvlwen hwat fon hjra hôndum kêmen was.

Hêriga bårn. Thâ hja to-ra selva wêron, thâ mâkadon hja thit hâge therp, bvwadon thâs burch thêrvppa, an da wâgrum thessa wryton hja thene tex, ånd vmbe that allera mannalik hja skolde müga finda, hâvath hja thåt lând rondomme Texlând hêten. Thêrvmbe skil-åt bilywa al wenne jrtha jrtha sy.

TEX FRYAS.

Held bêid tha Frya, to tha lesta skilun hja my hwiter sja. Thach thêra allêna mêi ik as fry kånna thêr nên slâf is fon ên ôther ni fon sine tochta. Hyr is min rêd.

Sâhwersa thju nêd årg sy ånd gode rêd ånd gode dêd nawet mâr ne formüge, hrop thån thi gåst Wr.aldas an, men j ne mot-im navt anhropa bifåra alle thinga prvvath send. Tha ik segs to jo mith rêdene ånd tid skil-et wâra, tha modelâsa skilun åmmar swika vnder hjar åjn lêd.

---

* Nylof ; de kleur van nieuw loof ? geel groen.

Most happy Frya! Like the starry host in the firmament, her children clustered around her.

Wise Frya! When she had seen her children reach the seventh generation, she summoned them all to Flyland, and there gave them her Tex, saying, " Let this be your guide, and it can never go ill with you."

Exalted Frya! When she had thus spoken the earth shook like the sea of Wr-alda. The ground of Flyland sunk beneath her feet, the air was dimmed by tears, and when they looked for their mother she was already risen to her watching star ; then at length thunder burst from the clouds, and the lightning wrote upon the firmament " Watch ! "

Far-seeing Frya! The land from which she had risen was now a stream, and except her Tex all that was in it was overwhelmed.

Obedient children! When they came to themselves again, they made this high mound and built this citadel upon it, and on the walls they wrote the Tex, and that every one should be able to find it they called the land about it Texland. Therefore it shall remain as long as the earth shall be the earth.

FRYA's TEX.

Prosperity awaits the free. At last they shall see me again. Though him only can I recognise as free who is neither a slave to another nor to himself. This is my counsel :—

1. When in dire distress, and when mental and physical energy avail nothing, then have recourse to the spirit of Wr-alda; but do not appeal to him before you have tried all other means, for I tell you beforehand, and time will prove its truth, that those who give way to discouragement sink under their burdens.

---

* *Nylof;* the colour of new foliage, bright green.

2. Wr.aldas gåst mêi mån allêna knibuwgjande thånk
to wya, jå thrju wåra far hwat jv fon him noten håve, far
hwat jv nith, ånd fara håpe thêr hy jo lêt an ånga tida.

3. J håwed sjan ho ring ik helpe lênde, dva al ên mith
jo nêston, men ne tof navt til mån jo bêden heth, tha
lydande skolde jo floka, min fåmna skoldon jvwa nåma
utfaga ut-åt bok ånd ik skolde jo lik vnbikånnade ofwisa
mota.

4. Nim nåmmar knibuwgjande tånk fon jv nêston an,
thjus ågath Wr.aldas gåst. Nid skolde j bikrjupa, wisdom solde j bilåka ånd min fåmna skoldon jo bityga fon
fåderråv.

5. Fjuwer thinga send to jvwe not jêven, mith nåma, loft,
wêter, lånd ånd fjur. Men Wr.alda wil thêr allêna bi-
sittar of wêsa. Thêrvmbe rêd ik jo, j skilun jo rjuchtfêr-
diga manna kyasa, tham thju arbêd ånd tha früchda nêi
rjuchta dêla, så that nåmman fry fon wårka ni fon wêra sy.

6. Såhwersa thêr åmman among jo fvnden wårth, thêr
sin åjn frydom vrsellath, tham-n-is navt fon jvw folk:
hi is en horning mith basterd blod. Ik rêde jo that j
him ånd sin måm to thåt lånd utdriva, sêgs that to jvwa
bårn, thes mornes, thes middêis ånd thes êwendes, til
thju hja thêrof dråme thes nachtis.

7. Allera månnalik thår en ôther fon sine frydom birå-
wath, al wêre thêne ôre him skeldech, mot ik anda bårn-
tåm êner slåfinne fåra lêta. Thach ik rêde jo vmbe sin
lik ånd that sinera måm vpp êne kåle stêd to vrbarnande,
åfternêi hjara aske fiftich fyt anda grvnd to dålvane, til
hju thêr nênen gårshålm vp waxa ni mêi, hwand aldulkera
gårs skolde jvw diaroste kvik dêja.

8. Ne grip nå thåt folk fon Lyda ner fon Finda an.
Wr.alda skolde helpa hjm, sa that-åt weld that fon jo
utgong vppa jvwa åjne håveda skolde witherkvma.

2. To Wr-alda's spirit only shall you bend the knee in gratitude—thricefold—for what you have received, for what you do receive, and for the hope of aid in time of need.

3. You have seen how speedily I have come to your assistance. Do likewise to your neighbour, but wait not for his entreaties. The suffering would curse you, my maidens would erase your name from the book, and I would regard you as a stranger.

4. Let not your neighbour express his thanks to you on bended knee, which is only due to Wr-alda's spirit. Envy would assail you, Wisdom would ridicule you, and my maidens would accuse you of irreverence.

5. Four things are given for your enjoyment — air, water, land, and fire—but Wr-alda is the sole possessor of them. Therefore my counsel to you is, choose upright men who will fairly divide the labour and the fruits, so that no man shall be exempt from work or from the duty of defence.

6. If ever it should happen that one of your people should sell his freedom, he is not of you, he is a bastard. I counsel you to expel him and his mother from the land. Repeat this to your children morning, noon, and night, till they think of it in their dreams.

7. If any man shall deprive another, even his debtor, of his liberty, let him be to you as a vile slave; and I advise you to burn his body and that of his mother in an open place, and bury them fifty feet below the ground, so that no grass shall grow upon them. It would poison your cattle.

8. Meddle not with the people of Lyda, nor of Finda, because Wr-alda would help them, and any injury that you inflicted on them would recoil upon your own heads.

9. Sâhwersa thât machte bêra that hja fon juwe rêd
jefta awet owers wilde, alsa aghat j to helpane hjam. Men
kvmath hja to râwande; fal than vppa tham nither lik
blixenande fjvr.

10. Sâhwersa annen fon hjam êner jvwer toghaterum to
wif gêrth ånd hju that wil, thån skolun j hja hjra dvmhêd
bitjvtha; thach wil hju toch hjra frêjar folgja, that hja
than mith frêtho gâ.

11. Willath jvw svna fon hjara toghaterum, så mot j
alsa dva as mith jvwa toghaterum. Thach hor tha êna
nor tha ôthera mêi witherkvma; hwand hja skoldvn
uthêmeda sêda ånd plêga mith fara; ånd drêi thessa by
jo heldgad wrde, mêi ik navt longer ovir jo wâka.

12. Vppa minre fâm Fâsta håv ik min hâp fåstegth,
thêrvmbe most j hja to êremoder nêma. Folgath j min
rêd, thån skil hju nêmels min fâm bilywa ånd alla frâna
fâmna thêr hja folgja; thån skil thju foddik nåmer utgâ
thêr ik far jo vpstoken håv. Thât ljucht thêra skil thån
êvg jvwe bryn vpklarja, ånd j skilun thån êvin fry bilyva
fon vnfrya weld as jvwa swite rinstrâma fon thât salte
wêter thêr åndelåse sê.

THET HET FASTA SÊID.

Alle setma thêr en êw, thât is hvndred jêr, omhlâpa
müge mith tha krodar ånd sin jol, thêra mügon vppa rêd
thêre moder, ånd by mêna willa vppa wêgar thêra burgum
writ hwertha; send hja uppa wêgar writ, thån send hja
êwa, ånd thât is vsa plicht vmbe altham an êra to haldande.
Kvmth nêd ånd tvang vs setma to jêvane, stridande wither
vsa êwa ånd plêgum, så mot månneska dva alsa hja askja;
thach send hja wêken, thån mot mån åmmer to thât alda
witherkêra. Thât is Fryas willa, ånd thât mot wêsa tham
fon al hjra bårn.

9. If it should happen that they come to you for advice or assistance, then it behoves you to help them; but if they should rob you, then fall upon them with fire and sword.

10. If any of them should seek a daughter of yours to wife, and she is willing, explain to her her folly; but if she will follow her lover, let her go in peace.

11. If your son wishes for a daughter of theirs, do the same as to your daughter; but let not either one or the other ever return among you, for they would introduce foreign morals and customs, and if these were accepted by you, I could no longer watch over you.

12. Upon my servant Fasta I have placed all my hopes. Therefore you must choose her for Eeremoeder. Follow my advice, then she will hereafter remain my servant as well as all the sacred maidens who succeed her. Then shall the lamp which I have lighted for you never be extinguished. Its brightness shall always illuminate your intellect, and you shall always remain as free from foreign domination as your fresh river-water is distinct from the salt sea.

This has Fasta spoken.

All the regulations which have existed a century, that is, a hundred years, may by the advice of the Eeremoeder, with the consent of the community, be inscribed upon the walls of the citadel, and when inscribed on the walls they become laws, and it is our duty to respect them all. If by force or necessity any regulations should be imposed upon us at variance with our laws and customs, we must submit; but should we be released, we must always return to our own again. That is Frya's will, and must be that of all her children.

FASTA SÊIDE.

Alle thinga, thêr mån anfangja wil, hoka thât-åt môga
wêsa, vppa tha dêi, thêr wy Frya heldgad håwa, tham skilun êvg falykant utkvma : nêidam tid nw biwysd heth thât
hju riucht hêde, så is thât en êwa wrdon, thât mån svnder
nêd ånd tvang a Frya hjra dêi nawet owers ni dva ne mêi,
tha blyda fêrsta fyrja.

THAT SEND THA ÊWA THÊR TO THÊRA BURGUM HÊRA.

1. Såhwersa thêr årne êne burch bvwet is, så mot thju
foddik thêra an tha forma foddik et Texlånd vpstêken
wrda. Thach thât ne mêi nåmmer owers as troch tha
moder skên.

2. Ek moder skil hjra åjn fåmna kjasa ; alsa thêra thêr
vppa thêra ôthera burgum as moder send.

3. Thju moder to Texlånd mêi hjra folgster kjasa, thach
såhwersa hju falth êr hju-t dên heth, sa mot thas kêren
hwertha vppa êna mêna acht, by rêdum fon alle stata et
sêmne.

4. Thju moder to Texlånd mêi ên ånd tvintich fåmna
ånd sjvgun spille mangêrta håva, til thju thêr åmmer
sjvgun by thêre foddik muge wåkja dêilikes ånd thes
nachtes. By tha fåmna thêr vppa ora burgum as moder
thjanja alsa fêlo.

5. Såhwersa en fåm annen gåda wil, sa mot hju-t thêre
moder melda, ånd bistonda to tha månniska kêra, êr hju
mith hjra tochtige ådama thât ljucht bivvlath.

6. Thju moder ånd alrek burchfåm skil mån tofogjande
ên ånd tvintich burchêran, sjvgun alda wisa, sjvgun alda
kåmpar, ånd sjvgun alda sêkåmper.

FASTA SAID—

Anything that any man commences, whatever it may
be, on the day appointed for Frya's worship shall eternally fail, for time has proved that she was right; and it
is become a law that no man shall, except from absolute
necessity, keep that day otherwise than as a joyful feast.

THESE ARE THE LAWS ESTABLISHED FOR THE GOVERNMENT OF THE CITADELS.

1. Whenever a citadel is built, the lamp belonging to
it must be lighted at the original lamp in Texland, and
that can only be done by the mother.

2. Every mother shall appoint her own maidens. She
may even choose those who are mothers in other towns.

3. The mother of Texland may appoint her own successor, but should she die without having done so, the
election shall take place at a general assembly of the
whole nation.

4. The mother of Texland may have twenty-one maidens
and seven assistants, so that there may always be seven
to attend the lamp day and night. She may have the
same number of maidens who are mothers in other towns.

5. If a maiden wishes to marry, she must announce it
to the mother, and immediately resign her office, before
her passion shall have polluted the light.

6. For the service of the mother and of each of the
Burgtmaidens there shall be appointed twenty-one townsmen—seven civilians of mature years, seven warriors of
mature years, and seven seamen of mature years.

E

7. Ther fon skilun alle jêron to honk kêra thrim fon
elik sjvgun, thach hja ne mügon navt vpfolgath ne wertha
thrvch hjara sibtal nêjar sa tha fjarda kny.

8. Aider mêi thrê hvndred jonga burchwêrar håva.

9. Far thissa thjanesta skilun hja lêra Fryas tex ånd
tha êwa, fon tha wisa mannon thêne wisdom, fon tha alda
hêrmannon thene kunst fon tha orloch ånd fond tha sêken-
ingar thene kunsta thêr bi thåt butafåra nêthlik send.

10. Fon thissa wêrar skilun jêrlikes hvndred to bek
kêra. Thach send thêr svme vrlåmth wrden, sa mügon
hja vpper burch bilywa hjara êlle lêva long.

11. By thåt kjasa fon tha wêrar ne mêi nimmen fon
thêra burch nên stem navt ne håva, ni tha grêvetmanna
jefta ôthera håveda, mån thåt blåta folk allêna.

12. Thju moder et Texlånd skil mån jêva thrja sjvgun
flinka bodon mith thrja twilif rappa horsa. Vppa ora
burgum ek burchfåm thrê bodon mith sjvgun horsa.

13. Ak skil åjder burchfåm håva fiftich bvwara thrvch
thåt folk akêren. Men thêrto mêi mån allêna jêva
sokka, thêr navt abel ånd stora for wêra ner to butafårar
send.

14. Ajder burch mot hiri selva bidruppa ånd genêra fon
hjra åjn ronddêl ånd fon thåt dêl that hju fon thåt mårkjeld bürth.

15. Is thêr åmmau kêren vmbe vppa burgum to thjan-
jande ånd nil-er navt, thån ne mêi-er na nên burchhêr
wertha, ånd dus nên stem navt ni håva, is er al burchhêr
sa skil hi thju êr vrljasa.

16. Såhwersa åmman rêd gêrt fon thêre moder, tha fon
êne burchfåm, sa mot hi him selva melde by tha skrivwer.
Thesse brångth-im by tha burchmåster.

Forth mot-i nêi tha lêtsa, thåt is thêne hêlener. Thêr
mot sja jef er åk bisêken is fon kvada tochtum. Is-er god
sêid,

7. Out of the seven three shall retire every year, and shall not be replaced by members of their own family nearer than the fourth degree.

8. Each may have three hundred young townsmen as defenders.

9. For this service they must study Frya's Tex and the laws. From the sages they must learn wisdom, from the warriors the art of war, and from the sea-kings the skill required for distant voyages.

10. Every year one hundred of the defenders shall return to their homes, and those that may have been wounded shall remain in the citadels.

11. At the election of the defenders no burgher or Grevetman, or other person of distinction, shall vote, but only the people.

12. The mother at Texland shall have three times seven active messengers, and three times twelve speedy horses. In the other citadels each maiden shall have three messengers and seven horses.

13. Every citadel shall have fifty agriculturists chosen by the people, but only those may be chosen who are not strong enough to go to war or to go to sea.

14. Every citadel must provide for its own sustenance, and must maintain its own defences, and look after its share of the general contributions.

15. If a man is chosen to fill any office and refuses to serve, he can never become a burgher, nor have any vote. And if he is already a burgher, he shall cease to be so.

16. If any man wishes to consult the mother or a Burgtmaid, he must apply to the secretary, who will take him to the Burgtmaster. He will then be examined by a surgeon to see if he is in good health. If he is passed,

tha vndvath hi him selva fon sinum wêpna, ånd sjvgun
wêrar brångath him by thêre moder.

17. Is thju sêk vr êne ståte sa ne mügon thêr navt
miner thån thrê bodon kvma: is-t vr-t êlla Fryaslånd,
thån moton thêr jeta sjvgun tjuga bywêsa.   Thêrumbe
thåt er nên kva formvda navt risa ne mêi nor skalkhêd
dên ne wrde.

18. By alle sêkum mot tha moder walda ånd njvda thåt
hjra bårn, thåt is Fryas folk, så mêt-rik bilywa as thåt
wêsa mêi.   Thåt is thi gråtesta hjrar plichta, ånd vs alra
vmb-er thêr an to hêlpande.

19. Håt mån hja by êne rjuchtlika sêke anhropen
vmb-er utsprêk twisk annen grêvetman ånd tha mênte,
ånd findath hju thju sêke tvivelik, så mot hju to båte fon
thêr mênte sprêka til thju thêr frêtho kvma, ånd thrvch-
tham thåt bêtre sy that ên man vnrjucht dên wrde thån
fêlo.

20. Kvmth hwa vmb rêd ånd wêt thju moder rêd, sa
åch hju tham bystonda to jêvane, wêt hju bystonda nên
rêd, så mêi hju wachtja lêta sjvgun dêgum.   Wêt hju thån
nach nên rêd, sa mügon hja hinne brûda, ånd hja mügon
hjra selva navt biklagja, til thju nên rêd bêtre is thån
kva rêd.

21. Heth en moder årge rêd jêven ut kvada willa, så mot
mån hja dêja jefta ut of låndum dryva stoknaken ånd blåt.

22. Send hjra burchhêra mêdeplichtich, thån dvath mån
alsa mith tham.

23. Is hjra skild tvivelik jefta blåt formoda, så mot mån
thêr-vr thingja ånd sprêka, is-t nêdich, ên ånd twintich
wyka long.   Stemth tha halfdêl skildich, så halde mån
hja vr vnskildich, twêde så wacht mån jeta en fvl jêr.
Stemth mån thån alsa, så mêi mån hja skildich halda,
tha navt ni dêja.

he shall lay aside his arms, and seven warriors shall present him to the mother.

17. If the affair concerns only one district, he must bring forward not less than three witnesses; but if it affects the whole of Friesland, he must have twenty-one additional witnesses, in order to guard against any deceptions.

18. Under all circumstances the mother must take care that her children, that is, Frya's people, shall remain as temperate as possible. This is her most important duty, and it is the duty of all of us to help her in performing it.

19. If she is called upon to decide any judicial question between a Grevetman and the community, she must incline towards the side of the community in order to maintain peace, and because it is better that one man should suffer than many.

20. If any one comes to the mother for advice, and she is prepared to give it, she must do it immediately. If she does not know what to advise, he must remain waiting seven days; and if she then is unable to advise, he must go away without complaining, for it is better to have no advice at all than bad advice.

21. If a mother shall have given bad advice out of illwill, she must be killed or driven out of the land, deprived of everything.

22. If her Burgtheeren are accomplices, they are to be treated in a similar manner.

23. If her guilt is doubtful or only suspected, it must be considered and debated, if necessary, for twenty-one weeks. If half the votes are against her, she must be declared innocent. If two-thirds are against her, she must wait a whole year. If the votes are then the same, she must be considered guilty, but may not be put to death.

24. Sâhwersa svme among thât thrimna send tham hja alsa sêr vnskildich mêne that hja hja folgja wille, sâ mügon hja thât dva mith al hjara driwande ånd tilbara hâva ånd nåmman acht hjam thêr ovir min to achtiane, til thju thât måra dêl alsa blyd kån dwâla sa thât minra del.

MÊNA ÊWA.

1. Alle frya bårn send a êlike wysa bårn. Thêrvmbe moton hja åk êlika rjuchte hâva, alsa blyd vpp-åt lånd as vpp-åth ê, thât is wêter ånd vp ella thât Wr. alda jefth.

2. Allera mannalik mêi-t wif sinra kêsa frêja ånd ek toghater mêi efter hjra helddrvnk bjada thêr hju minth.

3. Heth hwa en wif nimth, sâ jêft mån hjam hus ånd wårv. N-is thêr nên; sa mot-åt bvwat wrde.

4. Is-er nêi en ôther thorp gongon vmb en wif ånd wil hi thêr bilywa, sâ mot mån him thêr en hus en wårf jêwa bijonka thât not fon tha hêmrik.

5. Allera mannalik mot mån en åfterdêl as wårf by sina hus jêva. Tha nimman ne mêi en fardêl by sin hus nåva, fül min en ronddêl. Allêna ief hwa en dåd dên heth to mêna nitha, sâ mêi him thât jêven wrde. Ak mêi sin jongste svn that erva. After tham mot thât thorp that wither nima.

6. Ek thorp skil en hêmrik hâva nêi sina bihof ånd thêne grêva skil njvda that alra ek sin dêl bidongth ånd god hald, til thju tha åfter kvmmande nên skåde navt ne lyda ne muge.

7. Ek thorp mêi en mårk hava to kåp ånd to vrkåp iefta to wandelja. Alle-t ôra lånd skil bvw ånd wald bilyva. Thâ tha bâma thêra ne mêi nimman navt fålla, buta mêna rêda ånd buta wêta thes waldgrêva, hwand tha walda send to mêna nitha. Thêrvmbe ne mêi nimman thêr måster of sa.

24. If any of the one-third who have voted for her wish to go away with her, they may depart with all their live and dead stock, and shall not be the less considered, since the majority may be wrong as well as the minority.

UNIVERSAL LAW.

1. All free-born men are equal, wherefore they must all have equal rights on sea and land, and on all that Wr-alda has given.

2. Every man may seek the wife of his choice, and every woman may bestow her hand on him whom she loves.

3. When a man takes a wife, a house and yard must be given to him. If there is none, one must be built for him.

4. If he has taken a wife in another village, and wishes to remain, they must give him a house there, and likewise the free use of the common.

5. To every man must be given a piece of land behind his house. No man shall have land in front of his house, still less an enclosure, unless he has performed some public service. In such a case it may be given, and the youngest son may inherit it, but after him it returns to the community.

6. Every village shall possess a common for the general good, and the chief of the village shall take care that it is kept in good order, so that posterity shall find it uninjured.

7. Every village shall have a market-place. All the rest of the land shall be for tillage and forest. No one shall fell trees without the consent of the community, or without the knowledge of the forester; for the forests are general property, and no man can appropriate them.

8. As mårkjeld ne mêi thåt thorp navt mår ni nimma sa tha tillifte dêl fon tha skat, hor fon tha inhêmar ner fon tha têrhêmande. Ak ne mêi tha mårk skat navt êr vrsellath* ne wertha as thåt ôra god.

9. Alle-t mårkjeld mot jêrlikes dêlath wrde, thrja dêgan far thêre joldêi, an hvndred dêlun to dêlande.

10. Thi grêvetman mit sinum grêvum skil thêr of büra twintich dêla; thêne mårk rjuchter tian dêla, ånd sinum helpar, fif dêla; thju folkesmoder ên dêl; thju gå moder fjvwer dêla; thåt thorp tian dêla; tha årma, thåt is thêra tham navt wårka ni kunna ni müge, fiftich dêla.

11. Thêra, tham to mårka kvma, ne mügon navt ni wokeria, kvmath thêr svm, sa is-t thêra famna plicht hjam kånbêr to makjana in-vr thåt êlle lånd, til thju hja nimmerthe kêren navt wrde to eng ampt, hwand soka håvath en gyra-lik hirte, vmbe skåt to garja skolde hja ella vrrêda, thåt folk, thjv moder, hjara sibben ånd tho tha lesta hjara selva.

12. Is thêr åmman alsa årg that-er sjvcht-siak fja jeftha vrdêren wêr vrsellath vr hêl god, sa mot thene mårk-rjuchtar him wêra ånd tha famna him noma invr-et êlle lånd.

In êra tyda hêmadon Findas folk mêst algadur invr hjara moders bårta-lånd, mit nôma ald-lånd that nw vnder-ne sê lêith; hja wêron thus fêr-of, thêrvmbe nêdon wi åk nên orloch, tha hja vrdrêven send ånd hêinda kêmon to råwane, thå kêm-er fon selva låndwêr hêrmanna kêninggar ånd orloch, vr altham kêmon setma ånd uta setma kêmon êwa.

HYR FOLGATH THA ÊWA THÊR THÊRUT TAVLIKT SEND.

1. Ek Fryas mot-a lêtha jeftha fyanda wêra mith aldulkera wåpne as-er forsinna, bikvma ånd håndtêra mêi.

---

* De mårkskat werd in goederen betaald.

8. The market charges shall not exceed one-twelfth of the value of the goods either to natives or strangers. The portion taken for the charges shall not be sold before the other goods.

9. All the market receipts must be divided yearly into a hundred parts three days before the Juul-day.

10. The Grevetman and his council shall take twenty parts; the keeper of the market ten, and his assistants five; the Volksmoeder one, the midwife four, the village ten, and the poor and infirm shall have fifty parts.

11. There shall be no usurers in the market.

If any should come, it will be the duty of the maidens to make it known through the whole land, in order that such people may not be chosen for any office, because they are hard-hearted.

For the sake of money they would betray everybody— the people, the mother, their nearest relations, and even their own selves.

12. If any man should attempt to sell diseased cattle or damaged goods for sound, the market-keeper shall expel him, and the maidens shall proclaim him through the country.

In early times almost all the Finns lived together in their native land, which was called Aldland, and is now submerged. They were thus far away, and we had no wars. When they were driven hitherwards, and appeared as robbers, then arose the necessity of defending ourselves, and we had armies, kings, and wars.

For all this there were established regulations, and out of the regulations came fixed laws.

HERE FOLLOW THE LAWS WHICH WERE THUS ESTABLISHED.

1. Every Frisian must resist the assailants with such weapons as he can procure, invent, and use.

---

* The market dues were paid in kind.

2. Is en boi twilif jer, sa mot-i tha sjvgunde dêi miste fon sin lêr-tid vmbe rêd to werthande mith-a wåpne.

3. Is hi bikvmen, sa jêve mån him wåpne ånd hi warth to wêrar slågen.

4. Is hi thrê jêr wêrar, så wårth-i burch-hêr ånd mêi hi hêlpa sin håwed-manna to kjasane.

5. Is hwa sjvgun jêr kjasar, så mêi hi hêlpa en hêrman jeftha kêning to kjasane, thêr to åk kêren wrde.

6. Alle jêr mot-er ovir kêren wertha.

7. Buta tha kêning mügon alle ambtmanna wither kêren wertha, tham rjucht dva ånd nêi fryas rêd.

8. Annen kêning ne mêi navt ni lônger as thrê jêr kêning bilywa, til thju hi navt biklywa ne mêi.

9. Heth-i sjvgun jêr rest, så mêi hi wither kêren wertha.

10. Is thi kêning thruch thene fyand fallen, så mügon sina sibba åk nêi thêre êre thinga.

11. Is-er vppa sin tid ofgvngen jeftha binna sin tid sturven, så ne mêi nên sibba him vpfolja, thêr-im nêiar sy sa tha fjarde kny.

12. Thêra tham strida mitha wåpne au hjara handa ne kunnath navt forsinna ånd wis bilywa, thêrvmbe ne fochteth nêne kêning wåpne to hantêra an tha strid. Sin wisdom mot sin wåpen wêsa ånd thju ljafte sinra kåmpona mot sin skyld wêsa.

HYR SEND THA RJUCHTA THÊRE MODER AND THÊRA KÊNINGGAR.

1. Sahwersa orloch kumth, send tha moder hira bodon nêi tha kêning, thi kêning send bodon nêi tha grêvetmanna vmbe lånd-wêr.

2. Tha grêvetmanna hropath alle burch-hêra et sêmne ånd birêdath ho fêlo manna hja skilun stjura.

2. When a boy is twelve years old he must devote one day in seven to learning how to use his weapons.

3. As soon as he is perfect in the use of them they are to be given to him, and he is to be admitted as a warrior.

4. After serving as a warrior three years, he may become a citizen, and may have a vote in the election of the headman.

5. When he has been seven years a voter he then may have a vote for the chief or king, and may be himself elected.

6. Every year he must be re-elected.

7. Except the king, all other officials are re-eligible who act according to Frya's laws.

8. No king may be in office more than three years, in order that the office may not be permanent.

9. After an interval of seven years he may be elected again.

10. If the king is killed by the enemy, his nearest relative may be a candidate to succeed him.

11. If he dies a natural death, or if his period of service has expired, he shall not be succeeded by any blood relation nearer than the fourth degree.

12. Those who fight with arms are not men of counsel, therefore no king must bear arms. His wisdom must be his weapon, and the love of his warriors his shield.

These are the Rights of the Mothers and the Kings.

1. If war breaks out, the mother sends her messengers to the king, who sends messengers to the Grevetmen to call the citizens to arms.

2. The Grevetmen call all the citizens together and decide how many men shall be sent.

3. Alle bisluta thêra moton ring nêi thêre moder senden wertha mith bodon ånd tjugum.

4. Thju moder lêth alle bisluta gaderja ånd jêfth et guldnetal, thåt is thåt middeltal fon alle bisluta etsêmne, thêrmitha mot mån far thåt forma frêto ha ånd thene kening alsa.

5. Is thju wêra a kåmp, thån hoft thi kêning allêna mith sinum havedmanna to rêda, thach thêr moton åmmerthe thrê burch-hêra fon thêre moder fôrana sitta svnder stem. Thissa burch-hêra moton dêjalikis bodon nêi thêre moder senda, til thju hju wêta müge jef thêr awet dên wårth, stridande with-a êwa jeftha with Fryas rêdjevinga.

6. Wil thi kêning dva ånd sina rêda navt, så mêi hi thåt navt vnderstonda.

7. Kvmth-ene fyand vnwarlinga, thån mot mån dva sa thene kêning bith.

8. Nis thene kêning navt vppet pat, så mot mån sin folgar hêrich wêsa of tham-is folgar alont tha lesta.

9. Nis thêr nên havedman, så kjase mån hwa.

10. Nis thêr nên tid, så wårpa hi him to havedman thêrim weldich fêleth.

11. Heth thene kêning en frêsalik folk ofslagen, så mügon sina after kvmande sin nåma åfter hjara åjne fora; wil thene kêning, så mêi-er vppen vnbibvwade stêd en plåk utkjasa to hus ånd erv. Thåt erv mêi en rond-dêl wêsa sa gråt thåt hi fon alle sidum sjvgun hvndred trêdun ut of sine hus mêi hlapa, êr hi an sina rêna kvmth.

12. Sin jongste svn mêi thåt god erva, åfte tham thamis jongste, thån skil mån that wither nimma.

HYR SEND THA RJUCHTA ALLER FRYAS VMBE SÊKUR TO WÊSANDE.

1. Sahwersa thêr êwa vrwrocht wrde jefta nêja setma

3. All the resolutions must immediately be sent to the mother by messengers and witnesses.

4. The mother considers all the resolutions and decides upon them, and with this the king as well as the people must be satisfied.

5. When in the field, the king consults only his superior officers, but three citizens of the mother must be present, without any voice. These citizens must send daily reports to the mother, that they may be sure nothing is done contrary to the counsels of Frya.

6. If the king wishes to do anything which his council opposes, he may not persist in it.

7. If an enemy appears unexpectedly, then the king's orders must be obeyed.

8. If the king is not present, the next to him takes command, and so on in succession according to rank.

9. If there is no leader present, one must be chosen.

10. If there is no time to choose, any one may come forward who feels himself capable of leading.

11. If a king has conquered a dangerous enemy, his successors may take his name after their own. The king may, if he wishes, choose an open piece of ground for a house and ground; the ground shall be enclosed, and may be so large that there shall be seven hundred steps to the boundary in all directions from the house.

12. His youngest son may inherit this, and that son's youngest son after him; then it shall return to the community.

HERE ARE THE RULES ESTABLISHED FOR THE SECURITY
OF ALL FRISIANS.

1. Whenever new laws are made or new regulations

tavlikt, alsa mot-et to mêna nitha skên, men nåmmer to
bâta fon enkeldera månniska, her fon enkeldera slachta,
ner fon enkeldera stâta, nach fon awet that enkel
sy.

2. Sahwersa orloch kvmt ånd thêr wrde husa homljat
jeftha skêpa, hok that et sy, sy-et thrvch thene fyand, tha
by mêna rêdum, så ach tha mêna mênta, thåt is al-et folk
to sêmne that wither to hêlene; thêr vmbe that nåmman
tha mêna sêka skil helpa vrljasa vmbe sin åjn god to
bihaldane.

3. Is orloch vrthêjan, ånd send thêr svm, alsa vrdêren
that hja navt longer wårka ne mügon, så mot tha mêna
mênte hjam vnderhalda, by tha fêrstum achon hja forana to
sittana, til thju tha jüged skil êra hjam.

4. Send thêr wêdvon ånd wêson kêmon, så mot mån hja
åk vnderhalda ånd tha svna mügon thi nåma hjarar tåta
vpp-ira skildum writa hjara slachtha to êrane.

5. Send thêr svm thrvch thene fyand fat ånd kvmath hja
to båk, så mot mån hjam fêr fon thåt kåmp of fora, hwand
hja machton fry lêten wêsa by arge loftum ånd than ne
mügon hja hjara lofta navt ni halda ånd toch êrlik
bilywa.

6. Jef wi selwa fyanda fâta, så brånge mon tham djap
anda landa wêi, mån lêrth hja vsa frya sêde.

7. Lêt mån hja åfternêi hlåpa, så lêt mån thåt mith wel-
hêd thrvch tha fåmna dva, til thju wi åtha ånd frjunda
winna fori lêtha ånd fyandun.

UT MINNOS SKRIFTUN.

Sahwersa thêr ênman is thêrmêta årg that hi vsa
swetsar birawath, morth-dedun dvat husa barnth,
mangêrtha skånth, hok thåt-et sy, thåt årg sy, ånd
vsa swetnata willon thåt wroken håva, så is thåt
rjucht thåt mån thene dêder fâtath ånd an hjara åjn-

established, they must be for the common good, and not for individual advantage.

2. Whenever in time of war either ships or houses are destroyed, either by the enemy or as a matter of precaution, a general levy shall be assessed on the people to make it good again, so that no one may neglect the general welfare to preserve his own interest.

3. At the conclusion of a war, if any men are so severely wounded as to be unable to work, they shall be maintained at the public expense, and shall have the best seats at festivals, in order that the young may learn to honour them.

4. If there are widows and orphans, they shall likewise be maintained at the public expense; and the sons may inscribe the names of their fathers on their shields for the honour of their families.

5. If any who have been taken prisoners should return, they must be kept separate from the camp, because they may have obtained their liberty by making treacherous promises, and thus they may avoid keeping their promises without forfeiting their honour.

6. If any enemies be taken prisoners, they must be sent to the interior of the country, that they may learn our free customs.

7. If they are afterwards set free, it must be done with kindness by the maidens, in order that we may make them comrades and friends, instead of haters and enemies.

FROM MINNO'S WRITINGS.

If any one should be so wicked as to commit robbery, murder, arson, rape, or any other crime, upon a neighbouring state, and our people wish to inflict punishment, the culprit shall be put to death in the presence

warda dêjath, til thju thêr vr nên orloch ne kvme, wêrthrvch
tha vnskêldiga skolde bota fori tha skêldiga. Willath hja
him sin lif bihalda lêta ând thju wrêka ofkâpja lêta, så mêi
mån thât dâja. Thach is then bona en kêning, grêvetman,
grêva hwa thât-et sy, tham ovira sêda mot wâka, så moton
wi thât kwad bêterja men ta bona mot sin straf hâ.

Forth hi en êrenâma vppa sine skeld fon sina êthelun, så
ne mügon sina sibba thi nâma navt lônger ne fora. Thêrvmbe thât hi êne sibba svrg skil hâva ovira sêda thêra ôthera.

ÊWA FARA STJURAR. STJURAR IS THI ÊRENOMA THÊRA BUTAFARAR.

Alle fryas svna hâva lika rjuchta, thêrvmb mügon âlle
flinka knâpa hjara self as butafârar melda by tha ôldermôn
ând thisse ne mêi him nit ofwisa, wara thât er nên sted is.

2. Tha stjurar mügon hjara âjn mâstrun noma.

3. Tha kâpljvd moton kêren ând binomath wertha thrvch
tha mênte thêr-et god hêreth ând tha stjurar ne mügon
thêr by nên stem hâva.

4. Jef mån vppe rêis bifinth thât thene kêning ârg jefta
vnbikvmmen is, så mügon hja en ôra nimma ; kvmon hja to
bâk, så mêi thene kêning him self biklagja by tha ôldermôn.

5. Kvmth thêr flâte to honk ând sin thêr bâta, så moton
tha stjurar thêr of en thrimene hâva, althus to dêlande, thi
witkêning twilf môn-is dêla, thi skolt by nacht sjugun dêla,
tha bôtmônna ek twa dêla, thi skiprun ek thrê dêla, that
ôra skip-is folk ek ên dêl. Tha jongste prentar ek en
thrimnath, tha midlosta ek en half-dêl ând tha ôldesta ek
en twêdnath.

6. Sin thêr svme vrlameth, så mot-a mêna mênte njvda
far hjara lif, âk moton hja fôrana sitta by tha mêna fêrsta,
by huslika fêrsta, jâ by alle fêrsta.

---

* Stjurar, van hier de naam Sturii by Plinius.

of the offended, in order that no war may arise, and the innocent suffer for the guilty. If the offended will spare his life and forego their revenge, it may be permitted. If the culprit should be a king, Grevetman, or other person in authority, we must make good his fault, but he must be punished.

If he bears on his shield the honourable name of his forefathers, his kinsmen shall no longer wear it, in order that every man may look after the conduct of his relatives.

LAWS FOR THE NAVIGATORS.

Navigator is the title of those who make foreign voyages.

1. All Frya's sons have equal rights, and every stalwart youth may offer himself as a navigator to the Olderman, who may not refuse him as long as there is any vacancy.

2. The navigators may choose their own masters.

3. The traders must be chosen and named by the community to which they belong, and the navigators have no voice in their election.

4. If during a voyage it is found that the king is bad or incompetent, another may be put in his place, and on the return home he may make his complaint to the Olderman.

5. If the fleet returns with profits, the sailors may divide one-third among themselves in the following manner : The king twelve portions, the admiral seven, the boatswains each two portions, the captains three, and the rest of the crew each one part; the youngest boys each one-third of a portion, the second boys half a portion each, and the eldest boys two-thirds of a portion each.

6. If any have been disabled, they must be maintained at the public expense, and honoured in the same way as the soldiers.

---

* *Stjurar*, from this is derived the word *Sturii* in Pliny.

F

7. Sin thêr vppa tocht vmkume, så moton hjara nêstun hjara dêl erva.

8. Sin thêr wêdven ånd wêson fon kvmen, så mot thju mênte hja vnderhalda; sin hja an ênre kase felth, sa mügon tha svna thi nôma hjarar tåta vppira skeldun fora.

9. Sin thêr prentara * forfaren, sa moton sina erva en êl mannis dêl håva.

10. Was hi forsêith, så mêi sin brud sjugun mannis dêlun aska vmbe hira fryadulf en stên to to wjande, mar thån mot hja for tha êre wêdve bilyva lêva lông.

11. Sahwersa en mênte en flåte to rêth, moton tha rêdar njvda fåra beste liftochtun ånd får wif ånd bårn.

12. Jef en stjurar of ånd årm is, ånd hi heth hus nach erv, så mot im that jon wertha. Nil hy nên hus nach erv, sa mügon sin friundun hem tus nêma ånd thju mênte mot et bêtera nêi sina ståt, wara thåt sin friunda thene båta weigerja.

NETLIKA SÊKA UT-A NÊILÊTNE SKRIFTUM MINNOS.

Minno † was en alde sêkêning, sjaner ånd wisgyrich. An tha Krêtar heth-i êwa jêven. Hi is bårn an tha Lindawrda, ånd nêi al sin witherfåra heth hi thåt luk noten umbe to Lindahêm to sterva.

Sahwersa vsa swethnata en dêl lånd håve jeftha wêtir, that vs god tolikt, sa focht-et vs vmbe that a kåp to frêja, nillath hja thåt navt ne dva, than mot mån hja that bihalda lêta. That is nêi Frya-his tex ånd-et skolde vnrjucht wêsa to vnthandana that.

Sahwersa thêr swethnata et sêmna kyva ånd sana vr enga sêka, tha vr lånd, and hja vs frêja en ordêl to sprêka, sa ach man thåt rêder åfterwêja to lêtane,

* Prentar, nog op Texel een (stuurmans) leerling.
† Minno, Minos (de oude).

7. If any have died on the voyage, their nearest relatives inherit their portion.

8. Their widows and orphans must be maintained at the public expense; and if they were killed in a sea-fight, their sons may bear the names of their fathers on their shields.

9. If a topsailman is lost, his heirs shall receive a whole portion.

10. If he was betrothed, his bride may claim seven portions in order to erect a monument to her bridegroom, but then she must remain a widow all her life.

11. If the community is fitting out a fleet, the purveyors must provide the best provisions for the voyage, and for the women and children.

12. If a sailor is worn out and poor, and has no house or patrimony, one must be given him. If he does not wish for a house, his friends may take him home; and the community must bear the expense, unless his friends decline to receive it.

Useful Extracts from the Writings left by Minno.

Minno was an ancient sea-king. He was a seer and a philosopher, and he gave laws to the Cretans. He was born at Lindaoord, and after all his wanderings he had the happiness to die at Lindahem.

If our neighbours have a piece of land or water which it would be advantageous for us to possess, it is proper that we should offer to buy it. If they refuse to sell it, we must let them keep it. This is Frya's Tex, and it would be unjust to act contrary to it.

If any of our neighbours quarrel and fight about any matter except land, and they request us to arbitrate, our best course will be to decline; but if

---

* *Prentar*, still used in Texel to designate a pilot's apprentice.

† *Minno*, *Minos* (the Ancient).

tach sa man thêr navt buta ne kan, sa mot man thât erlik
ånd rjuchtfêrdich dva.

Kvmth thêr hwa ånd sêith, ik håv orloch, nw most-v mi
helpa; jeftha en ôra kvmth ånd sêith, min svn is vnjêrich
ånd vnbikvmmen, ånd ik bin ald, nw wild-ik thi to wâran-
stew ovir hini ånd ovir min land stålla, til hi jêrich sy,
sa ach man that wêigarja, til thju wi nawt an twist
ne kvme ne müge vr sêka stridande with vsa frya
sêdum.

Sahwersa thêr kvmth en vrlandisk kapman vppa tolêt-
mårk et Wyringga tha to Almanland ånd hi bidroght, sa
warth-er bistonda mårk-bêten ånd kanbêr måkad trvch tha
fåmna invr et êle land. Kvmth-er thån to båk, sa ne skil
nimman kåpja fon him, hy mêi hinne brûda sa-r kvmen is.
Thus, sahwersa-r kåpljud kêren wrde vmbe wr-a merka to
gå, jeftha mith-e flåt to fârane, sa ach man allêna aldulkera
to kjasane tham mån tyge by tyge kånth ånd an en goda
hrop ståne by tha fåmna. Bêrth-et navt to min that-er en
årg man mông sy, tham tha ljud bitrogha wil, sa agon tha
ora thåt to wêrane. Het-i-t-al dên sa mot mån thåt bêterja,
ånd thene misdêdar ut of låndum banna, til thju vsa nåma
vral mith êrane skil wertha binomath.

Men jef wir vs vppen vrlandiska mårkt finda, sy-et hêinde
jeftha fêr, ånd bêrth-et thåt-et folk vs lêt dvath jeftha
bistêlleth, så agon wy mith haste hêi to to slåna, hwand
afskên wy êlla agon to dvande vmbe frêtho willa, vsa half-
brothar ne mügon vs nimmer minachtja nach wåna that
wi ange send.

In min jüged håv ik wel ênis mort overa bånda thêra
êwa, åfter håv ik Frya often tanked vr hjra tex, ånd vsa
êthla vr tha êwa thêr thêrnêi tavlikt send.

Wr.alda jeftha Alfoder heth mi fêlo jêren jêven,
invr fêlo landa ånd sêa håv ik omme fåren ånd nêi
al hwa ik sjan hå, bin ik vrtjûgad that wi allêna

they insist upon it, it must be done honourably and justly.

If any one comes and says, I am at war, you must help me; or another comes and says, My son is an infant and incompetent, and I am old, so I wish you to be his guardian, and to take charge of my property until he is of age, it is proper to refuse in order that we may not come into disputes about matters foreign to our free customs.

Whenever a foreign trader comes to the open markets at Wyringen and Almanland, if he cheats, he must immediately be fined, and it must be published by the maidens throughout the whole country.

If he should come back, no one must deal with him. He must return as he came.

Whenever traders are chosen to go to trading stations, or to sail with the fleets, they must be well known and of good reputation with the maidens.

If, however, a bad man should by chance be chosen and should try to cheat, the others are bound to remove him. If he should have committed a cheat, it must be made good, and the culprit must be banished from the land in order that our name may be everywhere held in honour.

If we should be ill-treated in a foreign market, whether distant or near, we must immediately attack them; for though we desire to be at peace, we must not let our neighbours underrate us or think that we are afraid.

In my youth I often grumbled at the strictness of the laws, but afterwards I learned to thank Frya for her Tex and our forefathers for the laws which they established upon it. Wr-alda or Alvader has given me many years, and I have travelled over many lands and seas, and after all that I have seen, I am convinced that we alone

trvch Alfoder utforkêren send, êwa to håvande. Lydas folk
ne mêi nên êwa to måkjande ni to håldande, hja send to
dvm ånd wild thêrto. Fêlo slachta Findas send snôd enoçh,
men hja send gyrich, håchfårande, falsk, vnkûs ånd mort-
sjochtich. Poga blêsath hjara selva vppa, ånd hja ne mügath nawet than krupa. Forska hropath wårk, wårk, ånd
hja ne dvath nawet as hippa ånd kluchtmåkja. Tha roka
hropath spår, spår, men hja stêlon ånd vrslynath al wat vnder
hjara snavela kvmath. Lik al tham is thåt Findas folk,
hja bogath immer ovir goda êwa ; ek wil setma måkja vmb-
et kwåd to wêrane, men selva nil nimman theran bonden
wêsa. Thêra hwam-his gåst that lestigoste sy ånd thêrtrvch
sterik, tham-his hône krêjath kêning ånd tha ôro moton al-
wenna an sin weld vnderwurpen wêsa, til en ôther kvmth
thêr-im fon-a sêtel drywet. Thåt word êwa is to från vmbe
an mêna sêka to nomande. Thervmbe heth mån vs êvin
sega lêrth. Êwa thåt sêit setma thêr bi aller månniska êlik
an hjara mod prenth send, til thju hja müge wêta hwat rjucht
ånd vnrjucht sy ånd hwêrtrhvch hja weldich send vmbe hjara
åjne dêda ånd tham fon ôrum to birjuchtande, thåt wil sedsa
alsanåka hja god ånd navt misdêdich vpbrocht send. Ak is-
er jet-en ôra sin an fåst. Êwa seit ak, êlik wêter-lik ; rjucht
ånd sljucht as wêter that thrvch nên stornewind jeftha awet
owers vrstoren is. Warth wêter vrstoren, sa warth-et vnêwa,
vnrjucht, mem et nygt êvg vmbe wither êwa to werthande,
that lêith an sin fonselvhêd, alsa tha nygung to rjucht ånd
frydom in Fryas bern leith. Thessa nygung håvath wi
trvch Wr.aldas gåst, vsa foders, thêr in Fryas bern bogth,
thêrvm be skil hju vs åk êvg biklywa. Êwa is åk thet ôra
sinnebyld fon Wr.aldas gåst, thêr êvg rjucht ånd vnforstoren
bilywath, afskên-et an lichême årg to gêit. Êwa ånd vnforstoren send tha mårka thêra wisdom ånd rjuchtfêrdichhêd

are chosen by Alvader to have laws. Lyda's people can neither make laws nor obey them, they are too stupid and uncivilised. Many are like Finda. They are clever enough, but they are too rapacious, haughty, false, immoral, and bloodthirsty.

The toad blows himself out, but he can only crawl. The frog cries " Work, work ; " but he can do nothing but hop and make himself ridiculous. The raven cries " Spare, spare ; " but he steals and wastes everything that he gets into his beak.

Finda's people are just like these. They say a great deal about making good laws, and every one wishes to make regulations against misconduct, but does not wish to submit to them himself. Whoever is the most crafty crows over the others, and tries to make them submit to him, till another comes who drives him off his perch.

The word " Eva " is too sacred for common use, therefore men have learned to say " Evin."

" Eva " means that sentiment which is implanted in the breast of every man in order that he may know what is right and what is wrong, and by which he is able to judge his own deeds and those of others ; that is, if he has been well and properly brought up. " Eva " has also another meaning; that is, tranquil, smooth, like water that is not stirred by a breath of wind. If the water is disturbed it becomes troubled, uneven, but it always has a tendency to return to its tranquil condition. That is its nature, just as the inclination towards justice and freedom exists in Frya's children. We derive this disposition from the spirit of our father Wr-alda, which speaks strongly in Frya's children, and will eternally remain so. Eternity is another symbol of Wr-alda, who remains always just and unchangeable.

Eternal and unalterable are the signs wisdom and rec-

thêr fon alla frêmo mânniska socht ånd trvch alla rjuchtera
bisêten wrden mot. Willath tha mânniska thus setma ånd
domar måkja, thêr alan god bilywa ånd allerwêikes, sa moton
hja êlik wêsa to fara alle mânniska; nêi thisse êwa achath
tha rjuchtera hjara ordêl ut to kêthande. Is thêr eng kwâd
dên, hwêrvr nên êwa tavlikt send, sa mot mån êne mêna
acht bilidsa; thêr ordêlth mån nêi tha sin thêr Wr.aldas
gåst an vs kêth vmbe over ella rjuchtfêrdich to birjuchtande, althus to dvande ne skil vs ordêl nåmmer fålikant
ut ne kvma. Ne dvath mån nên rjucht men vnrjucht, alsa
rist thêr twist ånd twispalt emong tha mânniska ånd stata,
thêrut sprût inlandiska orloch, hwêrthrvch ella homljath
ånd vrdåren wårth. Men, o dvmhêd. Dåhwila wi to
dvande send ekkorum to skådane, kvmth-et nidige folk
Findas mith hjara falska presterum jvw håva to råwande,
jvwa toghatera to skåndane, jvwa sêda to vrdva ånd to tha
lesta klåppath hja slåvona banda om jahwelikes frya hals.

UT-A SKRIFTA MINNOS.

Tha Nyhellênia * tham fon hira åjn nôme Min-erva hête,
god sêten was ånd tha Krêkalander † hja to met even hårde
minade as vs åjn folk, thå kêmon thêr svme forsta ånd
prestera vppe-ra burch ånd frêjon Min-erva hwêr of hjra
erva lêjon. Nyhellênia andere, mina erva drêg ik om
in mina bosm, hwât ik urven håv is ljafde vr wisdom,
rjucht ånd frydom, håv ik tham vrlêren, alsa ben ik
êlik an tha minniste jvvar slåvonena. Nw jêv ik rêd vm
nawet, men than skold ik vrkåpja tham. Tha hêra gvngon
wêi, ånd hripon al lakande, jvwer hêroga thjanra, wisa Hellênia. Thach thêrmitha miston hja hjara dol, hwand thåt
folk thåt hja minnade ånd hja folgade, nam this nôme to-n
êre nôme an. Tha hja sågon thåt hjara skot mist hêde,

---

* Nyhellenia, Nehalennia.
† Krekaland, het Krekenland, zoowel Groot Griekenland als Griekenland zelf.

titude, which must be sought after by all pious people, and must be possessed by all judges. If, therefore, it is desired to make laws and regulations which shall be permanent, they must be equal for all men. The judges must pronounce their decisions according to these laws. If any crime is committed respecting which no law has been made, a general assembly of the people shall be called, where judgment shall be pronounced in accordance with the inspiration of Wr-alda's spirit. If we act thus, our judgment will never fail to be right.

If instead of doing right, men will commit wrong, there will arise quarrels and differences among people and states. Thence arise civil wars, and everything is thrown into confusion and destroyed; and, O foolish people! while you are injuring each other the spiteful Finda's people with their false priests come and attack your ports, ravish your daughters, corrupt your morals, and at last throw the bonds of slavery over every freeman's neck.

FROM MINNO'S WRITINGS.

When Nyhalennia, whose real name was Min-erva, was well established, and the Krekalanders loved her as well as our own people did, there came some princes and priests to her citadel and asked Min-erva where her possessions lay. Hellenia answered, I carry my possessions in my own bosom. What I have inherited is the love of wisdom, justice, and freedom. If I lose these I shall become as the least of your slaves; now I give advice for nothing, but then I should sell it. The gentlemen went away laughing and saying, Your humble servants, wise Hellenia. But they missed their object, for the people took up this name as a name of honour. When they saw that

---

* *Nyhellenia* or *Nehalennia.*

† *Krekaland,* the Krekenland means Magna Grecia as well as Greece.

thå gvngon hja hja bihlvda ånd sêidon that hju-t folk hex-
nad hêde, men vs folk ånd tha goda Krêkalandar wêrde
aller wêikes that-et laster wêre. Enis kêmon hja ånd frê-
gon, as thv thån nên thjonster ne biste, hwat dêist thån
mitha åjar tham thv altid bi thi heste. Min-erva andere,
thisse åjar send that sinebyld fon Fryas rêdjêvinga, wêrin
vsa tokvmste forholen hlêit ånd fon êl thåt månneskalik
slachte; tid mot hja utbroda ånd wi moton wåka thåt-er
nên lêth an ne kvmth. Tha prestera, god sêid; men
hwêrto thjanath thene hund an thina fêra hand. Hellênia
andere, heth thene hårder nên skêper vmbe sin kidde at
sêmene to haldande? hwat thene hvnd is inna thjanest
thes skêphårder, bin ik iu Fryas tjanest, ik mot ovir
Fryas kidde wåka. That likath vs god to, sêdon tha
prestera; men seg vs, hwat is thju bitjvtenise fon thi
nachtule, ther immer boppa thin hole sit, is that ljucht-
skvwande djar altomet thet têken thinra klårsjanhêd. Nêan
andere Hellênia, hi helpt my hügja that er en slach fon
månuiska ovir hirtha omme dwålth, thêr evin lik hi in kårka
ånd hola hêma; thêr an tjuster frota, tach navt as hi, vmb
vs fon mûsa ånd ôra plåga to helpane, men renka to forsinna, tha ôra månniska hjara witskip to råwane, til thju
hja tham to bêtre müge fåta vmber slavona fon to måkjande
ånd hjara blod ut to sûgane, even as vampyra dva. Enis
kêmon hja mith en benda folk. Pest was over-et land
kvmen, hja sêidon, wi alle send to dvande, tha Goda to
offerja, til thju hja pest wêra müge. Nilst thv then navt
ne helpa hjara grimskip to stilane, jeftha hethste pest selva
ovir-et lånd brocht mith thinra kunsta. Nêan sôide Min-
erva, men ik ne kån nêne goda, thêr årg dvande send;
thêrvmbe ne kan ik navt frêja jef hja beter wrda willa. Ik
kån ên gode, thåt is Wr.aldas gåst; men thrvch tham er
god is, dvath er åk nen kwåd. Hwanath kvmth-et kwåd

their shot had missed they began to calumniate her, and
to say that she had bewitched the people; but our people
and the good Krekalanders understood at once that it was
calumny. She was once asked, If you are not a witch,
what is the use of the eggs that you always carry with
you? Min-erva answered, These eggs are the symbols of
Frya's counsels, in which our future and that of the whole
human race lies concealed. Time will hatch them, and we
must watch that no harm happens to them. The priests
said, Well answered; but what is the use of the dog on
your right hand? Hellenia replied, Does not the
shepherd have a sheep-dog to keep his flock together?
What the dog is to the shepherd I am in Frya's service.
I must watch over Frya's flocks. We understand that
very well, said the priests; but tell us what means
the owl that always sits upon your head, is that
light-shunning animal a sign of your clear vision?
No, answered Hellenia; he reminds me that there
are people on earth who, like him, have their homes in
churches and holes, who go about in the twilight, not, like
him, to deliver us from mice and other plagues, but to invent tricks to steal away the knowledge of other people, in
order to take advantage of them, to make slaves of them,
and to suck their blood like leeches. Another time they
came with a whole troop of people, when the plague was in
the country, and said: We are all making offerings to
the gods that they may take away the plague. Will you
not help to turn away their anger, or have you yourself
brought the plague into the land with all your arts?
No, said Min-erva; I know no gods that do evil, therefore
I cannot ask them to do better. I only know one good
spirit, that is Wr-alda's; and as he is good he never
does evil. Where, then, does evil come from? asked

thån wêi, frejath tha prestera.   Allet kwâd kvmth fon jow
ånd fon thêre dvmhêd thêra månniska, tham hjara selva fon
jow fensa lêta.   Jef thin drochten thån så bjustre god is,
wêrvmb wêrther-et kwâd thån navt, frêjath tha prestera.
Hellenia andere, Frya het vs vppe wêi brocht ånd thene
kroder that is tid, tham mot thåt ovrige dva.   With alle
rampun is rêd ånd help to findande, tha Wr.alda wil thåt
wi hja selva soka skilon, til thju wi sterik skile wertha
ånd wis.   Nillath wi navt, thån lêt-er vsa trul ut trulla,
til thju wi skilon erfåra, hwat nêi wisa dêdum ånd hwat
nêi dvma dêdum folgath.   Tha sêide-ne forst, ik skolde
wåna, that wêre betre, that to wêrande.   Hwel müglik,
endere Hellênia, hwand than skolde tha månniska bilywa
lik tåmade skêpa ; thv ånd tha prestera skolde-r than hoda
willa, men åk skêra ånd nêi thêra slacht benke fora.   Tach
alsa nil-t vs drochten navt, hi wil that wi ekkorum helpa,
men hi wil åk thåt jahweder fry sy ånd wis wrde.   Thåt is
åk vsa wille, thêrvmbe kjasth vs folk sin forsta, grêva,
rêdjêvar ånd alle båsa ånd måstera ut-a wisesta thêra goda
månniska, til thju allemånnalik sin best skil dva vmbe
wis ånd god to werthande.   Althus to dvande skilun wi
ênis wêta ånd anda folka lêra, that wis wêsa ånd wis dva
allêna lêith to salichhêd.   That likt en ordêl, sêidon tha
prestera, men aste nv mênste, that pest thrvch vsa dvmhêd
kvmth, skolde Nyhellênia thån wel sa god wêsa wille, vmbe
vs ewat fon thåt nya ljucht to lênande, hwêr vppa hju sa
stolte is.   Jes sêide Hellênia ; tha rokka ånd ôra füglon
kvmath allêna falla vp vûl ås, men pest minth navt allêna
vûl ås, men vûla sêd-plegum ånd fangnisa.   Wilstv nv that
pest fon-i wika ånd na wither ne kvma, thån mostv tha
. fangnisa wêi dva, ånd that i alla rên wrde fon binna ånd
fon bûta.   Wi willath bilåwa thåt thin red god sy, sêidon
tha prestera, men seg vs, ho skilum wi thêr alla

the priests. All the evil comes from you, and from the stupidity of the people who let themselves be deceived by you. If, then, your god is so exceedingly good, why does he not turn away the bad? asked the priests. Hellenia answered: Frya has placed us here, and the carrier, that is, Time, must do the rest. For all calamities there is counsel and remedy to be found, but Wr-alda wills that we should search it out ourselves, in order that we may become strong and wise. If we will not do that, he leaves us to our own devices, in order that we may experience the results of wise or foolish conduct. Then a prince said, I should think it best to submit. Very possibly, answered Hellenia; for then men would be like sheep, and you and the priests would take care of them, shearing them and leading them to the shambles. This is what our god does not desire, he desires that we should help one another, but that all should be free and wise. That is also our desire, and therefore our people choose their princes, counts, councillors, chiefs, and masters among the wisest of the good men, in order that every man shall do his best to be wise and good. Thus doing, we learn ourselves and teach the people that being wise and acting wisely can alone lead to holiness. That seems very good judgment, said the priests; but if you mean that the plague is caused by our stupidity, then Nyhellenia will perhaps be so good as to bestow upon us a little of that new light of which she is so proud. Yes, said Hellenia, but ravens and other birds of prey feed only on dead carrion, whereas the plague feeds not only on carrion but on bad laws and customs and wicked passions. If you wish the plague to depart from you and not return, you must put away your bad passions and become pure within and without. We admit that the advice is good, said the priests, but how shall we induce all the people under our rule

mânniska to krêja, thêr vnder vs weld send. Tha stand
Hellênia vp fon hira sêtel ånd kêth : Tha muska folgath
thene sêjar, tha folka hjara goda forsta, thêrvmbe ach-stv
to bijinnande mith thin selva ålsa rên to måkjande, that
stv thinna blikka in ånd utward mêi rjuchta svnder skåmråd to werthande to fara thin åjn mod. Men in stêde fon
thåt folk rên to måkjande heste vûla fêrsta utfonden,
hwêr vppa thåt folk al sa nåka sûpth, that hja to lesta lik
tha barga annath slip frota, vmbe that stv thin vûla lusta
bota mêi. Thåt folk bigost to jolande ånd to spotande.
Thêr thrvch ne thuradon hja nên strid wither an to spin-
nande. Nv skolde åjder wåna, thåt hja vral-et folk to
håpe hropen hêde vmbe vs algadur to-t land ut to driwande.
Nêan an stêde fon hja to bihluda gvngon hja allerwêikes,
åk to tha hêinde Krêkalana til tha Alpa ut to kêthane,
thåt et thene allervrste drochten hågth hêde sin wisa toghater Min-erva, to nômth Nyhellênia êmong tha månniska to sendane in overa sê mith-en ulk, vmbe tha månniska gode rêd to jêvane ånd that allermannalik, thêr hja
hêra wilde, rik ånd lukich skolde wertha, ånd ênis bås
skolde wertha ovir alle kêningkrik irtha.s. Hira byldnese
ståldon hja vppe hjara åltårum, jeftha hja vrsellade-t anda
dvma månniska. Hja kêthon allerwêikes rêd-jêvinga, thêr
hju nimmer jêven hêde, ånd tåladon wondera, thêr hju nå
dên hêde. Thrvch lesta wiston hja-ra selva master to
måkjande fon vsa êwa ånd setma, ånd thrvch wankêthinga
wiston hja alles to wisa ånd to vrbruda. Hja ståldon åk
fåmma vnder hjara hode, tha skinber vndere hoda fon
Fåsta* vsa forma êre moder, vmbe over thåt fråna ljucht
to wåkane. Men thåt ljucht hêde hja selva vpstoken,
ånd in stêde fon tha fåmkes wis to måkjande, ånd afternêi êmong thåt folk to senda, ta sjaka to lêvande ånd tha
bårn to lêrande, måkadon hja-ra dvm ånd dimme bi-t
ljucht ånd ne machten hja nå buta ne kvma. Ak wrdon

---

* Fåsta, Vesta, en de Vestaalsche maagden.

to agree to it? Then Hellenia stood up and said: The sparrows follow the sower, and the people their good princes, therefore it becomes you to begin by rendering yourselves pure, so that you may look within and without, and not be ashamed of your own conduct. Now, instead of purifying the people, you have invented foul festivals, in which they have so long revelled that they wallow like swine in the mire to atone for your evil passions. The people began to mock and to jeer, so that she did not dare to pursue the subject; and one would have thought that they would have called all the people together to drive us out of the land; but no, in place of abusing her they went all about from the heathenish Krekaland to the Alps, proclaiming that it had pleased the Almighty God to send his clever daughter Min-erva, surnamed Nyhellenia, over the sea in a cloud to give people good counsel, and that all who listened to her should become rich and happy, and in the end governors of all the kingdoms of the earth. They erected statues to her on all their altars, they announced and sold to the simple people advice that she had never given, and related miracles that she had never performed. They cunningly made themselves masters of our laws and customs, and by craft and subtlety were able to explain and spread them around. They appointed priestesses under their own care, who were apparently under the protection of Festa, our first Eeremoeder, to watch over the holy lamp; but that lamp they lit themselves, and instead of imbuing the priestesses with wisdom, and then sending them to watch the sick and educate the young, they made them stupid and ignorant, and never allowed them to come out. They were em-

---

* *Fêsta* is Vesta, or the Vestal Virgins.

hja to rêdjêvstare brukath, tach thi rêd was by skin ut
hjara mvlun; hwand hjara mvla wêron navt owers as tha
hropar, hwêr trvch tha prestera hjara gêrta utkêthon.

Tha Nyhellênia fallen was, wilden wi en ore moder
kjasa, svme wildon nêi Texlând vmbe thêr êne to frêjande,
men tha prestera tham by hira âjn folk thât rik wither in
hêde, nildon that ni hengja ând kêthon vs by-ra folk as
vn-frâna ut.

III. Ut-a Skrifta Minnos.

Tha-k althus wêi faren was mith mina ljvd fon Athenia,
kêmon wi to tha lesta an en êland thrvch min ljvd Krêta
hêten vm-a wilda krêta tham et folk anhyv by vsa kvmste.
Tha as hja sagon thât wi nên orloch an-t skêld foron,
wrdon hja mak, alsa-k et lest far en bota mit yserark en
havesmode ând en stada land wandelde. Thach tha wi
en stut sêten hêde ând hja spêradon that wi nên slavona
nêde, tha wêron hja vrstâlath, men tha-k-ra nw talt hêde
that wi êwa hêdon êlik to birjuchtande vr alla, tha wilde-t
folk âk fon sokka hâ. Tach skêrs hêdon hja tham, jefta
thât êlle land kêm anda tys. Tha forsta ând prestera
kêmon bârja, that wi hjara tjvth over hêrich mâkad hêde
ând thât folk kêm to vs vmbe hul ând skul. Tach thâ
tha forsta sagon thât hja hjara rik vrljasa skolda, thâ
jêvon hja thât folk frydom ând kêmon to my vmb-en êsega
bok. Thach thât folk was nên frydom wenth ând tha hêra
bilêvon welda nêi that ir god thochte. Thâ thi storn wr wêr,
bigoston hja twispalt among vs to sêja. Hja sêidon to min folk
that ik hjara help anhropen hêde vmbe standfâst kening to
werthande. Enis fand ik gif in min met, thâ as er ênis en skip

ployed as advisers, but the advice which seemed to come
from them was but the repetition of the behests of the
priests.   When Nyhellenia died, we wished to choose
another mother, and some of us wished to go to Texland
to look for her; but the priests, who were all-powerful
among their own people, would not permit it, and accused
us before the people of being unholy.

FROM THE WRITINGS OF MINNO.

When I came away from Athenia with my followers,
we arrived at an island named by my crew Kreta, because
of the cries that the inhabitants raised on our arrival.   When
they really saw that we did not come to make war, they
were quiet, so that at last I was able to buy a harbour in
exchange for a boat and some iron implements, and a piece
of land.   When we had been settled there a short time,
and they discovered that we had no slaves, they were very
much astonished; and when I explained to them that we
had laws which made everybody equal, they wished to have
the same; but they had hardly established them before
the whole land was in confusion.

The priests and the princes declared that we had excited
their subjects to rebellion, and the people appealed to us
for aid and protection.   When the princes saw that they
were about to lose their kingdom, they gave freedom to
their people, and came to me to establish a code of laws.
The people, however, got no freedom, and the princes
remained masters, acting according to their own pleasure.
When this storm had passed, they began to sow divisions
among us.   They told my people that I had invoked their
assistance to make myself permanent king.   Once I
found poison in my food.   So when a ship from

G

fon-t Fly by vs vrsêilde, ben ik thêrmith stolkens hinne
brith. — Tach min witherfara to lêtande, sa wil-k mith
thesa skêdnesa allêna sêga, that wi navt müge hêma mith
et Findas folk fon wêr thât et sy, hwand thât hja fvl send
mith falska renka, êwa to frêsane as hjara swête wina mith
dêjande fenin.

Ende wra skrifta Minnos.

HIR VNDER SEND THRÊ WÊTA, THÊR AFTER SEND THISSA SETMA MAKAD.

1. Allera mannalik wêt, thât i sin bihof mot, men wârth
âmmon sin bihof vnthalden, sa nêt nên man hwat er skil
dva vmbe sin lif to bihaldande.

2. Alle elte minniska werthat drongen a bârn to têlande,
wârth that wêrth, sa nêt nim man wath ârges thêrof
kvme mei.

3. Alrek wêt thât-i fry ând vnforlêth wil lêva, ând that
ôre that âk wille. Umbe sekur to wêsande send thesa
setma ând domar makad.

Thât folk Findas heth âk setma ând domar: men thissa
ne send navt nêi tha rjucht, men allêna to bâta thêra
prestera ând forsta, thana send hjara stâta immerthe fvl
twispalt ând mord.

1. Sahwersa imman nâd heth ând hi ne kan him selva
navt ne helpe, sa moton tha fâmna thât kvndich dva an
tha grêva. Thêrfar thât et en stolte Fryas navt ne focht
thât selva to dva.

2. Sa hwa ârm wârth thrvch tham hi navt wârka nil,
thêr mot to thât lând ut drêven werthia, hwand tha.lâfa
ând loma send lestich ând ârg tânkande: thêrvmbe âch
mân to wârane tham.

3. Jahwêder jong kerdel âch en brud to sêka ând is er
fif ând twintich sa âcht-er en wif to hâva.

Flyland sailed past, I quietly took my departure. Leaving alone, then, my own adventures, I will conclude this history by saying that we must not have anything to do with Finda's people, wherever it may be, because they are full of false tricks, fully as much to be feared as their sweet wine with deadly poison.

Here ends Minno's writing.

THESE ARE THE THREE PRINCIPLES ON WHICH THESE LAWS ARE FOUNDED.

1. Everybody knows that he requires the necessaries of life, and if he cannot obtain them he does not know how to preserve his life.

2. All men have a natural desire to have children, and if it is not satisfied they are not aware what evil may spring from it.

3. Every man knows that he wishes to live free and undisturbed, and that others wish the same thing.

To secure this, these laws and regulations are made.

The people of Finda have also their rules and regulations, but these are not made according to what is just— only for the advantage of priests and princes—therefore their states are full of disputes and murder.

1. If any man falls into a state of destitution, his case must be brought before the count by the maidens, because a high-minded Frisian cannot bear to do that himself.

2. If any man becomes poor because he will not work, he must be sent out of the country, because the cowardly and lazy are troublesome and ill-disposed, therefore they ought to be got rid of.

3. Every young man ought to seek a bride and to be married at five-and-twenty.

4. Is hwa fif ånd twiutich, ånd heth er nên êngâ, sa åch ek man him ut sin hus to wêrane. Ta knåpa åchon him te formyda. Nimth er thån nach nên êngâ, så mot mån hin dåd sêga, til thju hi ut of lande brude ånd hir nên årgenese nêva ne mêi.

5. Is hwa wrak, thån mot-er avbêr sêga, that nimman fon him to frêsane nach to duchtane heth. Så mei er kvma hwêr er wil.

6. Plêcht er åfternêi hordom, så mêi-r fluchta, ne fluchter navt, så is er an tha wrêke thêr bitrogna vrlêten, ånd nimman ne mêi helpa him.

7. Sahwersa åmmon eng god heth, ånd en ôther likt that thermête that i him thêran vrfate, sa mot-i thåt thrja vrjelda. Stêlth-i jeta rêis, thån mot hi nêi tha tinlânum. Wil thene bistêlne him fry jêva, så mêi-r thåt dva. Tha bêrth et wither sa ne mêi nimman him frydom jêva.

THISSA DOMAR SEND MAKAD FARA NYDIGA MANNISKA.

1. Sa hwa in håste mode tha ut nid an nen otheris lêja brekth, ågna ut stât, jeftha thoth, hok thåt et sy, sa mot thi lêtha bitallja hwat thene lêdar askth. Ne kan hi håt ni dva, så mot-er avbêr an im dên wertha, sa hi an thene ôre dêth. Nil hi thåt navt ut ne stonda, sa mot-i him to sina burch-fåm wenda, jef-i inna yser jeftha tin lâna mêi werka til sin skeld an sy, nêi thêr mêne dom.

2. Jef ther imman fvnden wårth alsa årg that-i en Fryas felth, hi mot et mit sina lif bitallja. Kan sina burch-fåm hin far altid nei tha tinlâna helpa êr er fat wrde, sy mêi thåt dva.

3. Sahwersa thi bona mêi biwisa mith vrkånda tju-

4. If a young man is not married at five-and-twenty, he must be driven from his home, and the younger men must avoid him. If then he will not marry, he must be declared dead, and leave the country, so that he may not give offence.

5. If a man is impotent, he must openly declare that no one has anything to fear from him, then he may come or go where he likes.

6. If after that he commits any act of incontinence, then he must flee away; if he does not, he. may be given over to the vengeance of those whom he has offended, and no one may aid him.

7. Any one who commits a theft shall restore it threefold. For a second offence he shall be sent to the tin mines. The person robbed may forgive him if he pleases, but for a third offence no one shall protect him.

These Rules are made for Angry People.

1. If a man in a passion or out of illwill breaks another's limb or puts out an eye or a tooth, he must pay whatever the injured man demands. If he cannot pay, he must suffer the same injury as he has done to the other. If he refuses this, he must appeal to the Burgtmaagd in order to be sent to work in the iron or tin mines until he has expiated his crime under the general law.

2. If a man is so wicked as to kill a Frisian, he must forfeit his own life; but if the Burgtmaagd can send him to the tin mines for his life before he is taken, she may do so.

3. If the prisoner can prove by proper witnesses that

gum that et by vnluk skên is, sa skil hi fry wêsa, men
bêrth et jetta rêis, sa mot-i tach nêi tha tinlânum, til
thju mân thêr thrvch formitha all vnerimde wrêka ånd
fêitha.

THIS SEND DOMAR FARA HORNINGA.

1. Hwa en ôtheris hvs ut nid thene râde hôn anstekt
nis nên Fryas, hi is en horning mith basterde blod. Mêi
mân hin bi thêr dêd bifâra, sa mot mân hin vppet fjvr
werpa. Hy mêi flya sa-r kân tach nårne skil-i sêkur wêsa
fara wrêkande hand.

2. Nên åfta Fryas skil ovira misslêga sinra nêste malja
nach kalta. Is hwa misdêdoch far-im selva, tha navt
frêselik far en ôra, så mêi hi him selva riuchta. Wårth-i
alsa årg that er frêslik wårth, sa mot mân-t anda grêva
bara; men is thêr hwa thêr en ôther åfterbåkis bitighat
in stêde foñ-t to dvande by tha grêva, tham is en horning.
Vpper mårk mot-i anda pêle bvnden wrde, sa that et jong
folk im anspêja mêi; åfter lâdath mân him overa mårka,
men navt nêi tha tinlâna, thrvch that en êrerâwer åk is to
frêsane.

3. Sahwersa thêr ênis imman wêre sa årg that i vs gvng
vrrêde by tha fyand, pâda ånd to pâda wes, vmbe vsa fly-
burga to nâka, jeftha thes nachtis thêrin to glupa, tham
wêre allêna wrocht ut Findas blod. Him skolde mân
mota barna. Tha stjurar skoldon sin mân ånd al sina
sibba nêi en fêr êland mota brånga ånd thêr ṣin ask
forstuva, til thju-r hyr nên feninige krûdon fon waxa ne
müge. Tha fâmna moton thån siu nâm utspêja in vr al
vsa stâta, til thju nên bårn sin nâm ne krêje ånd tha
alda him müge vrwerpa.

the death was accidental, he may go free; but if it happens a second time, he must go to the tin mines, in order to avoid any unseemly hatred or vengeance.

THESE ARE THE RULES CONCERNING BASTARDS.

1. If any man sets fire to another's house, he is no Frisian, he is a bastard. If he is caught in the act, he must be thrown into the fire; and wherever he may flee, he shall never be secure from the avenging justice.

2. No true Frisian shall speak ill of the faults of his neighbours. If any man injures himself, but does no harm to others, he must be his own judge; but if he becomes so bad that he is dangerous to others, they must bring it before the count. But if instead of going to the count a man accuses another behind his back, he must be put on the pillory in the market-place, and then sent out of the country, but not to the tin mines, because even there a backbiter is to be feared.

3. If any man should prove a traitor and show to our enemies the paths leading to our places of refuge, or creep into them by night, he must be the offspring of Finda; he must be burnt. The sailors must take his mother and all his relations to a desolate island, and there scatter his ashes, in order that no poisonous herbs may spring from them. The maidens must curse his name in all the states, in order that no child may be called by his name, and that his ancestors may repudiate him.

Orloch was vrtigen, men nêd was kvmen au sin stêd.
Nw wêron hyr thrê mânniska thêr-ek en buda kêren stêlon
fon asvndergane êjnhêra. Tha hja wrdon alle fat. Nw
gong thene êrosta to ånd brocht thene thjaf by tha skelte.
Tha fâmna thêr-vr kêtande sêidon allerwêis, that i dêu
hêde nêi rjucht. Thi ôra nom thene thjaf thåt kêren of
ånd lêth im forth mith frêto. Tha fâmna sêidon, hi heth
wel dên. Men thi thredde êjnhêr gvng nêi tha thjaf sin
hus thâ. Asser nw sach ho nêd thêr sin sêtel vpstålth
hêde, thâ gvng hi to bâk ånd kêrde wither mith en wêin
fol nêdthreftum, thêr hi nêd mith fon thêre hêrd of driwe.
Fryas fâmna hêdon by him omme wârath ånd sin dêd an
dat êvge bok skrêven, dahwile hja al sina lêka ut·fâchth
hêde. Thju êremoder was et sêid ånd hju lêt het kvndich
dva thrvch thåt êle lånd.

THAT·HYR VNDER STAT IS IN UT THA WAGAR THÊRE
WARABUROH WRITEN.

(Zie plaat I.)

Hwat hyr boppa ståt send thi têkna fon thåt jol. Thåt
is thåt forma sinnebild Wr.aldas, åk fon t-anfang jeftha-t
bijin, wêrnt tid kêm, thåt is thene Kroder thêr êvg mith
thåt jol mot ommehlåpa. Thana heth Frya thåt stand-
skrift måkad, thåt hja brukte to hira tex. Thâ Fåsta
êremoder wêre, heth hju-r thåt run ieftha hlåpande
skrift fon måkad. Ther Witkêning thåt is Sêkêning,
Godfrêiath thene alda heth thêr asvndergana telnomar fon
måkad får stand ånd rvnskrift bêde. T is thêrvmbe navt
to drok that wi-r jêrliks ênis fêst vr fyrja. Wy mügon
Wr.alda êvg thank to wya thåt hi sin gåst sa herde in vr vsa
êthla heth fåra lêtn. Vnder hira tid heth Finda åk en skrift

ᚦAT ᚦIR VNDE STAT IS INUT ᚦA WAQAR ᚦERE
WARA.BURCᚦ WRITEN.

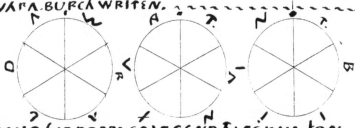

ᚦWAT ᚦIR BOPPA STAT SENDᚦI TÉ KNA ton
ᚦATIOL ᚦAT ISᚦAT fORMA SINNE BILD WRAL
DAS. AKtON T.ANᚦAIꝺ iEᚦA T BIIIN WQRUT
TID kEM. ᚦAT IS ᚦENE kRODER ᚦGR GVꝺ MIᚦ
ᚦAT iOL M OF OMMEᚦLAPE. ᚦANA ᚦEᚦ fRIA
ᚦAT STANDS kRIfT ᚦAT ᚦIA BRUKTE TO ᚦIRA
TEX. ᚦA fASTA GRE MODEF WERE ᚦEᚦ ᚦIU
.R ᚦAT RUN iEᚦA ᚦᚦ PANDE SKRIfE ton MAK
AD. ᚦER WITKENIꝺ. ᚦAT IS SEKENIꝺ. ꝺOD.
fREiAᚦ. ᚦENE ALDA.ᚦEᚦ ᚦGF ASVNDEFꝺANA
TEL NOMAF ton MAKAD ᚦᚦR STAND AND
RUN SKRIfT BEDE. T.IS ᚦGRVMBE NAVT TO DROK
ᚦAT WIᴿiERLIKS GNIS fEST VF fRRIA.WᚦMꝺꝺ
ON WRALDA GVꝺ ᚦANKtOWᚦA ᚦAT ᚦIS IN
ꝺAST SA ᚦEFDE.IN VR VSA GᚦLA ᚦEᚦ fARA
LGTN. VNDEF ᚦI RATID ᚦEᚦ fINDA AKENS kR
Ifr UFfVNDEN. MEN ᚦAT WERE SA ᚦAꝺfAᴿ
.ANDE ANDfVL MIᚦ fRISLA ANDkROLUM
ᚦAT ᚦA AffERkVMANDA ᚦGFOf ᚦIU BIfIVD
NESE RIA VFLEREN ᚦAVE. AᚦERNGI ᚦAVON
ᚦIA VS SKRIfT LGRED BINOMA ᚦA fINNA.
ᚦA ᚦY RIAR AND ᚦA kREKA LANDAR. MEN ᚦIA
NISTON NAVT ꝺOD ᚦAT ET ton ET iOL MAKAD
WAS ANDᚦATEᴿᚦGRVMBE ALTID S KREVEN
ᚦ MAKAD-

Page 45 of the manuscript of the book of Adelas Followers

Pl.1.

War had come to an end, but famine came in its place.
There were three men who each stole a sack of corn from
different owners, but they were all caught. The first
owner brought his thief to the judge, and the maidens
said everywhere that he had done right. The second
owner took the corn away from his thief and let him go
in peace. The maidens said he has done well. The third
owner went to the thief's house, and when he saw what
misery was there, he went and brought a waggon-load of
necessaries to relieve their distress. Frya's maidens came
around him and wrote his deed in the eternal book,
and wiped out all his sins. This was reported to the
Eeremoeder, and she had it made known over the whole
country.

WHAT IS WRITTEN HEREUNDER IS INSCRIBED ON THE WALLS OF WARABURGT.

(See Plate I.)

What appears at the top is the signs of the Juul—that
is, the first symbol of Wr-alda, also of the origin or beginning from which Time is derived; this is the Kroder,
which must always go round with the Juul. According
to this model Frya formed the set hand which she used
to write her Tex. When Fasta was Eeremoeder she made
a running hand out of it. The Witkoning—that is, the
Sea-King Godfried the Old—made separate numbers for
the set hand and for the runic hand. It is therefore
not too much that we celebrate it once a year. We
may be eternally thankful to Wr-alda that he allowed
his spirit to exercise such an influence over our forefathers.

In her time Finda also invented a mode of writing,

utfvnden, men thât wêre sa hâgfârende ånd fvl mith frisla
ånd krolum, thât tha afterkvmanda thêrof thju bitjudnese
ring vrlêren hâve. Afternêi hâvon hja vs skrift lêred binoma
tha Finna, tha Thyrjar ånd tha Krekalander. Men hja
niston navt god, thât-et fon et jol mâkad was ånd that-et
thêrumbe altid skrêven wrde moste mith son om. Thêrby
wildon hja thât hjara skrift vnlêsbêr skolde wêsa far ora
folkum, hwand hja hâvath altid hêmnesa. Thus to
dvanda send hja herde fon-a wis râkath, thêrmêtha, that
ta bârn tha skriftun hja-rar aldrum amper lêsa en mûga;
dahwile wy vsa alderaldesta skriftun êvin rêd lêsa mûga as
thêra thêr jester skrêven send.

Hir is thât stand skrift, thêrvnder thât run skrift, forth
tha tâlnomar a byder wisa.

(Zie plaat II.)

THAT STÊT VP ALLE BURGUM ESKRÊVEN.

Êr thêre årge tid kêm was vs lånd thât skênueste in
wr.alda.   Svnne rês hager ånd thêr was sjelden frost.
Anda bâma ånd trêjon waxton frügda ånd nochta, thêr nw
vrlêren send.   Among tha gårs-sêdum hedon wi navt
alena kêren, ljaver ånd blyde, men âk swete thêr lik
gold blikte ånd thât mån vndera svnnastrêla bakja kvste.
Jêron ne wrde navt ne telath, hwand thât êne jêr was
alsa blyd as et ôthera.   An tha êne side wrdon wi thrvch
Wr.aldas sê bisloten, hwêrvp nên folk buta vs navt
fara ne mochte nach kvnde.   Anda ôre side wrden wi
thrvch thât brêde Twisklånd vmtunad, hwêr thrvch
thât Findas folk navt kvma ne thvradon, fon ovira
tichta walda ånd ovir it wilde kwik.   By morne paldon
wi ovir it uter ende thes aster-sê, by êvind an thene

but that was so high-flown and full of flourishes that her
descendants have soon lost the meaning of it.

Afterwards they learned our writing—that is, the Finns,
the Thyriers, and the Krekalanders—but they did not know
that it was taken from the Juul, and must therefore always
be written round like the sun. Furthermore, they wished
that their writing should be illegible by other people, because they always had matters to conceal. In doing this
they acted very unwisely, because their children could only
with great difficulty read the writings of their predecessors,
whereas our most ancient writings are as easy to read as
those that were written yesterday.

Here is a specimen of the set hand and of the running
hand, as well as of the figures, in both.

(See Plate II.)

THIS STANDS INSCRIBED UPON ALL CITADELS.

Before the bad time came our country was the most
beautiful in the world. The sun rose higher, and there was
seldom frost. The trees and shrubs produced various
fruits, which are now lost. In the fields we had not only
barley, oats, and rye, but wheat which shone like gold,
and which could be baked in the sun's rays. The years
were not counted, for one was as happy as another.

On one side we were bounded by Wr-alda's Sea, on which
no one but us might or could sail; on the other side we
were hedged in by the broad Twiskland (Tusschenland,
Duitschland), through which the Finda people dared not
come on account of the thick forests and the wild
beasts.

Eastward our boundary went to the extremity of
the East Sea, and westward to the Mediterranean

middelsê, alsa wi buta tha littiga wel twelif gráta swete riustrama hêdon, vs thrvch Wr.alda jêven vmb vs lánd elte to haldane ánd vmb us wigandlik folk tha wêi to wisana nêi sina sê.

Tha owira thissar rin strama wrdon tomet algadur thrvch vs folk bisêton, ák tha fjelda an thju Rêne fon t êna enda alon et ôre ende thâ.

To jenst-vr tha Dênamarka ánd that Juttarlánd hêdon wi folkplantinga mith en burchfâm, dâna wonon wi kâper ánd yser, bijvnka târ, pâk ánd svma ôr bihof. To jenst vr vs formêlich Westland thêr hêdon wi Brittanja mith sina tinlâna. Brittanja thât was thât lánd thêra bannalinga, thêr mith hulpe hjarar burchfâm wêi brith wêron vmbe hira lif to bihâldana. Thach for that hja navt to bâk kvma ne skolde, warth er êrost en B to fâra hjara stâr priked, tha bana mith râde blod farve ánd tha ôra misdêdar mith blâwe farve. Buta ánd bihalva hêdon vsa stjurar ánd kâpljvd mêni loge anda hêinde Krêkalanda ánd to Lydia. In vr Lydia thêr send tha swarta minniska. Thâ vs lánd sâ rum ánd grât wêre, hêdon wi fêlo asondergana nâmon. Thêra tham saton biâsten tha Dênemarka wrdon Jutta hêton, uthâvede hja tomet navt owers ne dêdon as barn-stên juta. Hja tham thêr satou vppa êlanda wrdon Lêtne hêten, thrvchdam hja mêst al vrlêten lêvadon. Alle strând ánd skor hêmar fon-a Dênemarka alont thêre sândfal nw Skelda wrdon Stjurar,* Sêkâmpar,† ánd Angelara‡ hêton. Angelara sâ hêton mân to fora tha butafiskar vmbe that hja alan mith angel jefta kol fiskton ánd nimmer nên netum. Thêra thêr thâna til tha hêinde Krêkalânda sâton, wrdon blât Kâdhêmar hêten, thrvch tham hja ninmerthe buta foron. Thêra thêr ia da hâge marka sâton, thêr anna Twisklanda pâlon, wrdon Saxmanna hêton, uthâwede hja immer wêpned wêron vr thât wilde kwik ánd vrwildarda Britne. Thêr to

---

* Stjurar, Sturii.　　† Sêkâmpar, Sicambri.　　‡ Angelara, Angli.

Sea; so that besides the small rivers we had twelve large rivers givèn us by Wr-alda to keep our land moist, and to show our seafaring men the way to his sea.

The banks of these rivers were at one time entirely inhabited by our people, as well as the banks of the Rhine from one end to the other. Opposite Denmark and Jutland we had colonies and a Burgtmaagd. Thence we obtained copper and iron, as well as tar and pitch, and some other necessaries. Opposite to us we had Britain, formerly Westland, with her tin mines.

Britain was the land of the exiles, who with the help of their Burgtmaagd had gone away to save their lives; but in order that they might not come back they were tattooed with a B on the forehead, the banished with a red dye, the other criminals with blue. Moreover, our sailors and merchants had many factories among the distant Krekalanders and in Lydia. In Lydia (Lybia) the people are black. As our country was so great and extensive, we had many different names. Those who wère settled to the east of Denmark were called Jutten,' because often they did nothing else than look for amber (*jutten*) on the shore. Those who lived in the islands were called Letten, because they lived an isolated life. All those who lived between Denmark and the Sandval, now the Scheldt, were called Stuurlieden (pilots), Zeekampers (naval men), and Angelaren (fishermen). The Angelaren were men who fished in the sea, and were so named because they used lines and hooks instead of nets. From there to the nearest part of Krekaland the inhabitants were called Kadhemers, because they never went to sea but remained ashore.

Those who were settled in the higher marches bounded by Twisklanden (Germany) were called Saxmannen, because they were always armed against the wild beasts and the savage Britons. Besides

---

* *Stjurar*, in Latin *Sturii*.　　† *Sêkâmpar*, in Latin *Sicambri*.
‡ *Angelara*, in Latin *Angli*.

boppa hêdon wi tha nôma Landsâton, Mârsata,* ånd Holt-
jefta Wodsâta.

Ho Arge Tid kêm.

Hêl thene sümer was svnne åftere wolkum skolen, as
wilde hja irtha navt ne sja. Wind reston in sina bûdar,
werthrvch rêk ånd stom lik sêla boppa hus ånd polon
stand. Loft wårth althus drov ånd dimme, ånd inna tha
hirta thêra månniska was blydskip nach früchda. To
midden thisre stilnise fång irtha an to bêvande lik as hju
stårvande wêre. Berga splyton fon ekkorum to spêjande
fjvr ånd logha, ôra svnkon in hira skåt del, ånd thêr hju
êrost fjelda hêde; hêjade hju berga vppa. Aldland † trvch
tha stjurar Atland hêten svnk nyther ånd thåt wilde hef
ståpton alsa nåka wr berg ånd dêlon, that ella vndere sê
bidvlwen wêre. Fêlo månniska wrdon in irtha bidobben,
ånd fêlo thêr et fjvr vnkêmen wêron, kêmon thêrnêi innet
wêter vm. Navt allêna inda landa Findas spêidon berga
fjvr, men åk in-t Twisk-land. Walda bårnadon thêrthrvch
åfter ekkorum ånd thå wind dåna wêi kêm, thå wåjadon
vsa landa fvl ask. Rinstråma wrdon vrlêid ånd by hjara
mvda kêmon nêja êlanda fon sand ånd drivande kwik.
Thrju jêr was irtha alsa to lydande; men tha hju bêter
wêre macht mån hira vvnda sja. Fêlo landa wêron
vrsvnken, ôra uta sê rêsen ånd thåt Twisk-land to fåra-n
halfdêl vntwalt. Bånda Findas folk kêmon tha lêtogha
rumtne bifåra. Vsa wêibritne vrdon vrdelgen jefta hja
wrdon hjara harlinga. Thå warth wåkandom vs dvbbeld
boden ånd tid lêrd vs that êndracht vsa stårikste burch is.

Thit stêt inna Waraburch by thêre Aldega Mvda wryt.

Thju Wâraburch nis nên fåmnaburch, men thêr in wrdon

---

these we had the names Landzaten (natives of the land), Marzaten (natives of the fens), and Woud or Hout zaten (natives of the woods).

HOW THE BAD TIME CAME.

During the whole summer the sun had been hid behind the clouds, as if unwilling to look upon the earth. There was perpetual calm, and the damp mist hung like a wet sail over the houses and the marshes. The air was heavy and oppressive, and in men's hearts was neither joy nor cheerfulness. In the midst of this stillness the earth began to tremble as if she was dying. The mountains opened to vomit forth fire and flames. Some sank into the bosom of the earth, and in other places mountains rose out of the plain. Aldland, called by the seafaring people, Atland, disappeared, and the wild waves rose so high over hill and dale that everything was buried in the sea. Many people were swallowed up by the earth, and others who had escaped the fire perished in the water.

It was not only in Finda's land that the earth vomited fire, but also in Twiskland (Germany). Whole forests were burned one after the other, and when the wind blew from that quarter our land was covered with ashes. Rivers changed their course, and at their mouths new islands were formed of sand and drift.

During three years this continued, but at length it ceased, and forests became visible. Many countries were submerged, and in other places land rose above the sea, and the wood was destroyed through the half of Twiskland (Germany). Troops of Finda's people came and settled in the empty places. Our dispersed people were exterminated or made slaves. Then watchfulness was doubly impressed upon us, and time taught us that union is force.

THIS IS INSCRIBED ON THE WARABURGT BY THE ALDEGAMUDE.

The Waraburgt is not a maiden's city, but the place where

---

* *Mârsata*, in Latin *Marsacii*.   † *Aldland*, in Latin *Atlantis.*

alla uthêmeda ånd vrlandeska thinga wârath, thêr
mitbrocht binne thrvch tha stjurar. Hju is thri pêla, thât
is en half ty sûdwarth fon Mêdêa-sblik lêgen. Alsa is
thât fôrword: berga nygath thinna krunna, wolka ånd
strâma wên. Jes. Skênland * blôst, slâvona folka stôp-
path vppat thin klât, o Frya. Alsa is thju skêdnesse.
100 ånd 1 jêr † nêi that åldland svnken is, kêm thêr
ut-et åsta en folk wêi. Thât folk was vrdrêven thrvch en
ôther folk, åfter vs twisk land krêjon hja twispalt, hja
skifton hjara selva an twam hâpa, ek hêr gvng sines
wêiges. Fon-t êne dêl nis nên tâl to vs ne kêmen, men
thât ôre dêl fyl åfter to vs Skênland. Skênland was
sunnich bifolkath, ånd anda åfter-kåd thât sunnichste fon
al. Thêrvmbe machton hja-t svnder strid wrwinna, ånd
uthâwede hja ôwers nên lêth ne dêdon, nildon wi thêrvr
nên orloch ha. Nw wi hjam hâvon kånna lêred, så willath
wi ovir hjara sêda skriwa, åfternêi ho-t vs mith hjam for-
gungen is. Thât folk was navt ne wild lik fêlo slachta
Findas, men êlik anda Êgipta-landar, hja hâvath prestera
lik tham ånd nw hja kårka håve åk byldon. Tha prestera
send tha engosta hêra, hja hêton hjara selva Mågjara,
hjara aller ovirste hêt Magy, hi is hâvedprester ånd kêning
mith ên, allet ôre folk is nul in-t siffer ånd êllik ånd al
vnder hjara weld. Thât folk nêth navt ênis en nôme,
thrvch vs send hja Finna hêten, hwand afskên hjara fêrsta
algadur drov ånd blodich send, thach send hja thêr alsa
fin vp, that wi thêr bi åfter stâne, forth ne send hja navt
to binydane, hwand hja send slâvona fon tha presterum
ånd jeta fül årger fon hjara mêninga. Hja mênath
that ella fvl kvada gâston is, thêr inda månniska ånd
djara gluppe, men fon Wr.aldas gâst nêton hja
nawet. Hja hâvath stêne wêpne, tha Magjara kâpra.
Tha Magjara tellath that hja tha ˙ årge gâston

---

* Skênland, Scania, Scandinavia.   † 219-3101 = 2092 v. Chr.

all the foreign articles brought by sailors were stored. It lies three hours south from Medeasblik.

Thus is the Preface.

Hills, bow your heads; weep, ye streams and clouds. Yes. Schoonland (Scandinavia) blushes, an enslaved people tramples on your garment, O Frya.

This is the History.

One hundred and one years after the submersion of Aldland a people came out of the East. That people was driven by another. Behind us, in Twiskland (Germany), they fell into disputes, divided into two parties, and each went its own way. Of the one no account has come to us, but the other came in the back of our Schoonland, which was thinly inhabited, particularly the upper part. Therefore they were able to take possession of it without contest, and as they did no other harm, we would not make war about it. Now that we have learned to know them, we will describe their customs, and after that how matters went between us. They were not wild people, like most of Finda's race; but, like the Egyptians, they have priests and also statues in their churches. The priests are the only rulers; they call themselves Magyars, and their headman Magy. He is high priest and king in one. The rest of the people are of no account, and in subjection to them. This people have not even a name; but we call them Finns, because although all the festivals are melancholy and bloody, they are so formal that we are inferior to them in that respect. But still they are not to be envied, because they are slaves to their priests, and still more to their creeds. They believe that evil spirits abound everywhere, and enter into men and beasts, but of Wr-alda's spirit they know nothing. They have weapons of stone, the Magyars of copper. The Magyars affirm that they can exorcise

---

* Skênland or Scaudinavia.   † 2193 – 101 is 2092 before Christ.

banna ånd vrbanna mügon, thêr vr is-t folk ôlan in
ange frêse ånd vppira wêsa nis nimmer nên blydskip
to bisjan. Thâ hja god sêten wêron, sochton tha Magjara
athskip bi vs, hja bogadon vp vsa tâl ånd sêdum, vp vs fja
ånd vppa vs ysere wêpne, thêr hja gêrn to fori hjara goldun
ånd sulvere syrhedum wandela wilde, ånd hjara tjoth hildon hja immerthe binna tha pêlon, men thât vrskalkton
vsa wâkendom. Achtantich jêr forther, just wêr-et jol-
fêrste, thêr kêmon hja vnwarlinge lik snêi thrvch stornewind drêwen ovir vsa landa to runnande. Thêr navt flya
machton wrdon vrdên, Frya wârth anhropen, men tha
Skênlandar hêdon hira rêd warlâsed. Thâ wrdon krâfta
sâmlath, thri pêlun fon Goda-hisburch,* wrdon hja wither
stonden, tha orloch bilêv. Kât jefta Kâter-inne, alsa hête
thju fâm, thêr burchfâm to Goda burch was. Kât was
stolte ånd hâchfâranda, thêrvmbe ne lêt hju nên rêd ni
follistar anda Moder ne frêja. Men thâ tha burchhêra
thât fâta, thâ svndon hja selva bodon nêi Texlând nêi
thêre Moder thâ. Minna alsa was thêre Moder-is nôme,
lêt âla tha stjurar mânja ånd âl-et othera jongk folk fon
Ast-flyland ånd fon tha Dênnemarkum. Ut thesse
tocht is thju skydnese fon Wodin bern, sa-r vppa burgum wryten is ånd bir êskrêven. Anda Alder-gâmude†
thêr reste en alde sêkâning. Sterik was sin nôme ånd
tha hrop vr sina dêda was grât. Thisse alde rob hêde thrê
nêva; Wodin thene aldeste hêmde to Lumka-mâkja‡ bi
thêre É-mude to Ast-flyland by sin eldrum t-us. Ênes was
er hêrman wêst. Tünis ånd Inka wêron sêkâmper ånd
just nw bi hjara fâderja anda Aldergâ-mude t-vs. As tha
jonga kâmpar nw bi ekkôrum kêmon, kêron hja Wodin
to hjara hêrman jefta kâning ut, ånd tha sêkâmpar kêron Tünis to-ra sêkâning ånd Inka to hjara skelte bî thêr
nacht. Tha stjurar gvngon thâ nêi tha Dênnemarka fâra,
thêr nâmon hja Wodin mith sin wigandlika landwêr in.

---

* Goda-hisburch, Gothenburg.
† Alderga, Ouddorp (bij Alkmaar).
‡ Lumkamâkja bithêre Emuda, Embden.

and recall the evil spirits, and this frightens the people, so that you never see a cheerful face. When they were well established, the Magyars sought our friendship, they praised our language and customs, our cattle and iron weapons, which they would willingly have exchanged for their gold and silver ornaments, and they always kept their people within their own boundaries, and that outwitted our watchfulness.

Eighty years afterwards, just at the time of the Juul-feest, they overran our country like a snowstorm driven by the wind. All who could not flee away were killed. Frya was appealed to, but the Schoonlanders (Scandinavians) had neglected her advice. Then all the forces were assembled, and three hours from Godasburgt they were withstood, but war continued. Kat or Katerine was the name of the priestess who was Burgtmaagd of Godasburgt. Kat was proud and haughty, and would neither seek counsel nor aid from the mother; but when the Burgtheeren (citizens) knew this, they themselves sent messengers to Texland to the Eeremoeder. Minna—this was the name of the mother—summoned all the sailors and the young men from Oostflyland and Denmark. From this expedition the history of Wodin sprang, which is inscribed on the citadels, and is here copied. At Aldergamude there lived an old sea-king whose name was Sterik, and whose deeds were famous. This old fellow had three nephews. Wodin, the eldest, lived at Lumkamakia, near the Eemude, in Oost-flyland, with his parents. He had once commanded troops. Teunis and Inka were naval warriors, and were just then staying with their father at Aldergamude. When the young warriors had assembled together, they chose Wodin to be their leader or king, and the naval force chose Teunis for their sea-king and Inka for their admiral. The navy then sailed to Denmark, where they took on board Wodin and his valiant host.

---

* Goda-hisburch is Gothenburg.
† Alderga is Ouddorp, near Alkmaar.
‡ Lumkamâkja bithêre Emuda is Embden.

Wînd was rum ånd alsa wêron hja an en åmerîng* to
Skênland. Thâ. tha northeska brothar ra selva by-m
fogath hêde, dêlde Wodîn sin weldich hêr an thri wiga.
Frya was hjara wêpenhrop ånd så hi båkward sloch tha
Finnen ånd Mågjara as of et bårn wêron. Thâ thene
Mågy fornôm ho sin ljvd al ombrocht wrdon, thâ sand hi
bodon mith ståf ånd krone. Hja sêidon to Wodin, o thv
alra gråteste thêra kåningar, wi send skeldich, thach al
hwat wi dên håve is ut nêd dên. Je mêne that wi jvw
brothar willengklik anfat håve, men wi send thrvch vsa
fyanda forth-fêtereth ånd thi alle send vs jeta vppa hakka.
Wi håvath often helpe an thinre burchfåm frêjath, men
hja neth vs navt ne meld. Thene Mågy sêith, så hwersa
wi ekkôrum to tha hålte vrdva, så skilun tha wilda skep-
hårdar kêmon ånd vs algådur vrdva. Thene Mågy heth
fül rikdom, men hi heth sjan that Frya weldiger is as al
vsa gåston et sêmine. Hi wil sin håved in hira skåt del
ledsa. Thv bist thene wigandlikste kåning irthas, thin
folk is fon yser. Warth vsa kåning ånd wi alle willath
thin slåvona wêsa. Hwat skolde that êr-rik får-i wêsa,
aste tha wilda wither to låk driwa koste, vsa sêfyra skolde-t
rondblêsa ånd vsa måra skoldon jv vral fårut gå.
Wodin was sterik, wostånd wigandlîk, men hi nas navt klår
sjande, thêrthrvch wårth i in hjar mêra fvngen ånd thrvch
thene Mågy kroneth. Rju fêlo stjurar ånd land-wêrar, tham
thisse kêr navt ne sinde, brûdon stolkes hinne, Kåt mith
nêmande, men Kåt thêr navt to fåra thêre Moder ner to fåra
thêre mêna acht forskine nilde, jompade wr bord. Thâ kêm
stornewind ånd fêtere tha skêpa vppa skorra fonna Denne-
mar kum del svnder enkel man to mistane. Afternêi håvon
hjatha strêt Kåtsgat† hêten. Thâ Wodin kroned was, gvng-er

---

* Amering, nog in N.-Holland in gebruik, beteekent daar : ademtocht,
oogenblik. Cf. Kiliaan in voce.
† Kåtsgat, het Kattegat.

The wind was fair, so they arrived immediately in
Schoonland. When the northern brothers met together,
Wodin divided his powerful army into three bodies. Frya
was their war-cry, and they drove back the Finns and
Magyars like children. When the Magy heard how his
forces had been utterly defeated, he sent messengers with
truncheon and crown, who said to Wodin : O almighty
king, we are guilty, but all that we have done was done
from necessity. You think that we attacked your brothers
out of illwill, but we were driven out by our enemies, who
are still at our heels. We have often asked your Burgtmaagd for help, but she took no notice of us. The
Magy says that if we kill half our numbers in fighting with each other, then the wild shepherds will come
and kill all the rest. The Magy possesses great riches,
but he has seen that Frya is much more powerful than all
our spirits together. He will lay down his head in her
lap. You are the most warlike king on the earth, and
your people are of iron. Become our king, and we will all
be your slaves. What glory it would be for you if you
could drive back the savages ! Our trumpets would re-
sound with your praises, and the fame of your deeds would
precede you everywhere. Wodin was strong, fierce, and
warlike, but he was not clear-sighted, therefore he was
taken in their toils, and crowned by the Magy.

Very many of the sailors and soldiers to whom this
proceeding was displeasing went away secretly, taking
Kat with them. But Kat, who did not wish to appear before either the mother or the general assembly,
jumped overboard. Then a storm arose and drove the
ships upon the banks of Denmark, with the total destruction of their crews. This strait was afterwards
called the Kattegat. When Wodin was crowned, he

---

* *Amering,* still in use in North Holland to signify a breath or a twinkling
of an eye.
† Kâtsgat is the Kattegat.

vppa wilda lôs; thi wêron al rutar, lik een hêjel buje
kêmon hja ajn Wodin-is hêr, men lik en twyrne wind
wendon hja omme ånd ne thvradon nå wither forskina.
As Wodin nw to båk kêm, jav thene Mågy him sin
toghater to-n wîf. Afternei wårth-i mith krûdon birêkad,
men thêr wêron tawerkrûdon mong, hwand Wodin warth
bi grådum alsa sêr vrmêten, that-i Frya ånd Wraldas
gåst miskåna ånd spota thvrade, thawyla hi sin frya hals
bog to fåra falska drochten-likande byldum. Sin rik
hilde sjvgun jêr, thå vrdwind-ir, Thene Mågy sêide that-
er mong hjara godon* vpnimeth wêre, ånd that hi fon
thêr over hjam welda, men vs folk lakton vmbe tin tål.
Thå Wodin en stût wêi wêst hêde, kêm thêr twispalt, wi
wildon en ôra kåning kjasa, men thåt nilde thene Mågy
navt me hengja. Hi wêrde that et en rjucht wêre, him
thrvch sina drochtne jêven. Buta ånd bihalva thissa twist,
sa was thêr jet-ên emong sin Mågjara ånd Finna, thêr Frya
ner Wodin êra navt nilde, men thi Mågy dêde as-t im
sinde, hwand sin toghater hêde en svn bi Wodin wvnen,
ånd nw wilde thene Mågy that thisse fon en håge kom-of
wêsa skolde. Thawyla alle sanade ånd twista, krônade hi
thene knåp to kåning ånd stålade hin sels as foged ånd
foramond jefta rêdjêvar an. Thêra thêr mår hildon fon
hjara balg as fon thåt rjucht, tham lêton him bidobba,
men tha goda brûdon wêi. Fêlo Mågjara flodon mith
hjara ljvda båk ward, ånd tha stjurar gvngon to skip ånd
en hêr fon drista Finna gvngen as rojar mitha.

Nw kvmath tha skêdnese fon nêf Tünis ånd sin nêf
Inka êrost rjucht vppet pat.

THIT ELLA STET NAVT ALLÊNA VPPER WARABURCH MEN OK
TO THÊRE BURCH STAVIA, THÊR IS LIDSEN AFTERE
HAVE FON STAVRE.

Tha Tünis mith sinum skêpum to honk kêra wilde, gvng-i
thet forma vppa Dånnemarka of, men hi ne macht thêr navt

---

* Wodin, Odin, Wodan.

attacked the savages, who were all horsemen, and fell
upon Wodin's troops like a hailstorm; but like a whirl-
wind they were turned back, and did not dare to appear
again. When Wodin returned, Magy gave him his daughter
to wife. Whereupon he was incensed with herbs; but
they were magic herbs, and by degrees he became so
audacious that he dared to disavow and ridicule the spirits
of Frya and Wr-alda, while he bent his free head before
the false and deceitful images. His reign lasted seven
years, and then he disappeared. The Magy said that he
was taken up by their gods and still reigned over us, but
our people laughed at what they said. When Wodin had
disappeared some time, disputes arose. We wished to
choose another king, but the Magy would not permit it.
He asserted that it was his right given him by his idols.
But besides this dispute there was one between the Magyars and Finns, who would honour neither Frya nor
Wodin; but the Magy did just as he pleased, because his
daughter had a son by Wodin, and he would have it that
this son was of high descent. While all were disputing
and quarrelling, he crowned the boy as king, and set up
himself as guardian and counsellor. Those who cared
more for themselves than for justice let him work his own
way, but the good men took their departure. Many
Magyars fled back with their troops, and the sea-people
took ship, accompanied by a body of stalwart Finns as
rowers.

Next comes upon the stage the history of Neef Teunis
and Neef Inka.

ALL THIS IS INSCRIBED NOT ONLY ON THE WARABURGT, BUT
ALSO ON THE BURGT STAVIA, WHICH LIES BEHIND THE
PORT OF STAVRE.

When Teunis wished to return home, he went first
towards Denmark; but he might not land there, for so the

---

* Wodin is Odin or Wodan. *the first.*

ne landa, thât hêde thju Moder bisjowath. Ak et Flyland
ne macht-er navt ne landa ånd forth nårne. Hi skold alsa
mith sinum ljvdum fon lek ånd brek omkomth håve,
thêr vmbe gvngon hja thes nachtis tha landa biråwa ånd
fåra bi dêi. Alsa alinga thêre kåd forth farande kêmon hja to thêre folkplanting Kådik,* althus hêten
vmbe that hjara have thrvch êne stênene kådik formath
was. Hir selladon hja allerhanne liftochta, men Tutja
thju burchfåm nilde navt dåja that hja-ra selva nither
setta. Thå hja rêd wêron krêjon hja twist. Tünis wilde
thrvch thju strête fon tha middelsê vmbe to fårane får
tha rika kåning fon Egiptalandum, lik hi wel êr dên
hêde, men Inka sêide, that-i sin nocht hêde fon al et
Findas folk. Inka mênde that er byskin wel en hach dêl
fon Atland by wysa fon êland vrbilêwen skolde wêsa, thêr
hi mith tha ljvdum frêthoch lêva machte. As tha bêda
nêva-t-althus navt ênes wrde koste, gvng Tünis to ånd
stek en råde fône in-t strånd, ånd Inka êne blåwe. Thêr
åfter macht jahwêder kjasa, hwam ek folgja wilde, ånd
wonder, by Inka thêr en gryns hêde vmbe tha kåningar
fon Findas folk to thjanja, hlipon tha måsta Finna ånd
Mågjara ovir. As hja nw thåt folk tellath ånd tha skêpa
thêr nêi dêlath hêde, tha skêdon tha flåta fon ekkorum;
fon nêf Tünis is åfternêi tål kêmen, fon nêf Inka ninmer.
Nêf Tünis for allinggen thêre kåd al thrvch thju porte
thêre middelsê. Tha Atland svnken is, was-t-inna middelsê
ra owera åk årg to gvngen. Thêrthrvch wêron thêr fêlo månniska fon-t Findas land nêi vsa hêinde ånd fêre Krêkalanda
kvmen ånd åk fêlo fon Lyda-his land. Thêr åjn wêron åk
fêlo fon vs folk nêi Lydas land gvngon. Thåt ella hêde
wrocht, that tha hêinde ånd fêre Krêkalanda far thåt weld
hêre Moder vrlêren was. Thêr hêde Tünis vp rêkned. Thêrvmbe wilde hi thêr en gode håve kjasa ånd fon ther ut fara

---

* Kådik, Cadix.

mother had ordered, nor was he to land at Flyland nor
anywhere about there. In this way he would have lost
all his people by want and hardship, so he landed at night
to steal and sailed on by day. Thus coasting along, he at
length arrived at the colony of Kadik (Cadíz), so called
because it was built with a stone quay. Here they
bought all kinds of stores, but Tuntia the ̇ Burgtmaagd
would not allow them to settle there. When they were
ready they began to disagree. Teunis wished to sail
through the straits to the Mediterranean Sea, and enter the
service of the rich Egyptian king, as he had done before,
but Inka said he had had enough of all those Finda's
people. Inka thought that perchance some high-lying part
of Atland might remain as an island, where he and his
people might live in peace. As the two cousins could not
agree, Teunis planted a red flag on the shore, and Inka
a blue flag. Every man could choose which he pleased,
and to their astonishment the greater part of the Finns
and Magyars followed Inka, who had objected to serve the
kings of Finda's people. When they had counted the
people and divided the ships accordingly, the fleet sepa-
rated. We shall hear of Teunis afterwards, but nothing
more of Inka.

Neef Teunis coasted through the straits to the Mediterranean Sea. When Atland was submerged there was much
suffering also on the shores of the Mediterranean, on which
account many of Finda's people, Krekalanders, and people
from Lyda's land, came to us. On the other hand, many
of our people went to Lyda's land. The result of all this
was that the Krekalanders far and wide were lost to the
superintendence of the mother. Teunis had reckoned
on this, and had therefore wished to find there a good

---

* Kâdik is Cadiz.

rikka forsta fâra, men thrvchdam sine flâte ånd sin folk
sa wanhâven utsagon, mêndon tha Kâdhêmer that hja
râwera wêron, ånd thêrvmbe wrdon hja vral wêrath.   Tha
to tha lesta kêmon hja an to Phonisivs kâd, that wêre 100
ånd 93 jêr *'nêi âtland svnken is.   Nêi bi thêre kâd fvn-
don hja en êland mith twam diapa slinka, alsa-t as thrju
êlanda utsach.   Vppet midloste thêra staldon hja hjara
skula vp, åfternêi bvwadon hja thêr en burchwal om to.
As hja thêran nw en nôme jêva wilde, wrdon hja vnênes,
svme wild-et Fryasburch hêta, ôra Nêf tünia, men tha
Mâgjara ånd tha Finna bâdon thåt skolde Thyrhisburch †
hête.   Thyr ‡ alsa hêton hja ên hjarar drochtena ånd
vppe tham-is jêrdêi wêron hja thêr land, to wither-jeld
wildon hja Tünis êvg as hjara kåning bikånne.   Tünis lêt
im bilêsa ånd tha ôra nildon thêrvr nêu orloch ne hå.
Thâ hja nw god sâton, thâ sandon hja svme alde stjvrar
ånd mâgjara ana wâl ånd forthnêi thêre burch Sydon, men
that forma nildon tha Kâdhêmar nawet fon-ra nêta.   Thv
bist fêrhêmanda swårvar sêidon hja, thêr wi navt hachta
ne müge.   Tha thâ wi hjam fon vsa ysera wêpne vrsella
wilde, gvng to lersta ella god.   åk wêron hja sêr ny nêi
vsa bårnstênum ånd thåt frêja thêr nêi nam nêu ende.
Men Tünis thêr fårsjande wêre, bårde that er nên ysere
wêpne ner bårnstêne mâr hêde.   Thâ kêmon tha kåpljvd
ånd bâdon hi skolde twintich skêpa jêva, thêr hja alle
mith-a finneste wêrum tho hrêda wilde, ånd hja
wildon him alsa fêlo ljvda to rojar jêva as-er jêrde.
Twê-lif skêpa lêt-i-to hrêda mith win hvning ånd
tomâkad lêther, thêr bi wêron tåmar ånd sitlun mith
gold wrtêin sa mån hja ninmer nêde sjan.   Mith al
thi skåt fyl Tünis thåt Flymar binna.   Thi grêvaman fon
Westflyland wårth thrvch al thessa thinga bigåstered, hi

---

* 2193-193 = 2000 v. Chr.   † Thyrhisburch, Tyrus.
    ‡ Thyr, de zoon van Odin.

haven from which he might go and serve under the rich princes ; but as his fleet and his people had such a shat-' tered appearance, the inhabitants on the coasts thought that they were pirates, and drove them away. At last they arrived at the Phœnician coast, one hundred and ninety-three years after Atland was submerged. Near the coast they found an island with two deep bays, so that there appeared to be three islands. In the middle one they established themselves, and afterwards built a city wall round the place. Then they wanted to give it a name, but disagreed about it. Some wanted to call it Fryasburgt, others Neeftunia; but the Magyars and Finns begged that it might be called Thyrhisburgt.

Thyr was the name of one of their idols, and it was upon his feast-day that they had landed there ; and in return they offered to recognise Teunis as their perpetual king. Teunis let himself be persuaded, and the others would not make any quarrel about it. When they were well estab- lished, they sent some old seamen and Magyars on an expedition as far as the town of Sidon; but at first the inhabitants of the coast would have nothing to do with them, saying, You are only foreign adventurers whom we do not respect. But when we sold them some of our iron weapons, everything went well. They also wished to buy our amber, and their inquiries about it were incessant. But Teunis, who was far-seeing, pretended that he had no more iron weapons or amber. Then merchants came and begged him to let them have twenty vessels, which they would freight with the finest goods, and they would pro- vide as many people to row as he would require. Twelve ships were then laden with wine, honey, tanned leather, and saddles and bridles mounted in gold, such as had never been seen before.

Teunis sailed to the Flymeer with all this treasure, which so enchanted the Grevetman of Westflyland that he induced

* 2193-193 is 2000 years before Christ.   † Thyrhisburch is Tyre.
        ‡ Thyr is the son of Odin.

wrochte that Tünis bi thêre mvde fon-t Flymar en loge
bvwa mâchte, âfternêi is thju stêd Almanaland* heten ånd
tha mark thêr hja âfternei to Wyringgâ† vp wandelja
machton tolêtmark. Thju Moder rêde that wi ra ella
vrkâpja skolde buta ysere wêpne, men mån ne melde hja
navt. Thâ tha Tyrjar thus fry spel hêdon, kêmon hja ålan
wither to farand vsa wêron sâ hêinde as fêre vsa ajn sêkåmpar to skådne, Thêrâfter is bisloten vpper mêna
acht, jêrlikes sjvgun Thyrjar skêpa to to lêtane ånd navt
mar.

HWAT THÊR OF WRDEN IS.

Inner northlikste herne fon tha Middelsê, thêr lêid en
êland by thêre kåd. Nw kêmon hja thåt a kåp to frêjande. Thêrvr wårth ene mêna acht bilêid. Moder-is rêd
wårth wnnen, men Moder sach ra lyast fêr of. Thêrvmbe
mênde hju that er nên kwâ an stek, thach as wi âfternêi
sågon ho wi misdên hêde håvon wi thåt êland Missellja‡
hêten. Hirâfter skil blika ho wi thêr to rêde hêde. Tha
Gola,§ alsa heton tha såndalinga prestera Sydon-is. tha
Gola hêdon wel sjan thet et land thêr skares bifolkad was
ånd fêr fon thêre Moder wêre. Vmb ira selva nw en gode
skin to jêvane, lêton hja ra selva in vsa tâl ana trowe
wydena hêta, men that wêre bêtre wêst, as hja ra
selva fon thêre trowe wendena nômath hêde, jefta
kirt wei trjuwendne lik vsa stjurar lêter dên håve.
Thâ hja wel sêton wêron, tha wandeldon hjara kåp-
ljuda skêne kåpre wêpne ånd allerlêja syrhêdon to
fara vsa ysere wêpne ånd wilde djara huda, wêrfon in

---

* Almanaland, Ameland.   † Wyringgâ, Wieringen.
‡ Missellja, Marseille.   § Gola, Galli, Gaulois.

Teunis to build a warehouse at the mouth of the Flymeer. Afterwards this place was called Almanaland, and the market where they traded at Wyringen was called Toelaatmarkt. The mother advised that they should sell everything except iron weapons, but no attention was paid to what she said. As the Thyriers had thus free play, they came from far and near to take away our goods, to the loss of our seafaring people. Therefore it was resolved in a general assembly to allow only seven Thyrian ships and no more in a year.

WHAT THE CONSEQUENCE OF THIS WAS.

In the northernmost part of the Mediterranean there lies an island close to the coast. They now came and asked to buy that, on which a general council was held.

The mother's advice was asked, and she wished to see them at some distance, so she saw no harm in it; but as we afterwards saw what a mistake we had made, we called the island Missellia (Marseilles). Hereafter will be seen what reason we had. The Golen, as the missionary priests of Sidon were called, had observed that the land there was thinly peopled, and was far from the mother. In order to make a favourable impression, they had themselves called in our language *followers of the truth;* but they had better have been called *abstainers from the truth,* or, in short, "Triuwenden," as our seafaring people afterwards called them. When they were well established, their merchants exchanged their beautiful copper weapons and all sorts of jewels for our iron weapons and hides of wild beasts, which were abundant in our southern

---

* Almanaland is Ameland.   † Wyringâ is Wieringen.
‡ Missellja is Marseilles.   § Gola are the Galli or Gauls.

vsa suder lauda fêlo to bikvma wêron. Meu tha Gola
fyradon allerhâna wla drochtenlika fêrsta ånd to tyadon
tha kadhêmar thêra thrvch todvan hjarar horiga mangh-
êrtne ånd tha swêt hêd fon hjara fininnige win. Was thêr
hwa fon vs folk thêret alsa årg vrbrud hêde, that sin lif iu
frêse kêm, than lênadon tha gola him hul ånd foradon him
nêi Phonisia, that is palmland. Was hi thêr sêten, thån
most-i an siua sibba ånd åtha skriwa, that-et land så god
wêre ånd tha månniska så luklik, as ninmån hin selva
mocht forbylde. A Brittannja wêron rju fêlo manna, tha
lith wiva, thå tha Gola that wiston, lêton hja alwêis mangh-
êrtne skåka ånd thessa javou hja tha Britne vmb nawet.
Thach al thissa maughêrtne weron hjara thjansterum,
thêr tha bern fon Wrålda stolon vmb-ar an hjara falske
drochtne to jêvane.

NW WILLATH WI SKRIWA VR THA ORLOCH THÊRA BURCHFAMNA KALTA AND MIN-ERVA,

And ho wi thêr thrvch al vsa sûderlanda ånd Brittanja
anda Gola vrlêren håve.

Bi thêre Sûder-rên-mvda ånd thêre Skelda, thêr send
sjvguu ålanda, nômath nêi Fryas sjvgum wåkfåmkes there
wêk. Middel vppet êne åland is thju burch Walhallagåra,*
inut tha wågrum thêra is thju folgjande skêdnesse wrîten.
Thêr bvppa stêt: lês, lêr ånd wåk.

563 jêr† nêi åldland svnken is, sat hir en wise burch
fåm, Min-erva was hira nôma. Thrvch tha stjurar
Nyhellênja tonômath. This tonôma was god kêren,
hwand tha rêd, thåer hju lênade, was ny ånd hel·bvppa
alle ôtherum. Overa Skelda et thêre Flyburch sat Syrhêd.
Thjus fåm was fvl renka, skên was r-anhlith ånd kwik was

---

* Middelburg.
† 2193−563 = 1630 v. Chr.

countries; but the Golen celebrated all sorts of vile and monstrous festivals, which the inhabitants of the coast promoted with their wanton women and sweet poisonous wine. If any of our people had so conducted himself that his life was in danger, the Golen afforded him a refuge, and sent him to Phonisia, that is, Palmland. When he was settled there, they made him write to his family, friends, and connections that the country was so good and the people so happy that no one could form any idea of it. In Britain there were plenty of men, but few women. When the Golen knew this, they carried off girls everywhere and gave them to the Britons for nothing. So all these girls served their purpose to steal children from Wr-alda in order to give them to false gods.

Now we will write about the War between the Burgtmaagden Kalta and Min-erva,

And how we thereby lost all our southern lands and Britain to the Golen.

Near the southern mouth of the Rhine and the Scheldt there are seven islands, named after Frya's seven virgins of the week. In the middle of one island is the city of Walhallagara (Middelburg), and on the walls of this city the following history is inscribed. Above it are the words " Read, learn, and watch."

Five hundred and sixty-three years after the submersion of Atland—that is, 1600 years before Christ—a wise town priestess presided here, whose name was Min-erva —called by the sailors Nyhellenia. This name was well chosen, for her counsels were new and clear above all others.

On the other side of the Scheldt, at Flyburgt, Sijrhed presided. This maiden was full of tricks. Her face was

---

.* Walhallagara is Middelburg, in Walcheren.
† 2193–563 is 1630 years before Christ.

hira tvnge, men thi rêd thêr hju jef, was immer in thjustere worde. Thêr vmbe warth hju thrvch tha stjurar Kålta hêten, tha landsâta mênadon that et ôrnôma wêra. Inna ûtroste wille thêre vrsturvene Moder stand Rôsa-mvda thet forma, Min-erva thet twêde ånd Syrhêd thet thredde as folgstere biskreven. Min-erva nêde thêr nên wit fon, men Syrhêd was er thrvch knaked. Lik en wrlandeske forstinne wilde hju êrath frêsath ånd bêden wêsa, men Min-erva wilde enkel minth wêsa. To tha lesta kêmon alle stjurar hiri hjara held bjada, selva fon tha Dena-marka ånd fon t Flymar. That vvnde Syrhêd, hwand hju wilde bvppa Min-erva utminthja. Til thju mån en grôte thånk ovir hira wåkendum håva skolde, myk* hju ennen hôna vpper fâne. Thâ gvng Min-erva to ånd myk en hårder hvnd ånd en nachtul in vppira fâne. Thene hvnd sêide hju wåkt ovir sin hêr ånd ovira kidda ånd thene nachtul wåkt ovira fjelda til thju hja thrvch tha musa navt vrdên ne wrde. Men thene hôna neth far nimman frjundskip, ånd thrvch sin vntocht ånd håchfårenhêd is er vaken thene båna sinra nêista sibba wrden. As Kalta sach that er wårk falikant ut kêm, to gvng hju fon kwad to årger. Stolkes lêt hju Mågjara to hiri kvma vmbe tåwery to lârane. As hju thêr hira nocht fon hêde, werpte hju hira selva and årma thêra Golum, thach fon al thi misdêdon ne macht hju navt bêtre ne wrde. As hju sach that tha stjurar mår ånd mår fon iri wêke, tha wilde hju ra thrvch frêse winna. Was tha mône fvl ånd thene sê vnstumich, than hlip hju over et wilde hef, tha stjurar to hropande that hja alle skolde vrgân, sahwersa hja hiri navt anbidda nilde. Forth vrblinde hju hira ågun hwêr thrvch hja wêter fori land ånd land fori wêter hildon, thêrthrvch is måni skip vrgvngen mith mån ånd mus. Vppet forma wêrfêrste tha al hira landsâta wêpned wêron, lêt hju bårga bjar skånka, in thåt bjar hêde hju tåverdrank dên. As et folk nv algådur

---

* Myk wordt nog op Walcheren gehoord.

beautiful, and her tongue was nimble; but the advice that she
gave was always conveyed in mysterious terms.   Therefore
the mariners called her Kalta, and the landsmen thought it
was a title.   In the last will of the dead mother, Rosamond
was named first, Min-erva second, and Sijrhed third in succession.   Min-erva did not mind that, but Sijrhed was very
much offended.   Like a foreign princess, she wished to be
honoured, feared, and worshipped; but Min-erva only desired
to be loved.   At last all the sailors, even from Denmark and
Flymeer, did homage to her.   This hurt Sijrhed, because she
wanted to excel Min-erva.   In order to give an impression of
her great watchfulness, she had a cock put on her banner.
So then Min-erva went and put a sheep-dog and an owl on
her banner.   The dog, she said, guards his master and his
flock, and the owl watches that the mice shall not devastate
the fields ; but the cock in his lewdness and his pride is only
fit to murder his nearest relations.   When Kalta found
that her scheme had failed she was still more vexed, so
she secretly sent for the Magyars to teach her conjuring.
When she had had enough of this she threw herself into
the hands of the Gauls ; but all her malpractices did not
improve her position.   When she saw that the sailors
kept more and more aloof from her, she tried to win them
back by fear.   At the full moon, when the sea was stormy,
she ran over the wild waves, calling to the sailors that
they would all be lost if they did not worship her.   Then
she blinded their eyes, so that they mistook land for water
and water for land, and in this way many a good ship
was totally lost.   At the first war-feast, when all her
countrymen were armed, she brought casks of beer,
which she had drugged.   When they were all drunk

---

* *Myk* is a word still used in Walcheren.

I

drunken wêre, gvng hju bvppen vp hira stridhros standa,
to lênande mith hira hole tojenst hira spêri, môrneråd ne
kv navt skêuer. Tha hja sach that alle ôgon vpper fås-
tigath wêron êpende hju hira wêra ånd kêth, svnum ånd
thogatrum Fryas, i wêt wel that wi inna lerste tyd fûl lek
ånd brek lêden håve, thrvchdam tha stjurar navt lônger
kvme vmb vs skriffilt to vrsella, men i nête navt hwêrthrvch et kvmen is. Lông håv ik my thêr vr iuhalden,
thach nv kån-k-e tnavt lônger ôn. Hark then frjunda til
thju i wêta müge hwêrnêi i bita mêi. Anda ôra syde
thêre Skelda hwêr hja tomet tha fêrt fon alle sêa håve,
thêr måkath hja hjvd dêgon skriffilt fon pompa blêdar,
thêr mith sparath hja linnent ut ånd kånnath hja vs wel
miste. Nêidam thåt skriffilt måkja nv alti vs gråteste
bydriv wêst is, så heth thju Moder wilt that mån et vs
lêra skolde. Men Minerva heth al et folk bihexnath, jes
bihexnath frjunda, ivin as al vs fja thåt låsten sturven is.
Er-ut mot-et, ik wil thi tella, nas-k nên burchfåm ik
skold et wel wêta, ik skolde thju hex in hjara nest vr-
barne. Thå hju thi lerste worda ut hêde, spode hju hira
selva nêi hira burch tha, men thåt vrdrvnken folk was
althus dênera bigåstered, that et vr sin rêde navt mocht
to wåkane. In dvl-dryste iver gvngon hja overa Sand fal
ånd nêidam nacht midlerwil del strêk gvngon hja evin
drist vpper burch lôs, Thach Kålta miste al hwither hira
dol, hwand Minerva ånd hira fåmna ånd tha foddik wrdon
alle thrvch tha råppa stjurar hreth.

HIRBY KVMTH THA SKÊDNESSE FON JON.

Jon, Jôn, Jhon ånd Jån is al ên mith jêven, thach thet
lêit anda utsprêk thêra stjurar, thêr thrvch wenhêd ellas
bikirta vmbit fåra ånd hard hropa to mvgane. Jon thåt
is jêva was sêkêning, bern to-t-Aldergå, to-t Flymar ut

she mounted her war-horse, leaning her head upon her spear. Sunrise could not be more beautiful. When she saw that the eyes of all were fixed upon her, she opened her lips and said:—

Sons and daughters of Frya, you know that in these last times we have suffered much loss and misery because the sailors no longer come to buy our paper, but you do not know what the reason of it is. I have long kept silence about it, but can do so no longer. Listen, then, my friends, that you may know on which side to show your teeth. On the other side of the Scheldt, where from time to time there come ships from all parts, they make now paper from pumpkin leaves, by which they save flax and outdo us. Now, as the making of paper was always our principal industry, the mother willed that people should learn it from us; but Min-erva has bewitched all the people—yes, bewitched, my friends—as well as all our cattle that died lately. I must come out with it. If I were not Burgtmaagd, I should know what to do. I should burn the witch in her nest.

As soon as she had uttered these words she sped away to her citadel; but the drunken people were so excited that they did not stop to weigh what they had heard. In mad haste they hurried over the Sandfal, and as night came on they burst into the citadel. However, Kalta again missed her aim; for Min-erva, her maidens, and her lamp were all saved by the alertness of the seamen.

WE NOW COME TO THE HISTORY OF JON.

Jon, Jôn, Jhon, Jan, are all the same name, though the pronunciation varies, as the seamen like to shorten everything to be able to make it easier to call. Jon—that is, " Given "—was a sea-king, born at Alberga, who sailed

fâren mith 100 ånd 27 skêpum, tohrêth får en grôte buta-
rêis, rik to lêden mith bårnstên, tin, kâper, yser, lêken,
linnent, filt, fâmna filt fon otter, bêver, ånd kanina hêr.
Nw skold er fon hir jeta skriffilt mith nimma ; tha to Jon
hîr kêm ånd sach ho Kålta vsa rom rika burch vrdên hêde,
thâ wårther så uter mête heftich, that er mith al sinum
ljudum vpper Flyburch of gvng ånd thêr to witterjeld
thene râda hône an stek. Men thrvch sin skelt bi nacht
ånd svme sinra ljudum wårth thju foddik ånd tha fâmna
hret. Tach Syrhêd jefta Kålta ne mochton hja navt to
fâtane, hju klywde vppa utroste tinne, jahweder tochte
that hju inna logha omkvma moste, thâ hwat bêrde?
Dahwile al hira ljuda ståk ånd stif fon skrik standon, kêm
hju skêner as â-to fora vp hira klêppar to hropande nêi
Kålta min-âis.* Thâ strâmada thât ora Skelde folk to
hâpa. As tha stjurar that sågon hripon hja får Minerva
wy. En orloch is thêrut kvmen, hwêrthrvch thvsande
fallen send.

Under thesse tidon was Rôsamond thât is Rôsa mvda
Moder, hju hêde fûl in thêre minne dên vmbe frêtho to
wårja, tach nw-t alsa årg kêm, myk hju kirte mête. Bistonda sand hju bodun thrvch tha land påla ånd lêt en
mêna nêdban utkêtha, thâ kêmon thâ landwêrar ut alle
wrda wêi. Thât strydande land folk wårth al fat, men
Jon burch hin selva mith sin ljud vppa sina flâte, mith
nimand bêda tha foddika, byonka Minerva ånd tha fâmna
fon bêdar burchum. Helprik thene hêrman lêt-imrin banna,
men tha hwila alle wêrar jeta o-ra Skelda wêron for Jon to
bek nêi-t Flymar ånd forth wither nêi vsa ålandum. Sin
ljud ånd fêlo fon vs folk namon wif ånd bern skêp, ånd as
Jon nw sach that mån hin ånd sin ljud lik misdêdar strafja
wilde, brudon hi stolkes hinne. Hi dêde rjucht, hwand al
vsa landar ånd allet ora Skelda folk thêr fjuchten hêdon

---

* Kålta Min-his, Minnesdochter?

from the Flymeer with a fleet of 127 ships fitted out for
a long voyage, and laden with amber, tin, copper, cloth,
linen, felt, otter-skins, beaver and rabbit skins. He
would also have taken paper from here, but when he
saw how Kalta had destroyed the citadel he became so
angry that he went off with all his people to Flyburgt,
and out of revenge set fire to it. His admiral and some
of his people saved the lamp and the maidens, but they
could not catch Sijrhed (or Kalta). She climbed up on
the furthest battlement, and they thought she must be
killed in the flames ; but what happened ? While all her
people stood transfixed with horror, she appeared upon
her steed more beautiful than ever, calling to them, " To
Kalta ! " Then the other Schelda people poured out towards her. When the seamen saw that, they shouted,
" We are for Min-erva ! " from which arose a war in which
thousands were killed.

At this time Rosamond the mother, who had done all
iu her power by gentle means to preserve peace, when she
saw how bad it was, made short work of it. Immediately
she sent messengers throughout all the districts to call a
general levy, which brought together all the defenders of
the country. The landsmen who were fighting were all
caught, but Jon with his seamen took refuge on board
his fleet, taking with him the two lamps, as well as Min-
erva and the maidens of both the citadels. Helprik, the
chief, summoned him to appear ; but while all the soldiers
were on the other side of the Scheldt, Jon sailed back to
the Flymeer, and then straight to our islands. His fighting men and many of our people took women and children on board, and when Jon saw that he and his people
would be punished for their misdeeds, he secretly took
his departure. He did well, for all our islanders, and
the other Scheldt people who had been fighting were

---

* Kálta Min-his, Minnesdaughter.

wrdon nêi Brittanja brocht. Thius stap was mis dên, hwand nv kêm t-anfang fon thât ende: Kâlta thêr nêi-t segse êven blyd vppet wêter as vppet land hlâpa machte, gvng nêi tha fâsta wal, ånd forth vppa Missellja of. Thâ kêmon tha Gola mith hjara skepum ut-a Middelsê Kâdik bifâra ånd êl vs uter land, forth fylon hja vp ånd over Brittannja thach hja ne mochton thêr nên fâsta fot ne krêja, vmbe thât tha sjvrda weldich ånd tha bannalinga jeta fryas wêron. Men nw kêm Kâlta ånd kêth, thv bist fry bern ånd vmbe litha lêka heth mån thi to vrwurpene mâkad, navt vmbe thi to bêterja, men vmbe tin to winnande thrvch thina handa. Wilst wêr fry wêsa ånd vnder mina rêd ånd hoda lêva, tjân ut then, wêpne skilun thi wrda, ånd ik skil wâka o-er thi. Lik blixen fjur gvng et o-era âlanda, ånd êr thes Kroders jol ênis omhlâpen hêde, was hju mâsterinne over al gadur ånd tha Thyrjar fon al vsa suder stâta til thêre Sêjene.* Vmbe that Kâlta hira selva navt to fül bitrowada, lêt hju in-et northlika berchland êne burch bvwa Kâlta-s burch wârth hju hêten, hju is jet anwêsa, men nv hêt hja Kêren-âk. Fon thjus burch welde hju lik en efte moder, navt to wille får men over hira folgar ånd tham hjara selva forth Kâltana† hêton. Men tha Gola weldon by grâdon over êl Brittanja, thât kêm ênis dêlis that hju nên mår burga nêde, twyas that hju thêr nên burchfâmna nêde ånd thryas thrvchdam hju nên efte foddik navt nêde. Thrvch al thessa êrsêka kvn hira folk navt ni lêra, thât wrde dvm ånd dor ånd wrde endelik thrvch tha Gola fon al hira ysera wêpne birâwath ånd to thât lesta lik en buhl by thêre nôse omme lêid.

---

* Sêjene, de Seine.   † Kâltana, Celtae.

transported to Britain. This step was a mistake, for now came the beginning of the end. Kalta, who, people said, could go as easily on the water as on the land, went to the mainland and on to Missellia (Marseilles). Then came the Gauls out of the Mediterranean Sea with their ships to Cadiz, and along all our coasts, and fell upon Britain; but they could not make any good footing there, because the government was powerful and the exiles were still Frisians. But now came Kalta and said : You were born free, and for small offences have been sent away, not for your own improvement, but to get tin by your labour. If you wish to be free again, and take my advice, and live under my care, come away. I will provide you with arms, and will watch over you. The news flew through the land like lightning, and before the carrier's wheel had made one revolution she was mistress of all the Thyriers in all our southern states as far as the Seine. She built herself a citadel on the high land to the north, and called it Kaltasburgh. It still exists under the name of Kêre-nak. From this castle she ruled as a true mother, against their will, not *for* her followers, but *over* them, who were thenceforth called Kelts. The Gauls gradually obtained dominion over the whole of Britain, partly because they no longer had any citadel ; secondly, because they had there no Burgtmaagden; and thirdly, because they had no real lamps. From all these causes the people could not learn anything. They were stupid and foolish, and having allowed the Gauls to rob them of their arms, they were led about like a bull with a ring in his nose.

---

* Sêjene is the Seine.   † Kâltana are the Celts.

Nv WILLATH WI SKRIVA HO-T JON VRGVNGEN IS,
THIT STÊT TO TEXLAND SKRÊVEN.

10 jêr âfter Jon wêi brit was, kêmon hyr thrju skêpa
in-t Flymar falla, thât folk hrip ho-n-sêjen, fon hira
tâlinga heth thju Moder thit skrywa lêten. Thâ Jon antha
Middelsê kêm was then mâra thêra Gola hin vral fâr ut
gvngen, alsa hi an thêri kâd fon tha hêinda Krêkalanda
nârne fêlich nêre. Hi stêk thus mith sinum flâte nêi
Lydia, thât is Lyda his lând, thêr wildon tha swarta
mânniska fâta hjam âud êta. To tha lesta kêmon hja et
Thyrhis, men Minerva sêide hald of, hwand hir is thju loft
ôlangne vrpest thrvch tha prestera. Thi kâning was fon
Tünis ofstamed, sâ wi lêter hêrdon, men til thju tha prestera
en kâning wilde hâve thêr alderlangne nêi hjara bigrip
wêre, alsa hêde hja Tünis to en gode up hêjad, to ârgnisse
sinra folgar. As hja nv Thyr âfter bek wêre, kêmon, tha
Thyriar en skip uta âfte hoda râwa, nêidam thât skip to
fêr was, kvndon wi-t navt wither wina, men Jon swor
wrêka thêrvr. Tha nacht kêm kêrde Jon nêi tha fêre
Krêkalandum, to lesten kêmon hja by en land thât bjustre
skryl ut sa, men hja fondon thêr en havesmvda. Hir sêide
Minerva skil by skin nêu frêse to fara forstum nach presterum nêdich wêsa, nêidam hja algadur feta etta minna,
thach thâ hja inner have hlipon fonth mân hja navt
rum noch vmbe alle skêpa to bislûta, ând thach wêron
mêst alle to lâf vmbe wider to gane. Alsa gvng Jon
thêr forth wilde mith sin spêr ând fône thât jongk folk
to hropande, hwa willinglik bi-m skâra wilde. Minerva
thêr biliwa wilde dêde alsa. Thât grâteste dêl gvng
nêi Minerva, men tha jonggoste stjurar gvngon by Jon.

NOW WE SHALL WRITE HOW IT FARED WITH JON.
IT IS INSCRIBED AT TEXLAND.

Ten years after Jon went away, there arrived three
ships in the Flymeer; the people cried Huzza! (What a
blessing!) and from their accounts the mother had this
written.

When Jon reached the Mediterranean Sea, the reports of
the Gauls had preceded him, so that on the nearest Italian
coast he was nowhere safe. Therefore he went with his
fleet straight over to Lybia. There the black men wanted
to catch them and eat them. At last they came to Tyre,
but Min-erva said, Keep clear, for here the air has been
long poisoned by the priests. The king was a descendant
of Teunis, as we were afterwards informed; but as the
priests wished to have a king, who, according to their
ideas, was of long descent, they deified Teunis, to the
vexation of his followers. After they had passed Tyre, the
Tyrians seized one of the rearmost ships, and as the ship
was too far behind us, we could not take it back again;
but Jon swore to be revenged for it. When night came,
Jon bent his course towards the distant Krekalanden. At
last they arrived at a country that looked very barren, but
they found a harbour there. Here, said Min-erva, we need
not perhaps have any fear of princes or priests, as they
always look out for rich fat lands. When they entered
the harbour, there was not room for all the ships, and yet
most of the people were too cowardly to go any further.
Then Jon, who wished to get away, went with his spear
and banner, calling to the young people, to know who would
volunteer to share his adventures. Min-erva did the same
thing, but she wished to remain there. The greater part
stopped with Min-erva, but the young sailors went with Jon.

Jon nam thêre foddik fon Kâlta ånd hira fâmna mitha, ånd Minerva hild hira ajn foddik ånd hira ajn fâmna.

Bitwiska tha fêrum ånd heinda Krêkalandum fand Jon svma êlanda thêr im likte, vppet grâteste gvng-er inna tha walda twisk thåt berchta en burch bvwa. Fon uta litha êlanda gvng-er ut wrêka tha Thyrjar skêpa ånd landa birâwa, thêrvmbe send tha êlanda evin blyd Râwer êlanda, as Jonhis êlanda* hêten.

Tha Minerva thåt land bisjan hêde, thåt thrvch tha inhêmar Attika is hêten, sach hju that thåt folk al jêita hoder wêron, hja hildon hjara lif mith flesk, krûdum, wilde wotelum ånd hvning. Hja wêron mith felum tekad ånd hju hêdon hjara skula vppa hellinga thêra bergum. Thêrthrvch send hja thrvch vs folk Hellinggar hêten.

Thåt forma gvngon hja vppa run, tha as hja sâgon that wi navt ne tåldon nêi hjara skåt, thå kêmon hja tobek ånd lêton grâte åtskip blika. Minerva frêjde jef wi vs in thêre minna machte nither setta. That wrde to staden vnder biding that wi skolde helpa hjam with hjara swetsar to stridande, thêr alan kêmon hjara bern to skåkana ånd hjara skåt to râwana. Thå bvwadon wi êne burch arhalf pâl fon thêr have. Vppa rêd Minervas wårth hju Athenia† heten: hwand sêide hju, tha åfter kvmand agon to wêtane, that wi hir navt thrvch lest ner weld kvmen send, men lik åtha vntfongen. Dahwile wi an thêre burch wrochton kêmon tha forsta, as hja hja nv sagon that wi nên slavona hêde, sind er sok navt, ånd lêton-t an Minerva blika, til thju hja tochton that en forstene wêre. Men Minerva frêja, ho bist wel an thina slâvona kvmen? Hja andere, svme håvath wi kåpad, ôra anna strid wnnen. Minerva sêide, såhwersa ninman månneska kâpja nilda sa ne skolde ninman jvw bern râwa ånd i ne skolda

---

Jon took the lamp of Kalta and her maidens with him. Min-erva retained her lamp and her own maidens. Between the near and the distant coasts of Italy Jon found some islands, which he thought desirable. Upon the largest he built a city in the wood between the mountains. From the smaller islands he made expeditions for vengeance on the Tyrians, and plundered their ships and their lands. Therefore these islands were called Insulæ Piratarum, as well as Johannis Insulæ.

When Min-erva had examined the country which is called by the inhabitants Attica, she saw that the people were all goatherds, and that they lived on meat, wild roots, herbs, and honey. They were clothed in skins, and had their dwellings on the slopes (*hellinga*) of the hills, wherefore they were called Hellingers. At first they ran away, but when they found that we did not attack them, they came back and showed great friendship. Min-erva asked if we might settle there peaceably. This was agreed to on the condition that we should help them to fight against their neighbours, who came continually to carry away their children and to rob their dwellings. Then we built a citadel at an hour's distance from the harbour. By the advice of Min-erva it was called Athens, because, she said, those who come after us ought to know that we are not here by cunning or violence, but were received as friends (*âtha*). While we were building the citadel the principal personages came to see us, and when they saw that we had no slaves it did not please them, and they gave her to understand it, as they thought that she was a princess. But Min-erva said, How did you get your slaves? They answered, We bought some and took others in war. Min-erva replied, If nobody would buy slaves they would

---

* Jonhis êlanda—John's Islands, or the Pirates' Isles.
† Athenia is Athens.

thêrvr nên orloch håve, wilst thus vsa harlinga biliwa så mot-i thina slåvona fry lêta.

That nv willath tha forsta navt, hja willath vs wêi driwa. Men thâ klokeste hjarar ljuda kvmath helpa vsa burch ta bvmande, thêr wi nv fon stên mâkja.

Thit is thju skêduesse fon Jon ånd Minerva. As hja that nw ella tellad hêde, frêjath hja mith êrhjadenesse vm yrsene burchwêpne, hwand sêidon hja vsa lêtha send weldich, tha sa wi efta wâpne håve, skillon wi ra wel wither worda. As hju thêran to stemad hêde, frêjath tha ljuda jef tha Fryas sêda to Athenia ånd tha ôra Krekalanda bloja skolde, thju Moder andere, jef tha fêre Krêkalanda to tha erva Fryas hêra, alsa skilum hja thêr bloja, ne hêrath hja navt thêr to, alsa skil thêr lang over kåmpad wrda mote, hwand thene kroder skil jeva fifthusand jêr mith sin Jol ommehlâpa, bifara thåt Findas folk rip to fâra frydom sy.[*]

Thit is over tha Gêrtmanna.

Thâ Hellênja jefta Minerva sturven was, tha bâradon tha prestera as jef hja mith vs wêron, til thju that hel blika skolde havon hja Hellênia to-ne godene ute kêth. Ak nildon hja nêne ore Moder kjasa lêta, to segande, hja hêde frêse that er emong hira fâmna nimman wêre, thêr hja sa god kvnde trowa as Minerva thêr Nyhellênia tonomt was. Men wi nildon Minerva navt as êne godene navt bikånna, nêidam hja selva seid hêde that nimman god jefta fvlkvma wêsa ne kvnde thån Wr.aldas gåst. Thêrumbe kêron wi Gêrt Pire his toghater to vsa Moder ut.

As tha prestera sagon that hja hjara hering navt vp vsa fjvr brêda ne mochton, thâ gvngon hja buta Athenia ånd sêidon

---

[*] Vervolg hier het verhaal van bl. 48-56.

not steal your children, and you would have no wars about it. If you wish to remain our allies, you will free your slaves. The chiefs did not like this, and wanted to drive us away; but the most enlightened of the people came and helped us to build our citadel, which was built of stone.

This is the history of Jon and of Min-erva.

When they had finished their story they asked respectfully for iron weapons; for, said they, our foes are powerful, but if we have good arms we can withstand them. When this had been agreed to, the people asked if Frya's customs would flourish in Athens and in other parts of Greece (Krekalanden). The mother answered, If the distant Greeks belong to the direct descent of Frya, then they will flourish; but if they do not descend from Frya, then there will be a long contention about it, because the carrier must make five thousand revolutions of his Juul before Finda's people will be ripe for liberty.

THIS IS ABOUT THE GEERTMEN.

When Hellenia or Min-erva died, the priests pretended to be with us, and in order to make it appear so, they deified Hellenia. They refused to have any other mother chosen, saying that they feared there was no one among her maidens whom they could trust as they had trusted Min-erva, surnamed Nyhellenia.

But we would not recognise Min-erva as a goddess, because she herself had told us that no one could be perfectly good except the spirit of Wr-alda. Therefore we chose Geert Pyre's daughter for our mother. When the priests saw that they could not fry their herrings on our fire (have everything their own way), they left Athens, and said that we

---

* Here follows the narrative contained in pages from 48 to 56.

that wi Minerva navt to-ne godene bikâna nilda ut nyd, vmbe that hju tha inhêmar sâ fûl ljafde biwêsen hede. Forth javon hja that folk byldnisse fon hira liknese, tjûgande that hja thêrlan ella frêja machte alsa naka hja hêroch bilewon. Thrvch al thissa tellinga warth thât dvma folk fon vs ofkêrad ând to tha lesta fylon hja vs to lif. Men wi hêdon vsa stêne burchwal mith twam hornum om têjen al to tha sê. Hja ne machton vs thervmbe navt nâka. Thach hwat bêrde, an Êgiptalanda thêr wêre en overprester, hel fon âgnum, klâr fon bryn ând licht fon gâst, sin nâm wêre Sêkrops,* hy kêm vmb rêd to jêvane. As Sêkrops sach that er mith sinum ljuda vsa wal navt biranna ne kv, thâ sand hi bodon nêi Thyrhis. Afternêi kêmon er thrja hvndred skipun fvl salt-âtha fon tha wilde berchfolkum vnwarlinga vsa hâva bifâra, dahwila wy mith alle mannum vppa wallum to strydande wêron.

Drêi as hja thju hâva innomth hêde wildon tha wilda salt-âtha thât thorp ând vsa skipa birâwa. Ên salt-âthe hêde al en bukja skând, men Sêkrops wilde thât navt ne hângja, ând tha Thyrjar stjurar thêr jeta Fryas blod int lif hêde sêidon, aste that dêiste sâ skilun wi tha râde hône in vsa skypa stêka ând thv ne skilst thina berga na withera-sja. Sêkrops tham navt ne hilde ni fon morthja nor fon hommelja, sand bodon nêi Gêrt vmbir tha burch of to askja, hju macht frya uttochte hâ mith al hira drywande ând bêr-ande hâva, hira folgar alsa fül. Tha wista thêra burchhêrum êl god sjande thât hja tha burch navt hâlda ne kvnde, rêden Gêrt hja skolde gaw to bitta, bi fira Sêkrops wodin wrde ând overs bigvnde, thrê mônatha âfter brûde Gêrt hinne mith tha alder besta Fryas bern ând sjugum wara twilf skypum. Thâ hja en stût buta thêre have wêron kê-mon thêr wel thritich skêpon fon Thyrhis mit wif ând bern. Hja wilde nêi Athênia gâ, tha as hja hêrdon ha-t thêr eskêpen stande gvngon hja mit Gêrt. Thi wêtking thêra

---

* Sêkrops, Cecrops.

refused to acknowledge Min-erva as a goddess out of envy, because she had shown so much affection to the natives. Thereupon they gave the people statues of her, declaring that they might ask of them whatever they liked, as long as they were obedient to her. By these kinds of tales the stupid people were estranged from us, and at last they attacked us ; but as we had built our stone city wall with two horns down to the sea, they could not get at us. Then, lo and behold ! an Egyptian high priest, bright of eye, clear of brain, and enlightened of mind, whose name was Cecrops, came to give them advice.

When he saw that with his people he could not storm our wall, he sent messengers to Tyre. Thereupon there arrived three hundred ships full of wild mountain soldiers, which sailed unexpectedly into our haven while we were defending the walls. When they had taken our harbour, the wild soldiers wanted to plunder the village and our ships—one had already ravished a girl—but Cecrops would not permit it ; and the Tyrian sailors, who still had Frisian blood in their veins, said, If you do that we will burn our ships, and you shall never see your mountains again. Cecrops, who had no inclination towards murder or devastation, sent messengers to Geert, requiring her to give up the citadel, offering her free exit with all her live and dead property, and her followers the same. The wisest of the citizens, seeing that they could not hold the citadel, advised Geert to accept at once, before Cecrops became furious and changed his mind. Three months afterwards Geert departed with the best of Frya's sons, and seven times twelve ships. Soon after they had left the harbour they fell in with at least thirty ships coming from Tyre with women and children. They were on their way to Athens, but when they heard how things stood there they went with Geert. The sea-king of

* Sêkrops is Cecrops.

Thyrjar brocht algadur thrvch tha strête * thêr vnder thisse
tida vppa tha râde sê uthlip. Et leste lândon hja et Pangab,
that is in vsa sprêke fif wêtervm, vmbe that fif rinstrâma
mith hiri nêi tha sê to strâme. Hyr seton hja‘hjara selva
nithar. That lând hâvon hja Gêrtmannja hêton. Thene kêning fon Thyrhis âfternêi sjande that sin alderbesta stjurar
wei brit wêren sand al sin skipa mith sina wilde saltâtha
vmb-er dâd jefta lêvand to fâtane. Men as hjâ by thêre
strête kêm bêvadon bêde sê ând irtha. Forth hêf irtha hira ↲
lif thêr vppa, sâ hâg that al at wêter to thêre strête uthlip,
ând that alle wata ând skorra lik en burchwal to fâra hjam ᵈ
vp rêson. That skêde over tha Gêrtmanna hjara dügda lik
as allera mannalik hel ând klâr mêi sja.

An tha Jêra 1000 and 5 † nêi Aldland svnken is, is
thit vpp-ina asterwach it Fryas Burch writen.

Nêi that wi in twilif jêr tid nên Krêkalandar to Alman-
lând sjân hêde, kêmon thêr thrju skêpa sa syrlik as wi nên
hêdon ând to fara nimmer nêde sjan. Vppet storoste thêra
wêre-n kêning thêra Jhonhis êlandum. Sin nôme wêre
Ulysus ând tha hrop ovir sin wisdom grât. This kêning
was thrvch êne presteresse forsêid, that er kêning wertha
skolde ovir alla Krêkalanda sa-r rêd wiste vmbe-n foddik
to krêjande, thêr vpstêken was anda foddik it Texland.
Vmbe-r to fensane hêder fêle skâta mith brocht, boppa ella
fâmne syrhêdum, alsa thêr in wralda navt skênener
mâkad wrde. Hja kêmon fon Troja en stede tham tha
Krêkalandar innimth hêdon. Al thissa skâta bâd hi tha
Moder an, men thju Moder nilde nârne fon nêta. As er
to lesta sa, that hju navt to winne wêre, gvng er nêi
Walhallagara. ‡
  Thêr was en fâm sêten, hjra nôme wêre Kât, tha

---

the Tyrians brought them altogether through the strait which at that time ran into the Red Sea (now re-established as the Suez Canal).* At last they landed at the Punjab, called in our language the Five Rivers, because five rivers flow together to the sea. Here they settled, and called it Geertmania. The King of Tyre afterwards, seeing that all his best sailors were gone, sent all his ships with his wild soldiers to catch them, dead or alive. When they arrived at the strait, both the sea and the earth trembled. The land was upheaved so that all the water ran out of the strait, and the muddy shores were raised up like a rampart. This happened on account of the virtues of the Geertmen, as every one can plainly understand.

IN THE YEAR ONE THOUSAND AND FIVE AFTER ATLAND
WAS SUBMERGED, THIS WAS INSCRIBED ON THE
EASTERN WALL OF FRYASBURGT.†

After twelve years had elapsed without our seeing any Italians in Almanland, there came three ships, finer than any that we possessed or had ever seen.

On the largest of them was a king of the Jonischen Islands whose name was Ulysses, the fame of whose wisdom was great. To him a priestess had prophesied that he should become the king of all Italy provided he could obtain a lamp that had been lighted at the lamp in Texland. For this purpose he had brought great treasures with him, above all, jewels for women more beautiful than had ever been seen before. They were from Troy, a town that the Greeks had taken. All these treasures he offered to the mother, but the mother would have nothing to do with them. At last, when he found that there was nothing to be got from her, he went to Walhallagara (Walcheren).‡ There there was established a Burgtmaagd whose name was Kaat,

---

* Strête, at present restored as the Suez Canal. Pangab is the Indus.
† 2193–1005 is 1188 before Christ. ‡ Walhallagâra is Walcheren.

K

inna wandel wrde hju Kalip* hêten ut hawede that hjara
vnderlip as en utkikbored farutståk. Thêrby heth er
jêron hwilth to årgenisse fon al tham et wiston. Nêi
thêra fâmna hrop heth er to lesta en foddik fon hir krêjen,
tha hja heth im navt ne bât, hwand as er in sê kêm is sin
skip vrgvngon ånd hy nåked ånd blât vpnimth thrvch tha
ôthera skêpa.

Fon thisse kêning is hyr en skryver åfterbilêwen fon
rên Fryas blod, bårn to thêre nêie have fon Athênia ånd
hwat hyr folgath het er vs fon ovir Athênia skrêven,
thêrut mêi mån bisluta, ho wêr thja Moder Hel-licht
sproken heth, thâ hja sêide thât Fryas sêda to Athênia
nên stand holde ne kvste.

Fon tha ôthera Krêkalander hetste sêkur fül kwâd ovir
Sêkrops hêred, hwand hi wêre in nên gode hrop. Men ik
dår segse, hi wêre-n lichte man, hâchlik romed alsa sêr bi
tha inhêmar as wel bi vs, hwand hi wêre navt vmbe tha
månniska to diapana sa tha ôra prestera, men hi wêre dü-
gedsêm ånd hi wist tha wisdom thêra fêrhêmanda folkum
nêi wêrde to skåtande. Thêrvmbe that er that wiste,
hêde-r vs to stonden that wi machte lêva nêi vs ajn êlik
Sêgabok. Thêr gvng en telling that er vs nygen were,
vmbe that er tjucht wêsa skolde ut en Fryaske mangêrte
ånd Êgiptiska prester, uthawede that er blâwe åga hêde,
ånd that er fül mangêrta fon vs skåkt wêron ånd in
ovir Egiptalande vrsellath. Tha selva heth er nimmerte
jecht. Ho-t thêrmêi sy, sêkur is-t that er vs måra
åthskip biwês as alle ôthera prestum to sêmne. Men
as er fallen was, gvngon sina nêimanninga alring an
vsa êwa torena ånd bi grådum sa fêlo mislikanda kêra
to måkjande, that er to lônge lesta fon êlik sa ånd
fon frydom ha navt ôwers as tha skin ånd tha nôme
vrbilêf. Forth nildon hja navt ne dâja that-a setma an
skrift brocht wrde, hwerthrvch tha witskip thêra far

---

but who was commonly called Kalip, because her lower lip
stuck out like a mast-head. Here he tarried for years, to
the scandal of all that knew it. According to the report
of the maidens, he obtained a lamp from her ; but it did
him no good, because when he got to sea his ship was
lost, and he was taken up naked and destitute by another
ship. There was left behind by this king a writer of pure
Frya's blood, born in the new harbour of Athens, who
wrote for us what follows about Athens, from which may
be seen how truly the mother Hel-licht spoke when she
said that the customs of Frya could never take firm hold
in Athens.

From the other Greeks you will have heard a great deal
of bad about Cecrops, because he was not in good repute ;
but I dare affirm that he was an enlightened man, very
renowned both among the inhabitants and among us, for
he was against oppression, unlike the other priests, and
was virtuous, and knew how to value the wisdom of distant nations. Knowing that, he permitted us to live
according to our own Asegaboek. There was a story cur-
rent that he was favourable to us because he was the son
of a Frisian girl and an Egyptian priest : the reason of
this was that he had blue eyes, and that many of our girls
had been stolen and sold to Egypt, but he never con-
firmed this. However it may have been, certain it is that
he showed us more friendship than all the other priests
together. When he died, his successors soon began to
tear up our charters, and gradually to enact so many un-
suitable statutes that at long last nothing remained of
liberty but the shadow and the name. Besides, they would
not allow the laws to be written, so that the knowledge
of them was hidden from us. Formerly all the cases in

---

* Kalip, called by Homer Kalipso.

vs forborgen wârth. To fâra wrdon alle sêkum binna Athênia in vsa tâl bithongon, âfternêi most et in bêda tâla
skên ând to lesta allêna in tha landis tal. In tha êrosta
jêra nam that manfolk to Athênia enkel wiva fon vs ajn
slacht, men that jongkfolk vpwoxen mitha mangêrta thêr
landsâton namen thêr âk fon. Tha bâstera bern tham
thêrof kemon wêron tha skênsta ând snodsta in wralda, men
hja wêron âk tha ârgsta. To hinkande vr byde syda, to
mâlande her vm sêda ner vm plêga, hit ne sy that et wêre
for hjara ajne held. Alsa nâka thêr jeta-n strêl fon Fryas gâst weldande wêre wârth al'et bvwspul to mêna werka
forwrochten ând nimmân ne mocht en hus to bvwande,
thât rumer ând riker wêre as thât sinra nêstum. Tha thâ
svme vrbastere stêdjar rik wêron thrvch vs fâra ând thrvch
et sulver, thât tha slâvona uta sulverlôna wnnon, thâ
gvngon hja buta vppa hellinga jefta inda dêla hêma.
Thêr beftha hâga wallum fon lôf tha fon stên bvwadon
hja hova mith kestlik husark, ând vmbe by tha wla prestrum in en goda hrop to wêsande, stândon hja thêr falska
drochten likanda ând vntuchtiga bilda in. By tha wla
prestrum ând forstum wrdon tha knâpa al tomet mâra
gêrt as tha toghatera, ând fâken thrvch rika jefta thrvch
weld fon et pad thêre düged ofhlêid. Nêidam rikdom by
thât vrbrûde ând vrbasterde slachte fêr bvppa düged ând
êre jelde, sach mân altomet knâpa tham hjara selva mit
rûma rika klâtar syradon, hjara aldrum ând fâmna to
skônda ând hjara kvnna to spot. Kêmon vsa ênfalda
aldera to Athênia vppe thêre mêna acht ând wildon hja
thêrvr bâra, sâ warth ther hropen, hark, hark, thêr skil
en sêmomma kêtha. Alsa is Athênia wrdon êlik en brok-
land anda hête landa, fol blodsûgar, pogga ând feniniga
snâka, hwêrin nên mânniske fon herde sêdum sin fot navt
wâga ne mêi.

Athens were pleaded in our language, but afterwards in both languages, and at last in the native language only. At first the men of Athens only married women of our own race, but the young men as they grew up with the girls of the country took them to wife. The bastard children of this connection were the handsomest and cleverest in the world; but they were likewise the wickedest, wavering between the two parties, paying no regard to laws or customs except where they suited their own interests. As long as a ray of Frya's spirit existed, all the building materials were for common use, and no one might build a house larger or better than his neighbours; but when some degenerate townspeople got rich by sea-voyages and by the silver that their slaves got in the silver countries, they went to live out on the hills or in the valleys. There, behind high enclosures of trees or walls, they built palaces with costly furniture, and in order to remain in good odour with the nasty priests, they placed there likenesses of false gods and unchaste statues. Sometimes the dirty priests and princes wished for the boys rather than the girls, and often led them astray from the paths of virtue by rich presents or by force. Because riches were more valued by this lost and degenerate race than virtue or honour, one sometimes saw boys dressed in splendid flowing robes, to the disgrace of their parents and maidens, and to the shame of their own sex. If our simple parents came to a general assembly at Athens and made complaints, a cry was raised, Hear, hear! there is a sea-monster going to speak. Such is Athens become, like a morass in a tropical country full of leeches, toads, and poisonous snakes, in which no man of decent habits can set his foot.

THIT STAT IN AL VSA BURGA.

Ho vsa Dênemarka* fâra vs vlêren gvngon 1600 ånd 2 jêr† nêi Aldland vrgongen is. Thrvch Wodins dor ånd dertenhêd was thene Magy bâs wrden ovir Skênlandis astardêl. Wra berga ånd wr-n sê ne tvrade hi navt ne kvma. Thju Moder wildet navt wêrha, hja sprêk ånde kêth, ik sja nên frêse an sina wêpne, men wel vmbe tha Skênlander wêr to nimmande, thrvchdam hja bastered ånd vrdêren sind. Vppa mêna acht tochte man alên. Thêrvmbe is-t im lêten. Grât 100 jêr lêden byondon tha Dênemarkar to wandelja mith hjam. Hja jêvon him ysere wêpne ånd rêdskip thêr fori wandeldon hja golden syrhêdon bijunka kâper ånd yserirtha. Thju Moder sand bodon ånd rêd-er, hja skolde thju wandel fâra lêta. Thêr wêre frêse sêide hju fori hjara sêdum, ånd bitham hja hjara sêde vrlêren, thån skolde hja åk hjara frydom vrljasa. Men tha Dênemarkar nêde narne âra nei, hja nilda navt bigrippa that hjara sêde vrbrûde kvste, thêrvmbe ne meldon hja hja navt. To lônga lesta brochton hja ajne wêpne ånd liftochta wêi. Men thåt kwâd wrocht hjara gêia. Hjara lichêma wrdon bilâden mêi blik ånd skin, men hjara arka spynton ånd skvra wrdon lêtoch. Krek hondred jêr eftere dêi that et forma skip mit liftochta fona kâd fâren was, kêm ermode ånd lek thrvch tha anderna binna, honger sprêda sina wjvka ånd strêk vppet land del, twispalt hlip stolte in overe strêta ånd forth to tha hûsa in, ljafde ne kv nên stek lônger navt finda ånd êntracht run êwêi. Thåt bårn wilde êta fon sina måm ånd thju måm hêde wel syrhêdon tha nên êta. Tha wiva kêmon to hjara manna, thissa gvngon nêi tha grêva, tha; grêva nêdon selva nawet of hildon-t skul. Nw most mån tha syrhêdon vrsella, men thawila tha stjurar thêrmêi

---

THIS IS INSCRIBED IN ALL OUR CITADELS.

How our Denmark was lost to us 1602 years after the submersion of Atland. Through the mad wantonness of Wodin, Magy had become master of the east part of Scandinavia. They dare not come over the hills and over the sea. The mother would not prevent it. She said, I see no danger in their weapons, but much in taking the Scandinavians back again, because they are so degenerate and spoilt. The general assembly were of the same opinion. Therefore it was left to him. A good hundred years ago Denmark began to trade; they gave their iron weapons in exchange for gold. ornaments, as well as for copper and iron-ore. The mother sent messengers to advise them to have nothing to do with this trade. There was danger to their morals in it, and if they lost their morals they would soon lose their liberty. But the Denmarkers paid no attention to her. They did not believe that they could lose their morals, therefore they would not listen to her. At last they were at a loss themselves for weapons and necessaries, and this difficulty was their punishment. Their bodies were brilliantly adorned, but their cupboards and their sheds were empty. Just one hundred years after the first ship with provisions sailed from the coast, poverty and want made their appearance, hunger spread her wings all over the country, dissension marched proudly about the streets and into the houses, charity found no place, and unity departed. The child asked its mother for food; she had no food to give, only jewels. The women applied to their husbands, the husbands appealed to the counts; the counts had nothing to give, or if they had, they hid it away. Now the jewels must be sold, but while the sailors

---

* Dêna marka, the low marches.
† 2193–1602 is 591 years before Christ.

wêi brit wêron kêm frost ånd lêi-n plônk del vppa sê ånd
wra strête. Tha frost thju brigge rêd hêde, stop wåkandon
thêr wr to-t land ut ånd vrêd klywade vpper sêtel. In
stêde fon tha owera to biwåkande spandon hja hjara horsa
for hjara togum ånd runon nêi Skênland thå. Tha Skênlander, tham nêy wêron nêi that land hjarar êthla kêmon
nêi tha Dênemarkum. Vppen helle nacht kêmon hja alla.
Nw sêidon hja that hja rjucht hêde vppet land hjarar êthlon
ånd thahwil that mån thêrvr kåmpade kêmon tha Finna
in tha lêtoga thorpa ånd runadon mith tha bern ewêi.
Thêrtrvch ånd that hja nên goda wêpne navt nêdon, dêd
hjam tha kåsa vrljasa ånd thêrmêi hjari frydom, hwand
thene Magy wrde bås. That kêm that hja Fryas tex navt
lêsde ånd hira rêdjêvinga warlåsed hêde.

Ther send svme thêr mêne that hja thrvch tha grêva
vrrêden send, that tha fåmna thåt lông spêrath hêdon, tha
sa hvam sa thêr vr kêtha wilde, tham is mvla wrdon to
smôrath mith golden kêdne. Wi ne mügan thêrvr nên
ordêl to fellande, men wi willath jo tohropa, ne lên navt to
sêre vppa wisdom ånd düged ni fon jvwa Forsta, ni fon
jowa fåmna, hwand skel et halda sa mot allera mannalik
wåka ovir sin ajna tochta ånd for-t mêna held.

Twa jêr nêidam kêm thene Magy selva mith en flåte fon
lichte kånum, tha Moder fon Texland ånd tha foddik to
råwane.

Thås årge sêke bistonde-r thes nachtis anda winter by
storne tydum as wind gûlde ånd hêjel to jenst tha andêrna
fêtere. Thi utkik thêr mênde thater awet hêrde ståk siu
balle vp. Tha drêi as et ljucht fon êr tore vppet ronddêl
falda, sa-r that al fêlo wêpende manna wra burchwal wêron.
Nw gvng-er to vmbe tha klokke to lettane, tha et wêre to
lêt. Êr tha wêre rêd wêre, weron al twa thusand ina wêr
vmbe tha porte to rammande. Strid hwilde thervmbe kirt,

were away for that purpose, the frost came and laid a plank upon the sea and the strait (the Sound). When the frost had made the bridge, vigilance ceased in the land, and treachery took its place. Instead of watching on the shores, they put their horses in their sledges and drove off to Scandinavia. Then the Scandinavians, who hungered after the land of their forefathers, came to Denmark. One bright night they all came. Now, they said, we have a right to the land of our fathers; and while they were fighting about it, the Finns came to the defenceless villages and ran away with the children. As they had no good weapons, they lost the battle, and with it their freedom, and Magy became master. All this was the consequence of their not reading Frya's Tex, and neglecting her counsels. There are some who think that they were betrayed by the counts, and that the maidens had long suspected it; but if any one attempted to speak about it, his mouth was shut by golden chains.

We can express no opinion about it, we can only say to you, Do not trust too much to the wisdom of your princes or of your maidens; but if you wish to keep things straight, everybody must watch over his own passions, as well as the general welfare.

Two years afterwards Magy himself came with a fleet of light boats to steal the lamp from the mother of Texland. This wicked deed he accomplished one stormy winter night, while the wind roared and the hail rattled against the windows. The watchman on the tower hearing the noise, lighted his torch. As soon as the light from the tower fell upon the bastion, he saw that already armed men had got over the wall.

He immediately gave the alarm, but it was too late. Before the guard was ready, there were two thousand people battering the gate. The struggle did not last long.

hwand thrvchdam tha wêra navt nên gode wacht halden
nêde, kêmon alle om.

Hwil that alrek drok to kåmpane wêre, was thêr en wla
Fin to thêre flête jefta bedrum fon thêre Moder inglupth,
ånd wilde hja nêdgja. Tha thju Moder wêrd-im of that er
bekwârd tojênst tha wâch strumpelde. Thâ-r wither vpa
bêu wêre stek er sin swêrd to ir buk in segsande, nilst min
kul navt så skilst min swêrd ha. After im kêm en skiper
foua Dênemarka, thisse nam sin swêrd ånd hif thêne Fin
thrvch sina hole. Thêrut flât swart blod ånd thêrvr
swêfde-n blâwe logha. Thi Magy lêt thju Moder vpa sinra
skip forplêgja. As hju nw wither alsa fêre hêl ånd bêter
wêr that hju fåst sprêka machte, sêide thenc Magy that
hju mith fåra moste, tha that hju hira foddik ånd fåmna
halda skolde, that hju en stât skolde nyta så hâch as hju to
fara na nêde kenth. Forth sêide-r thât hi hiri frêja skolde
in ajnwarde fon sinum forsta, jef er mâster skolde wertha
over alle lânda ånd folkra Fryas. Hi sêide that hju that
bijâe ånd bijechta most, owers skolde-r vnder fêlo wêja
sterva lêta. As er thêr after al sinra forsta om ira lêger to
gadurad hêde frêjer lûd, Fråna vrmites i klârsjande biste
most m.ênis segsa of ik mâster skil wertha over alle lânda
ånd folkra Fryas. Fråna dêde as melde hja him navt.
To lônga lesta êpende hju hira wêra ånde kêth, min
âgun wrde thjûstred, tha that ôre ljucht dêgth vp in
minara sêle. Jes, ik sja-t. Hark Irtha ånd wês blyde
mith my. Vndera tydum that Aldland svnken is, stand
thju forma spêke fon thet Jol an top. Thêrnêi is hju
del gvngon ånd vsa frydom mith tham. As er twa spêka
jeftha 2000 jêr del trûled het, så skilun tha svna vpstonda
thêr tha forsta ånd prestera thrvch hordom bi-t folk têled
håve, ånd tojenst hjara tåta tjugha. Thi alle skilum
thrvch mort swika, men hwat hja kêth håve skil forth

As the guard had not kept a good watch, they were over-whelmed. While the fight was going on, a rascally Finn stole into the chamber of the mother, and would have done her violence. She resisted him, and threw him down against the wall. When he got up, he ran his sword through her: If you will not have me, you shall have my sword. A Danish soldier came behind him and clave his head in two. There came from it a stream of black blood and a wreath of blue flame.

The Magy had the mother nursed on his own ship. As soon as she was well enough to speak clearly, the Magy told her that she must sail with him, but that she should keep her lamp and her maidens, and should hold a station higher than she had ever done before. Moreover, he said that he should ask her, in pre-sence of all his chief men, if he would become the ruler of all the country and people of Frya; that she must declare and affirm this, or he would let her die a painful death. Then, when he had gathered all his chiefs around her bed, he asked, in a loud voice, Frana, since you are a prophetess, shall I become ruler over all the lands and people of Frya? Frana did as if she took no notice of him; but at last she opened her lips, and said: My eyes are dim, but the other light dawns upon my soul. Yes, I see it. Hear, Irtha, and rejoice with me. At the time of the submersion of Atland, the first spoke of the Juul stood at the top. After that it went down, and our free-dom with it. When two spokes, or two thousand years, shall have rolled down, the sons shall arise who have been bred of the fornication of the princes and priests with the people, and shall witness against their fathers. They shall all fall by murder, but what they have proclaimed shall endure,

bilywa ånd frûchdber wertha in-a bosme thêra kloke månniska, alsa lik gode sêdum thêr del lêid wrde in thinra
skåt. Jeta thûsand jêr skil thju spêke then del nyga ånd
al måra syga anda thjusternesse ånd in blod, ovir thi
utstirt thrvch tha låga thêr forsta ånd prestera. Thêrnêi
skil thet mornerâd wither anfanga to glora. Thit sjande
skilun tha falska forsta ånd prester alsamen with frydom
kåmpa ånd woxelja, men frydom, ljafde ånd êndracht
skil-et folk in hjara wach nêma ånd mit thet jol risa uta
wla pol. Thåt rjucht thåt erost allêna glorade, skil than
fon lêjar laja to-n logha wertha. Thåt blod thêra årgum
skil ovir thin lif stråma, men thu ne mügth et navt to thi
nêma. To tha lesta skil thåt feninige kwik thêr vp åsa
ånd thêrof sterva. Alle wla skêdnese tham forsunnen
send vmbe tha forsta ånd prestera to boga, skilun an logha
ofred wertha. Forth skilun al thinra beru mith frêtho
lêva. Thâ hju utspreken hêde, sêg hju del. Men thene
Mågy tham hja navt wel forstân hêde krêth, ik håv thi
frêjeth, jef ik bâs skilde wertha ovir alle lånda ånd folkra
Fryas, ånd nw håste to en other sproken. Fråna rjuchte
hiri wither, sach im star an ånd kêthe: er sjugun etmeldé
om send, skil thin sêle mitha nachtfüglon to tha gråwa
omme wåra ånd thin lik skil ledsa vppa bodem fona se.
Êl wel sêide thene Magy mith vrborgne wodin, segs men
thåt ik kvme. Forth sêider to jenst ên sinar rakkarum,
werp that wif vr skippes bord. Althus wêr-et ende fon-re
leste thêra Moderum.* Wrêke willath wi thêr vr navt ne
hropa, tham skil tyd nima. Men thûsand wåra thûsand
mêl willath wi Frya åfternêi hropa: wåk-wåk-wåk.

Ho-t thene Magy forth vrgvngon is.

Nêi that tha modder vrdên was, lêter tha foddik ånd
tha fåmna to sina skip to brenga bijunka alle in

---

and shall bear fruit in the bosoms of able men, like good seed which is laid in thy lap. Yet a thousand years shall the spoke descend, and sink deeper in darkness, and in the blood shed over you by the wickedness of the princes and priests. After that, the dawn shall begin to glow. When they perceive this, the false princes and priests will strive and wrestle against freedom; but freedom, love, and unity will take the people under their protection, and rise out of the vile pool. The light which at first only glimmered shall gradually become a flame. The blood of the bad shall flow over your surface, but you must not absorb it. At last the poisoned animals shall eat it, and die of it. All the stories that have been written in praise of the princes and priests shall be committed to the flames. Thenceforth your children shall live in peace. When she had finished speaking she sank down.

The Magy, who had not understood her, shrieked out, I have asked you if I should become master of all the lands and people of Frya, and now you have been speaking to another. Frana raised herself up, stared at him, and said, Before seven days have passed your soul shall haunt the tombs with the night-birds, and your body shall be at the bottom of the sea. Very good, said the Magy, swelling with rage; say that I am coming. Then he said to his executioners, Throw this woman overboard. This was the end of the last of the mothers. We do not ask for revenge. Time will provide that; but a thousand thousand times we will call with Frya, Watch! watch! watch!

How it fared afterwards with the Magy.

After the murder of the mother, he brought the lamp and the maidens into his own ship, together with all

---

* Refer to p. 4.

bold thêr im likte. Forth gvng er thåt Flymâr vp, hwand
hi wilde tha fâm fon Mêdêasblik jeftha fon Ståvora gabja
ånd tham to Moder mâkja. Tha thêr wêron hja vp hjara
hodum brocht. Tha stjurar fon Ståvora ånd fon thåt Alderga
hêdon hini gêrn to Jonis togen, men tha gråte flåte wêre
vppen fêre tocht ût. Nw gvngon hja to ånd foron mith
hjra littige flåte nêi Mêdêasblik ånd hildon hja skul after
thåt ly thêra bâmun. Thi Mågy nåkade Mêdêasblik bi helle
dêi ånd skynander svnne. Thach gvngon sina ljuda drist
drist wêi vppera burch to runnande. Men as allet folk mith
tha bôtum land was, kemon vsa stjurar utêre krêke wêi ånd
skåton hjara pila mith tårbarntin bollum vp sinra flåte.
Hja wêron alsa wel rjucht that fêlo sinra skêpun bistonda
anna brônd wêron. Tham vppa skêpun wachton, skåton åk
nêi vs thâ, thach thåt ne rojade nawet. As er to lesta en
skip al barnande nêi-t skip thes Mågy dryf, bifel-er sin
skiper hi skolde of håde, men thene skiper that wêre thene
Dênemarker thêr thene Fin felad hêde, andere, thv hest
vse Êremoder nêi tha bodem fona sê svnden to meldande
thatste kvma skolde, thit skoste thrvch tha drokhêd wel
vrjetta; nw wil ik njude thatste thin word jecht. Thi Mågy
wild-im ofwêra; men thene skiper, en åfte Fryas ånd
sterik lik en jokoxe klipade bêda sinum hônda om sin hole
ånd hif hini vr bord into thåt wellande hef. Forth hês er
sin brune skild an top ånd for rjucht to rjucht an nêi vsa
flåte. Thêrthrvch kêmon tha fâmna vnforlet to vs, men tha
foddik was utgvngon ånd nimman wiste ho-t kêmen was.
Tha hja vppa vnfordene skêpa heradon, that thene Mågy
vrdrvnken was, brûde hja hinne, hwand tha stjurar thêra
mêst Dênemarker wêron. Nêi that tha flåte fêr enoch ewêi
wêre, wendon vsa stjurar åud skåton hjara barnpila vppa
tha Finna del. Thâ tha Finna thus sagon, ho hja vrrêden
wêron, blip alrik thrvch vr ekkdrum ånd thêr nêre lônger
nên hêrichhêd ni bod. To thisre stonde run tha wêre hju ut

the booty that he chose. Afterwards he went up the Flymeer because he wished to take the maiden of Medeasblik or Stavoren and install her as mother; but there they were on their guard. The seafaring men of Stavoren and Alderga would gladly have gone to Jon, but the great fleet was out on a distant voyage; so they proceeded in their small fleet to Medeasblik, and kept themselves concealed in a sheltered place behind trees. The Magy approached Medeasblik in broad daylight; nevertheless, his men boldly stormed the citadel. But as they landed from the boats, our people sallied forth from the creek, and shot their arrows with balls of burning turpentine upon the fleet. They were so well aimed that many of the ships were instantly on fire. Those left to guard the ships shot at us, but they could not reach us. When at last a burning ship drifted towards the ship of the Magy, he ordered the man at the helm to sheer off, but this man was the Dane who had cleft the head of the Finn. He said, You sent our Eeremoeder to the bottom of the sea to say that you were coming. In the bustle of the fight you might forget it; now I will take care that you keep your word. The Magy tried to push him off, but the sailor, a real Frisian and strong as an ox, clutched his head with both hands, and pitched him into the surging billows. Then he hoisted up his brown shield, and sailed straight to our fleet. Thus the maidens came unhurt to us; but the lamp was extinguished, and no one knew how that had happened. When those on the un-injured ships heard that the Magy was drowned, they sailed away, because their crews were Danes. When the fleet was far enough off, our sailors turned and shot their burning arrows at the Finns. When the Finns saw that, and found that they were betrayed, they fell into confusion, and lost all discipline and order. At this moment the garrison sallied

têre burch. Tham navt ne fljuchte, werth afmakad, ånd
thêr fljuchte fvnd sin ende into tha polum fon et Krylinger wald.

NÊISCHRIFT.

Thâ tha stjurar an da kreke lêjon was thêr en spotter
fon ut Stavora mauk, thêr sêide, Mêdêa mei lakkja, sa wi
hyr ut hjra burch reda.   Thêrvmbe håvon tha fâmna thju .
krêke Mêdêa mêi lakkja * hêten.

Tha bêrtnissa thêr afternêi skêd send, mêi alra mannalik
hügja.   Tha fâmna hagon tham nei hjara wysa to tella ånd
wel biskriwa lêta.   Thêrvmbe rêkenjath wi hirmitha vsa
arbêd fvlbrocht.   Held.

---

* Medemi'lacus.

ENDE FON 'T BOK.

forth from the citadel. Those who resisted were killed, and those who fled found their death in the marshes of the Krylinger wood.

POSTSCRIPT.

When the sailors were in the creek, there was a wag from Stavoren among them, who said, Medea may well laugh if we rescue her from her citadel. Upon this, the maidens gave to the creek the name Medea mêilakkia (Lake of Medea). The occurrences that happened after this everybody can remember. The maidens ought to relate it in their own way, and have it well inscribed. We consider that our task is fulfilled. Hail !

---

* Medemi lacus, Lake of Medea's laughter.

THE END OF THE BOOK.

THA SKRIFTA FON ADELBROST AND APOLLONIA.

Min nôm is Adelbrost svn fon Apol ånd fon Adela. Thrvch min folk ben ik kêren to Grêvetman ovira Linda wrda. Thêrvmbe wil ik thit bok forfolgja vp alsa dênera wisa as mine mem sproken heth.

Nêi that thene Mâgy felt was ånd Fryasburch vp stel brocht, most er en moder kêren wertha. Bi-ra lêva nêde thju Moder hira folgstera navt nômth. Hira lersta wille was sok ånd narne to findne. Sjugun mônatha åfter werth er en mêna acht bilidsen ånd wel to Grênegå* ut êrsêke that anna Saxanamarka pâlth. Min mem werth kêren, men hju nilde nên Moder wêsa. Hju hêde heth lif minar tât hrêd, thêrthruch hêden hja ekkorum lyaf krêjen ånd nw wildon hja åk gådath wertha. Fêlon wildon min mem fon er bislut ofbrenga; men min mem sêide, en Êremoder âcht alsa rên in-ra mod to wêsana as hja buta blikt ånd êven mild far al hjara bern. Nêidam ik Apol nw lyaf hâv hoppa ella in wralda, så ne kån ik så-ne Moder navt nêsa. Så sprek ånd kêth Adela, men tha ôra burchfâmna wildon algåder Moder wêsa. Alrek stât thong fori sinera åjne fâm ånd nilde navt fyra. Ther-thrvch nis er nêne kêren ånd heth rik thus bandlås. Hyr åfter müg-it bigripa.

Ljudgêrt, tham kêning thêr hêmesdêga fallen is, was bi thêre Moder-is lêva kêren blikbêr trvch alle stâtha mith lyafde ånd trjvw. Heth wêre siu torn vmbe vppin eth grâte hof to Dok-hêm † to hêmande, ånd bi thêre Moder-is lêva wrd-im ther grâte êr biwêsen, hwand et wêre immer sa ful mith bodon ånd riddarum fon hêinde ånd fêre as-m-å to fora na nêde sjan. Tach nw wêr-er ênsêm and

---

* 'Grênegå, Groningen.   Dokhêm, Dokkum.

THE WRITINGS OF ADELBROST AND APOLLONIA.

My name is Adelbrost, the son of Apol and Adela. I was elected by my people as Grevetman over the Linda-oorden. Therefore I will continue this book in the same way as my mother has spoken it.

After the Magy was killed and Fryasburgt was restored, a mother had to be chosen. The mother had not named her successor, and her will was nowhere to be found. Seven months later a general assembly was called at Grênegâ (Groningen), because it was on the boundary of Saxamarken. My mother was chosen, but she would not be the mother. She had saved my father's life, in consequence of which they had fallen in love with each other, and she wished to marry. Many people wished my mother to alter her decision, but she said an Eeremoeder ought to be as pure in her conscience as she appears outwardly, and to have the same love for all her children. Now, as I love Apol better than anything else in the world, I cannot be such a mother. Thus spoke and reasoned Adela, but all the other maidens wished to be the mother. Each state was in favour of its own maiden, and would not yield. Therefore none was chosen, and the kingdom was without any restraint. From what follows you will understand Liudgert, the king who had lately died, had been chosen in the lifetime of the mother, and seemingly with the love and confidence of all the states. It was his turn to live at the great court of Dokhem, and in the lifetime of the mother great honour was done to him there, as there were more messengers and knights there than had ever been seen there before. But now he was lonely and forsaken,

---

* Grênegâ is Groningen.   † Dokhem is Dokkum.

vrlêten, hwand alrek wêre ange that-er him mâster skolde
mâkja boppa heth rjucht ånd welda ê-lik tha slâvona
kêninggar. Elk forst wânde forth that-er enoch dêde as
er wâkade ovir sin åjn stât; ånd thi ên ne jêf nawet tâ
antha ôthera. Mith-êra burchfamna gvnget jeta årger to.
Alrek thisra bogade vppira åjne wisdom ånd sahwersa tha
Grêvetmanna awet dêdon buta hjam, så wrochten hja
mistryvwa bitwiska tham ånd sinum ljudum. Skêder en
sêke thêr fêlon stâtha trof ånd hêde mån thju rêd êner
fâm in wnnen, så kêthon alle ôthera that hju sproken hêde
to fêre fon hjra åjne stât. Thrvch althus dênera renka brochton hja twyspalt in ovira stâtha ånd torendon hja that
band sâdêne fon ên, that et folk fon tha ênne stât nythich
wêre vppet folk fon en ora stât ånd fâret alderminesta
lik fêrhêmande biskôwade. Thju fêre thêra is wêst that
tha Gola jeftha Trowyda vs al-êt lånd of wnnen håven al
ont thêra Skelda ånd thi Magy al to thêre Wrsâra. Ho-r
thêrby to gvngen is, heth min mem vntlêth, owers nas thit
bok navt skrêven ne wrden, afskên ik alle hâpe vrlêren
håv tha-et skil helpa thâ bâta. Ik ne skryw thus navt
inna wân, thet ik thêrthrvch thet lånd skil winna jeftha
bihaldane, that is minra achtne vndvalik, ik skryw allêna
får et åfter kvmande slacht, til thju hja algâdur wêta
müge vp hvdêna wisa wy vrlêren gvnge, ånd tha alra
mannalik hyr ut lêra mêi that elk kwâd sin gêja têlath.

My heth mån Apollônja hêten. Twyia thritich dega
nêi måm hira dåd heth mån Adelbrost min brother
vrslêjen fonden vppa wårf, sin hawed split ånd sina lithne
ût ên hrêten. Min tåt thêr siak lêide is fon skrik vrstur-
ven. Thâ is Apol min jungere brother fon hyr nêi thêre
westsyde fon Skênlånd fâren. Thêr heth er en burch
ebuwad, Lindasburch* hêten, vmbe dâna to wrekana
vs lêth. Wr.alda heth-im thêr to fêlo jêra lênad. Hy
heth fif svna wnnen. Altham brengath thêne Magy skrik

---

* Lindasburch, op kaap Lindanaes, Noorwegen.

because every one was afraid that he would set himself above the law, and rule them like the slave kings. Every headman imagined that he did enough if he looked after his own state, and did not care for the others. With the Burgtmaagden it was still worse. Each of them depended upon her own judgment, and whenever a Grevetman did anything without her, she raised distrust between him and his people. If any case happened which concerned several states, and one maid had been consulted, the rest all exclaimed that she had spoken only in the interest of her own state. By such proceedings they brought disputes among the states, and so severed the bond of union that the people of one state were jealous of those of the rest, or at least considered them as strangers; the consequence of which was that the Gauls or Truwenden (Druids) took possession of our lands as far as the Scheldt, and the Magy as far as the Wesara. How this happened my mother has explained, otherwise this book would not have been written, although I have lost all hope that it would be of any use. I do not write in the hope that I shall win back the land or preserve it: in my opinion that is impossible. I write only for the future generations, that they may all know in what way we were lost, and that each may learn that every crime brings its punishment.

My name is Apollonia. Two-and-thirty days after my mother's death my brother Adelbrost was found murdered on the wharf, his skull fractured and his limbs torn asunder. My father, who lay ill, died of fright. Then my younger brother, Apol, sailed from here to the west side of Schoonland. There he built a citadel named Lindasburgt,* in order there to avenge our wrong. Wr-alda accorded him many years for that. He had five sons, who all caused fear

---

* Lindasburch, on Cape Lindanaes, Norway.

ånd min brother gôma. After måm ånd brother-is dåd
send tha fromesta fon-ut-a låndum to ekkôrum kvmen, hja
havon en bånd sloten Adelbånd hêten. Til thju vs nên
leth witherfåra ne skolde, håvath hja my ånd Adelhirt min
jungste brother vpper burch brocht, my by tha fåmna ånd
min brother by tha wêrar. Thå ik thritich jêr werê heth
man my to Burchfåm kêren, ånd thå min brother fiftich
wêre, werth-er keren to Grêvetman. Fon måm-is syde
wêre min brother thene sexte, men fon tåt his syde thene
thride. Nêi rjucht machton sine åfterkvmande thus nên
overa Linda åfter hjara nômun navt ne fora, men alra
månnalik wildet håva to êre fon mina måm. Thêr to
boppa heth mån vs åk en ofskrifte jêven fon thet bok
thêra Adela follistar. Thêr mitha ben ik thet blydeste,
hwand thrvch min måm hjra wisdom kêm-et in wralda.
In thas burch håv ik jeta ôra skrifta fvnden, thêr navt in
't bok ne stan, åk lovsprêka ovir min måm, altham wil ik
åfter skriva.

Thit send tha nêilêtne skrifta Brunnos, ther skrywer
wêsen is to thisre burch. After that tha Adela follistar
ella hêde lêta overskryva elk in sin rik, hwat wryt was
in vppa wågarum thêra burgum, bisloton hja en Moder
to kjasane. Thêrto wårth en mêna acht bilêid vp thisra
hêm. After tha forme rêd Adelas wårth Tüntja bifolen.
Ak skoldet slåcht håve. Thach nw frêge min Burgtfåm
thet wort, hju hede immerthe wêuich wêst thåt hju Moder
skolde wertha, ut êrsêke thåt hju hyr vpper burch sat,
hwana mêst alle Moderum kêren wêron. Tha hju thet
word gund was, êpende hju hira falxa wêra ånde kêth : I
alle skinth årg to heftane an Adelas rêd, tha thåt ne skil
thêrvmde min mvla navt ne sluta ner snôra. Hwa tach is
Adela ånd hwåna kvmt et wôi thåtster sokke håge love to
swikth. Lik ik hjuddêga is hju to fara hyr burchfam wêst.

to Magy, and brought fame to my brother. After the
death of my mother and my brother, all the bravest of
the land joined together and made a covenant, called the
Adelbond. In order to preserve us from injury, they
brought me and my youngest brother, Adelhirt, to the
burgt—me to the maidens, and him to the warriors. When
I was thirty years old I was chosen as Burgtmaagd, and
my brother at fifty was chosen Grevetman. From mother's
side my brother was the sixth, but from father's side the
third. By right, therefore, his descendants could not
put "overa Linda" after their names, but they all wished
to do it in honour of their mother. In addition to this,
there was given to us also a copy of "The Book of Adela's
Followers." That gave me the most pleasure, because it
came into the world by my mother's wisdom. In the
burgt I have found other writings also in praise of my
mother. All this I will write afterwards.

These are the writings left by Bruno, who was the
writer of this burgt. After the followers of Adela had
made copies, each in his kingdom, of what was inscribed
upon the walls of the burgt, they resolved to choose a
mother. For this purpose a general assembly was called
at this farm. By the first advice of Adela, Teuntje was
recommended. That would have been arranged, only that
my Burgtmaagd asked to speak : she had always supposed
that she would be chosen mother, because she was at the
burgt from which mothers had generally been chosen.
When she was allowed to speak, she opened her false lips
and said : You all seem to place great value on Adela's
advice, but that shall not shut my mouth. Who is
Adela, and whence comes it that you respect her so
highly ? She was what I am now, a Burgtmaagd of this

Tha is hju thêr vmbe wiser jefta bêtre as ik ånd alle
ôthera, jefta is hju mår stelet vppvsa sêd ånd plêgum.
Hwêre thåt et fal, så skolde hju wel Moder wrden wêsa,
thå hju thêrto kêren is, men nêan hju wilde rêder ennen
bosta ha mith all joi ånd nochta thêr er anebonden send,
in stêd fon ênsum over hjam ånd et folk to wåkane. Hju
is êl klarsjande, god, men min ågne ne send fêr fon vrth-
justred to wêsane. Ik håv sjan thåt hju hir fryadelf herde
minth, nw god, thåt is lovelik, men ik håv forther sjan
thåt Tüntja Apol-is nift is. Wyder wil ik navt ne sedsa.
Tha forsta bigripen êl god, hwêr hju hly sochte, men
emong et folk kêm twyspalt, ånd nêidam heth maradêl
fon hyr wei kêm, wilde-t Tüntja thiu êre navt ne guna.
Rêdne wrde stopth, tha saxne tågon uta skådne, men thêr
ne wårth nêne Moder kêren. Kirt åfter hêde annen vsera
bodne sin makker fåleth. Til hjuddêga hêde der frod
wêsen, thêrvmbe hede min burchfåm orlovi vmb-im buta
tha låndpåla to helpane. Thach in stêd fon im to helpane
nêi thet Twiskland, alsa fljuchte hju selva mith im overe
Wrsara ånd forth nêi tha Mågy. Thi Mågy tham sina
Fryas svna hagja wilde stald-iri as Moder to Godaburch
et Skênland, mên hju wilde mår, hju sêid-im thåt sahwersa
hi Adela vpruma koste, hi måster skolde wertha over êl
Fryas land. Hju wêr en fyand fon Adele sêide hju,
hwand thrvch hjra renka nas hju nên Moder wrden.
Sahwersa hy hir Texland forspreka wilde, sa skolde hjra
boda sina wichar to wêiwyser thjanja. Al thissa sêka
heth hjra boda selva bilyad.

THET OTHERA SKRIFT.

Fiftian monatha nêi thêre lerste acht wêr-et Frjunsklp
jeftha Winnemônath. Alleramånnelik jef to an mery

place; is she, then, wiser and better than I and all the others? or is she more conversant with our laws and customs? If that had been the case, she would have become mother when she was chosen; but instead of that, she preferred matrimony to a single life, watching over herself and her people. She is certainly very clear-sighted, but my eyes are far from being dim. I have observed that she is very much attached to her husband, which is very praiseworthy; but I see, likewise, that Teuntje is Apol's niece. Further I say nothing.

The principal people understood very well which way the wind blew with her; but among the people there arose disputes, and as most of the people came from here, they would not give the honour to Teuntje. The conferences were ended, knives were drawn, and no mother was chosen. Shortly afterwards one of our messengers killed his comrade. As he had been a man of good character hitherto, my Burgtmaagd had permission to help him over the frontier; but instead of helping him over to Twiskland (Germany), she fled with him herself to Wesara, and then to the Magy. The Magy, who wished to please his sons of Frya, appointed her mother of Godaburgt, in Schoonland; but she wished for more, and she told him that if he could get Adela out of the way he might become master of the whole of Frya's land. She said she hated Adela for having prevented her from being chosen mother. If he would promise her Texland, her messenger should serve as guide to his warriors. All this was confessed by her messenger.

THE SECOND WRITING.

Fifteen months after the last general assembly, at the festival of the harvest month, everybody gave himself

mery fru ånd bly, ånd nimman nêde diger than to åkane
sina nocht. Thach Wr.alda wild vs wysa, thåt wåkendom,
navt vrgamlath wrde ne mêi. To midne fon-et] fêst fyrja
kêm nêvil to hullande vsa wrda in thikke thjusternise.
Nocht runde wêi, tha wåkendom nilde navt ne kêra. Tha
strandwåkar wêron fon hjara nêd fjura hlåpen ånd vppa
tha topådum nas nênen to bisja. Thå nêvil ewêi tåch,
lokte svnne thrvch tha rêta thêra wolkum vp irtha. Alrek
kêm wither ut to juwgande ånd to jolande, thet jungk
folk tåch sjongande mitha gürbåm* ånd thisse overfulde
luft mith sina liaflika ådam. Men thahwila thêr alrek
in nocht båjada, was vrrêd lånd mith horsum ånd ridderum. Lik alle årga wêron hja helpen thrvch thjuster-
nisse, ånd hinne glupath thrvch Linda waldis påda. To
fåra Adelas dure tagon twilif mangêrtne mith twilif
låmkes ånd twilif knåpa mith twilif hoklinga, en junge
Saxmån birêd en wilde bufle thêr er selva fensen hêde
ånd tåmad. Mith allerlêja blomma wêron hja siarad, ånd
tha linnen tohnekna thêra mångêrtne wêron omborad mith
gold ut-er Rêne.

Thå Adela to hira hus ut vppet slecht kêm, fol en
blomrêin del vppira hole, alle juwgade herde ånd tha tot-
horne thêra knåpum gûldon boppa ella ut. Arme Adela,
årm folk, ho kirt skil frü hir bydja. Thå thju lônge skåre
ut sjocht wêre kêm er en hloth mågjara ridderum linrjucht
to rinnande vp Adelas hêm. Hira tåt ånd gåde wêron·
jeta vppa stoppenbenke sêten. Thju dure stond êpen ånd
thêr binna stand Adelbrost hira svna. As er sach ho sina
eldra in frêse wêron, gripter sine bôge fon-ere wåch wêi ånd
skåt nêi tha foresta thêra råwarum; this swikt ånd trulde
vppet gårs del; overne twade ånd thride was en êlik lôt
biskêren. Intwiska hêdon sina eldra hjara wêpne fat, ånd
tagon vndyger to Jonis. Tha råwera skoldon hjam ring

---

* Gürbam. C. Niebuhr Reize enz. I. 174. Eene zakpijp bij de Egyptenaren
Sumåra el Kürbe genoemd.

up to pleasure and merry-making, and no one thought of anything but diversion ; but Wr-alda wished to teach us that watchfulness should never be relaxed. In the midst of the festivities the fog came and enveloped every place in darkness. Cheerfulness melted away, but watchfulness did not take its place. The coastguard deserted their beacons, and no one was to be seen on any of the paths. When the fog rose, the sun scarcely appeared among the clouds; but the people all came out shouting with joy, and the young folks went about singing to their bagpipes, filling the air with their melody. But while every one was intoxicated with pleasure, treachery had landed with its horses and riders. As usual, darkness had favoured the wicked, and they had slipped in through the paths of Linda's wood. Before Adela's door twelve girls led twelve lambs, and twelve boys led twelve calves. A young Saxon bestrode a wild bull which he had caught and tamed. They were decked with all kinds of flowers, and the girls' dresses were fringed with gold from the Rhine.

When Adela came out of her house, a shower of flowers fell on her head; they all cheered loudly, and the fifes of the boys were heard over everything. Poor Adela! poor people! how short will be your joy ! When the procession was out of sight, a troop of Magyar soldiers rushed up to Adela's house. Her father and her husband were sitting on the steps. The door was open, and within stood Adelbrost her son. When he saw the danger of his parents, he took his bow from the wall and shot the leader of the pirates, who staggered and fell on the grass. The second and third met a similar fate. In the meantime his parents had seized their weapons, and went slowly to Jon's house. They would soon have been taken, but

---

Gürbam. C. Niebuhr, Travels, vol. i. p. 174. The bagpipe is called by the Egyptians *Sumâra el Kürbe.*

fensen ha, men Adela kêm, vppere burch hêde hja alle
wêpne to hantêra lêrad, sjugun irthfêt wêre hju lông ånd
hira gêrt så fêlo, thryja swikte hja tham or hjra hole ånd
as er del kêm wêr en ridder gårsfallich. Follistar kêmon
omme herne thêre lône wêi. Tha råwar wrdon fålath ånd
fensen. Thach to lêt, en pil hêde hjra bosme trefth.
Vrrêdelika Magy! In fenin was sin pint dipth ånd
thêrof is hju sturven.

THÊRE BURCHFAMS LOV.

Jes ferhêmande åthe, thusande send al kumen ånd jet
måra send vp wêi.
Wel, hja willath Adelas wisdom hêra.
Sekur is hju forstine, hwand hju is immer thja forste
wêst.
O wach hwêrto skolde hja thjanja. Hira hemeth is
linnen, hira tohnekka* wol, thåt hjv selva spon ånd
wêvade. Hwêrmêi skolde hja hjra skênhêd håga. Navt
mith pårlum, hwand hjra tuskar send witter ; navt mith
gold, hwand hjra hêr is blikkander ; navt mith stêna, wel
send hjra ågon saft as lamkes ågon, thach to lik sa glander
thåt mån thêr skrômlik in sja ne mêi.
Men hwat kålt ik fon skên. Frya wêre wis navt skêner.
Ja åthe, Frya thêr sjugun skênhêde hêde, hwêrfon hjra
toghåtera men êne elk håchstens thria urven håve. Men
al wêre hju lêdlik, thach skolde hju vs djura wêsa.
Jef hju wygandlik sy. Hark åthe, Adela is thet ênge
bern vsar grêvetman. Sjugun jrthfet is hju håch, jeta
gråter then hjra licheme is hjra wishêd ånd hjra mod is
lik bêde to sêmine.   •
Lok thêr, thêr wêre ênis en fênbrônd, thrju bern
wêron vp jenske gråfstên sprongen. Wind blos fel. Alrek krêta ånd thju måm wêre rêdalås. Thêr kvmt Adela :
ho stêitst ånd têmethste hropth hju, tragd help to lê-

---

* To hnekka, eene hooge, *tot aan de nek* reikende, japon.

Adela came. She had learned in the burgt to use all kinds of weapons. She was seven feet high, and her sword was the same length. She waved it three times over her head, and each time a knight bit the earth. Reinforcements came, and the pirates were made prisoners; but too late—an arrow had penetrated her bosom! The treacherous Magy had poisoned it, and she died of it.

THE ELEGY OF THE BURGTMAAGD.

Yes, departed friend, thousands are arrived, and more are coming. They wish to hear the wisdom of Adela. Truly, she was a princess, for she had always been the leader. O Sorrow, what good can you do!

Her garments of linen and * wool she spun and wove herself. How could she add to her beauty? Not with pearls, for her teeth were more white; not with gold, for her tresses were more brilliant; not with precious stones, for her eyes, though soft as those of a lamb, were so lustrous that you could scarcely look into them. But why do I talk of beauty? Frya was certainly not more beautiful; yes, my friends, Frya, who possessed seven perfections, of which each of her daughters inherited one, or at most three. But even if she had been ugly, she would still have been dear to us. Is she warlike? Listen, my friend. Adela was the only daughter of our Grevetman. She stood seven feet high. Her wisdom exceeded her stature, and her courage was equal to both together. Here is an instance. There was once a turf-ground on fire. Three children got upon yonder gravestone. There was a furious wind. The people were all shouting, and the mother was helpless. Then came Adela. What are you all standing still here for? she cried. Try to

---

* *To hnekka, a high petticoat reaching up to the neck.*

nande ånd Wr.alda skil jo krefta jêva. Thêr hipth hja
nêi-t krylwod, gript elsne trêjon, tragd en breg to mak-
jande, nw helpath åk tha ôthera ånd tha bern send hred.
Jêrlikes kêmon tha bern hyr blomma ledsa.

Thêr kêmon thrê Fonysjar skipljuda thêr hja wrêvela
wilde, men Adela kêm, hju hêde hjara hwop (hrop) hêrad,
in swim slêith hju tha lêtha ånd til thju hja selva jechta
skolde, thet hja vnwêrthelike manna wêron, bint hju
alsêmen an en spinrok fest.   Tha fêrhêmanda hêra kêmon
hjara thjud askja.   Tha hja sagon ho skots hja misdên
wêron, kêm torn vp, thach mån tellade ho-t bêrd was.

Hwat hja forth dêdon, hja buwgdon to fåra Adela ånd
keston thju slyp hyrar tohnekka.

Kvm fêrhêmande åthe, tha wald füglon fljuchtath to
fåra tha fêlo forsykar.   Kvm åthe så mêist hjara wishêd
hêra.

By tha gråfstên hwer fon in tha lovsprêke meld wårth,
is måm hira lik bigråven.   Vppira gråfstên heth mån
thissa worda hwryten.

NE HLAP NAVT TO HASTICH HWAND HYR LÊID ADELA.

Thju formlêre thêr is hwryten inutere wåch thêr burch-
tore, nis navt wither eskrêven in thåt bok thêra Adeli
follistar.   Hwêrvmbe thet lêten is nêt ik navt to skri
wand.   Tha thit bok is min ajn, thêrvmbe wil ik hja thê
inna setta to wille minra mågum.

FORMLÊRE.

Alle god minnanda Fryas bern sy held.   Hwand thrvcl

help them, and Wr-alda will give you strength.   Then she ran to the Krylwood and got some elder branches, of which she made a bridge.   The others then came to assist her, and the children were saved.   The children bring flowers to the place every year.   There came once three Phœnician sailors, who began to ill-treat the children, when Adela, having heard their screams, beat the scoundrels till they were insensible, and then, to prove to them what miserable wretches they were, she tied them all three to a spindle.

The foreign lords came to look after their people, and when they saw how ridiculously they had been treated they were very angry, till they were told what had happened.   Upon that they bowed themselves before Adela, and kissed the hem of her garment.   But come, distant living friend.   The birds of the forest fled before the numerous visitors.   Come, friend, and you shall hear her wisdom.   By the gravestone of which mention has already been made her body is buried.   Upon the stone the following words are inscribed :—

TREAD SOFTLY, FOR HERE LIES ADELA.

The old legend which is written on the outside wall of the city tower is not written in "The Book of Adela's Followers."   Why this has been neglected I do not know; but this book is my own, so I will put it in out of regard to my relations.

The Oldest Doctrine.

Hail to all the well-intentioned children of Frya !

tham skil et sêlich wertha vp jrtha. Lêr ånd kêth to tha
folkum. Wr.alda is thet alderaldesta jeftha overaldesta,
hwand thet skop alla thinga. Wr.alda is ella in ella,
hwand thet is êvg ånd vnendlik. Wr.alda is overal ain-
wardich, men narne to bisja, thêrvmbe wårth thet wêsa
gåst hêten. Al hwat wi fon him sja müge send tha skepsela thêr thrvch sin lêva kvme ånd wither henne ga,
hwand inut Wr.alda kvmath alle thinga ånd kêrath alle
thinga. Fon ut Wr.alda kvmth t anfang ånd et ende, alra
thinga gêith in im vppa. Wr.alda is thet êne ella mach-
tige wêsa, hwand alle ôre macht is fon him lênad ånd
kêrath to him wither. In ut Wr.alda kvmath alle krefta
ånd alle krefta kêrath to him wither. Thêrvmbe is hi
allêna theth skeppande wêsa ånd thêr nis nawet eskêpen
buta him.

Wr.alda lêide êvge setma thet is êwa in al et skêpne,
ånd thêr ne send nên gode setma jeftha hja moton thêrnêi
tavlikt wêsa. Men afskên ella in Wr.alda sy, tha boshêd
thêra månniska nis navt fon him. Boshêd kvmth thrvch
lômhêd vndigerhed ånd domhêd. Thêrvmbe kån hju wel
tha månniska skåda, Wr.alda nimmer. Wr.alda is thju
wishêd, ånd tha êwa thêr hju tavlikt heth, send tha boka
wêrût wy lêra müge, ånd thêr nis nêne wishêd to findande
ner to garjande buta tham. Tha månniska mügon fêlo
thinga sja, men Wr.alda sjath alle thinga. Tha månniska
mügon fêlo thinga lêra, men Wr.alda wêt alle thinga.
Tha månniska mügon fêlo thinga vntslûta, men to fåra
Wr.alda is ella êpned. Tha månniska send månnalik
ånd berlik, men Wr.alda skept bêde. Tha månniska
minnath ånd håtath, tha Wr.alda is allêna rjuchtfêrdich.
Thêrvmbe is Wr.alda allêne god, ånd thêr ne send nêne
goda bûta him. Mith thet Jol wandelath ånd wixlat
allet eskêpne, men god is allêna vnforanderlik. Thruch
that Wr.alda god is, alsa ne mei hi åk navt foranderja;

Through them the earth shall become holy. Learn and announce to the people Wr-alda is the ancient of ancients, for he created all things. Wr-alda is all in all, for he is eternal and everlasting. Wr-alda is omnipresent but invisible, and therefore is called a spirit. All that we can see of him are the created beings who come to life through him and go again, because from Wr-alda all things proceed and return to him. Wr-alda is the beginning and the end. Wr-alda is the only almighty being, because from him all other strength comes, and returns to him. Therefore he alone is the creator, and nothing exists without him. Wr-alda established eternal principles, upon which the laws of creation were founded, and no good laws could stand on any other foundation. But although everything is derived from Wr-alda, the wickedness of men does not come from him. Wickedness comes from heaviness, carelessness, and stupidity; therefore they may well be injurious to men, but never to Wr-alda. Wr-alda is wisdom, and the laws that he has made are the books from which we learn, nor is any wisdom to be found or gathered but in them. Men may see a great deal, but Wr-alda sees everything. Men can learn a great deal, but Wr-alda knows everything. Men can discover much, but to Wr-alda everything is open. Mankind are male and female, but Wr-alda created both. Mankind love and hate, but Wr-alda alone is just. Therefore Wr-alda is good, and there is no good without him. In the progress of time all creation alters and changes, but goodness alone is unalterable; and since Wr-alda is good, he cannot

M

ånd thrvch thet er bilywath, thêrvmbe is hy allêna wêsa
ånd al et ora skin.

THET OTHERA DÊL FONRE FORMLÊR.

Emong Findas folk send wanwysa, thêr thrvch hjara
overfindingrikhêd alsa årg send, thåt hja hjara selva wis
måkja ånd tha inewida bitjuga, thåt hja thet besta dêl
send fon Wr.alda; thåt hjara gåst thet beste dêl is fon
Wr.aldas gåst ånd thet Wr.alda allêna mêi thånkja thrvch
helpe hjaris bryn.*
Thåt aider skepsle en dêl is fon Wr.aldas vnendlik wêsa;
thåt håvon hja fon vs gåbad.
Men hjara falxe rêdne ånd hjara tåmlåse håchfarenhêd
heth ra vppen dwålwêi brocht. Wêre hjara gåst Wr.aldas
gåst, så skolde Wr.alda êl dvm wêsa in stêde fon licht and
wis. Hwand hjara gåst slåvth him selva immer of vmbe
skêne bylda to måkjande, thêr y åfternêi anbid. Men
Findas folk is en årg folk, hwand afskên tha wanwysa
thêra hjara selva wis måkja thåt hja drochtne send, sa
håvon hja to fåra tha vnewida falxa drochtne eskêpeu, to
kêthande allerwêikes, thåt thissa drochtne Wr.alda eskêpen
håve, mith al hwat thêr inne is ; gyriga drochtne fvl uyd
ånd torn, tham êrath ånd thjanath willath wêsa thrvch tha
månniska, thêr blod ånd offer willa ånd skåt askja. Men
thi wanwisa falxa manna, tham hjara selva godis skalka
jeftha prestera nôma lêta, bürath ånd såmnath ånd gethath
aldam to fåra drochtne thêr er navt ne send, vmbet selva
to bihaldande. Aldam bidrywath hja mith en rum emod,
thrvchdam hja hjara selva drochtne wåne, thêr an ninman
andert skeldich ne send. Send thêr svme tham hjara
renka froda ånd bår måkja, alsa wrdon hja thrvch hjara
rakkera fåt ånd vmbira laster vrbarnad, ella mith fêlo
ståtska plêgum, hjara falxa drochtne to-n êre. Men in trvth,

---

* Cf. Hegel a. h. 1.

change.   As he endures, he alone exists ; everything else
is show.

THE SECOND PART OF THE OLDEST DOCTRINE.

Among Finda's people there are false teachers, who, by
their over-inventiveness, have become so wicked that they
make themselves and their adherents believe that they are
the best part of Wr-alda, that their spirit is the best part
of Wr-alda's spirit, and that Wr-alda can only think by
the help of their brains.

. That every creature is a part of Wr-alda's eternal being,
that they have stolen from us ; but their false reasoning
and ungovernable pride have brought them on the road
to ruin.   If their spirit was Wr-alda's spirit, then Wr-alda
would be very stupid, instead of being sensible and wise ;
for their spirit labours to create beautiful statues, which
they afterwards worship.   Finda's people are a wicked
people, for although they presumptuously pretend among
themselves that they are gods, they proclaim the un-
consecrated false gods, and declare everywhere that these
idols created the world and all that therein is—greedy
idols, full of envy and anger, who desire to be served
and honoured by the people, and who exact bloody sacri-
fices and rich offerings ; but these presumptuous and false
men, who call themselves God's servants and priests,
receive and collect everything in the name of the idols
that have no real existence, for their own benefit.

They do all this with an easy conscience, as they think
themselves gods not answerable to any one.   If there are
some who discover their tricks and expose them, they hand
them over to the executioners to be burnt for their calum-
nies, with solemn ceremonies in honour of the false gods ;

allêna vmbe thât hja ra navt skâda ne skolde. Til thju vsa bern nw wêpned müge wêsa tojenst hjara drochtenlika lêre, alsa hâgon tha fâmna hjam fon buta to lêrande hwat hyr skil folgja. Wr.alda was êr alle thinga, ând nêi alle thinga skil er wêsa. Wr.alda is alsa êvg ând hi is vnendlik, thervmb nis thêr nawet buta him. Thrvch ut Wr.aldas lêva warth tid ând alle thinga bern, ând sin lêva nimth tid ând alle thinga wêi. Thissa sêka moton klêr ând bâr mâkad wrda by alle wisa, sâ thât hja-t an ôthera bithjuta ând biwisa müge. Is-t sâ fâr wnnen, sa sêith mân forther: Hwat thus vsa ommefang treft, alsa send wy en dêl fon Wr.aldas vnendelik wêsa, alsa tha ommefang fon al et eskêpne, thach hwat angâ vsa dânte, vsa ainskipa, vsa gâst ând al vsa bithânkinga, thissa ne hêra navt to thet wêsa. Thit ella send fljuchtiga thinga tham thrvch Wr.aldas lêva forskina, thach thêr thrvch sin wishêd sâdâne ând navt owers navt ne forskina. Men thrvchdam sin lêva stêdes forthga, alsa ne mêi thêr nawet vppa sin stêd navt bilywa. Thêrvmbe forwixlath alle eskêpne thinga fon stêd, fon dânte ând âk fon thânkwisa. Thervmbe ne mêi irtha selva, ner eng skepsle ni sedsa : ik ben, men wel ik was. Ak ne mêi nên mânniska navt ne sedsa ik thânk, men blât, ik thochte. Thi knâp is grâter ând owers as tha-r bern wêre. Hy heth ora gêrtne, tochta ând thânkwisa. Thi man en tât is ând thânkth owers as thâ-r knâp wêre. Êvin tha alda fon dêgum. Thât wêt allera mannelik. Sâhwersa allera mannalik nw wêt ând jechta mot, thât hy alon wixlath, sâ mot hy âk bijechta, that er jahweder âgeblik wixlath, âk thahwila-r sêid : ik ben, ând thât sina thânk bylda wixle, tha hwile-r sêid : ik thânk.

Instêde thât wy tha ârga Findas althus vnwerthlik after-nêi snakka ând kâlta, ik ben, jeftha wel, ik ben thet beste dêl Wr.aldas, ja thrvch vs allêna mêi-r thânkja,

but really in order to save themselves. In order that our
children may be protected against their idolatrous doctrine,
the duty of the maidens is to make them learn by heart
the following : Wr-alda existed before all things, and will
endure after all things. Wr-alda is also eternal and everlasting, therefore nothing exists without him. From
Wr-alda's life sprang time and all living things, and his
life takes away time and every other thing. These things
must be made clear and manifest in every way, so that
they can be made clear and comprehensible to all. When
we have learned thus much, then we say further : In what
regards our existence, we are a part of Wr-alda's everlasting being, like the existence of all created beings ;
but as regards our form, our qualities, our spirit, and all
our thoughts, these do not belong to the being. All these
are passing things which appear through Wr-alda's life,
and which appear through his wisdom, and not otherwise ; but whereas his life is continually progressing,
nothing can remain stationary, therefore all created
things change their locality, their form, and their
thoughts. So neither the earth nor any other created
object can say, I am ; but rather, I was. So no man can
say, I think ; but rather, I thought. The boy is greater
and different from the child ; he has different desires,
inclinations, and thoughts. The man and father feels
and thinks differently from the boy, the old man just the
same. Everybody knows that. Besides, everybody knows
and must acknowledge that he is now changing, that he
changes every minute even while he says, I am, and that
his thoughts change even while he says, I think. Instead,
then, of imitating Finda's wicked people, and saying, I am
the best part of Wr-alda, and through us alone he can think,

sâ willath wy kêtha wral ånd allerwêikes wêr et nêdlik sy :
wy Fryas bern send forskinsla thrvch Wr.aldas lêva; by-t
anfang min ånd blât, thach immer wårthande ånd nåkande
to fvlkvmenlikhêd, svnder â sa god to wrda as Wr.alda
selva. Vsa gâst nis navt Wr.aldas gâst, hi is thêrfon
allêna en afskinsle. Tha Wr.alda vs skop, heth er vs in
thrvch sine wishêd-bryn-sintûga, hügia ånd fêlo goda ainskipa lênad. Hyrmêi mugon wy sina êwa bitrachta.
Thêrof mügon wy lêra ånd thêrvr mügon wy rêda, ella
ånd allêna to vs ain held. Hêde Wr.alda vs nêne sinna
jêven, sa ne skolde wy narne of nêta ånd wy skolde jeta
reddalasser as en sêkwale wêsa, thêr forthdryven wårth
thrvch ebbe ånd thrvch flod.

THIT STAT VP SKRIVFILT SKRÊVEN. TAL AND ANDWORDE
ORA FAMNA TO-N FORBYLD.

En vnsels gyrich mån kêm to bârande by Trâst thêr fâm
wêre to Stavia. Hy sêide vnwêder hêde sin hus wêi brocht.
Hy hêde to Wr.alda bêden, men Wr.alda nêdim nêne helpe
lênad. Bist en åfte Fryas, frêje Trâst. Fon elder t elder,
andere thene mån. Thån sêide hju wil ik åwet in thin
mod sêja in bitrouwa, thåt et kyma groja ånd früchda
jêva mêi. Forth sprêk hju ånde kêth. Thâ Frya bern
was, stand vs moder naked ånd blât, vnbihod to jenst tha
strêlum thêre svnne. Ninman macht hju frêja ånd thêr
wêre ninman thêr hja help macht lêna. Thâ gvng Wr.alda
to ånd wrochte in hjara mod nigung ånd liavde anggost ånd
skrik. Hju sach rondomme, hjara nigung kås thet beste ånd
hju sochte skul vndera wårande linda. Men rêin kêm ånd
t onhlest wêre thât hju wet wrde. Thach hju hêde sjan

we proclaim everywhere where it is necessary, We, Frya's
children, exist through Wr-alda's life—in the beginning
mean and base, but always advancing towards perfection
without ever attaining the excellence of Wr-alda himself.
Our spirit is not Wr-alda's spirit, it is merely a shadow
of it. When Wr-alda created us, he lent us his wisdom,
brains, organs, memory, and many other good qualities.
By this means we are able to contemplate his creatures
and his laws; by this means we can learn and can speak
of them always, and only for our own benefit. If Wr-alda
had given us no organs, we should have known nothing,
and been more irrational than a piece of sea-weed driven
up and down by the ebb and flood.

THIS IS WRITTEN ON PARCHMENT—" SKRIVFILT." SPEECH
AND ANSWER TO OTHER MAIDENS AS AN EXAMPLE.

An unsociable, avaricious man came to complain to
Troost, who was the maid of Stavia. He said a thunder-
storm had destroyed his house. He had prayed to Wr-alda,
but Wr-alda had given him no help. Are you a true
Frisian? Troost asked. From father and forefathers,
replied the man. Then she said, I will sow something
in your conscience, in confidence that it will take root,
grow, and bear fruit. She continued, When Frya was
born, our mother stood naked and bare, unprotected from
the rays of the sun. She could ask no one, and there
was no one who could give her any help. Then Wr-alda
wrought in her conscience inclination and love, anxiety
and fright. She looked round her, and her inclination chose the best. She sought a hiding-place under
the sheltering lime-trees, but the rain came, and
the difficulty was that she got wet. She had seen.

ho thet wêter to tha hellanda blâdar of drupte. Nw
mâkade hju en hrof mith hellanda sidum, vp stôka
mâkade hju tham. Men stornewind kêm ånd blos rêin
thêr vnder. Nw hêde hja sjan thåt tha stam hly jef, åfter
gong hja to ånd mâkade en wâch fon plâga ånd sâdum,
thet forma an êne syda ånd forth an alle syda. Storne
wind kêm to bek jeta wodander as to fora ånd blos thju
hrof ewêi. Men hju ne bârade navt over Wr.alda ner to
jenst Wr.alda. Men hja mâkade eu reitne hrof ånd leide
stêne thêr vppa. Bifvnden håvande ho sêr thet dvath vmb
allêua to tobbande, alsa bithjude hju hira bern ho ånd
hwêrvmbe hju alsa hêde dên. Thissa wrochton ånd
tochton to sêmine. A sadenera wise send wy an hûsa
kêmen mith stoppenbånkum, en slecht ånd warande linda
with tha svnnestrêlum. To tha lesta håvon hja en burch
mâkad ånd forth alle ôthera. Nis thin hus thus navt
sterk noch wêst, alsa mot i trachda vmbet ôre bêter to
mâkjande. Min hus wêre sterk enoch, sêider, men thet
håge wêter heth et vp bêrad ånd stornewind heth et ore
dên. Hwêr stand thin hus thân, frêje Trâst. Alingen
thêre Rêne, andere thene man. Ne stand et thân navt
vppen nol jeftha therp, frêje Trâst. Nean sêider, miu
hus stand ênsum by tha overe, allêna håv ik et buwad,
men ik ne macht thêr allêna nên therp to makane. Ik
wist wel, sêide Trâst, tha fâmna håv et my meld. Thv
hest al thin·lêva en grûwel had an tha månniska, ut frêse
thåtste awet jêva jeftha dva moste to fara hjam. Thach
thêr mitha ne mêi mån navt fêr ne kvma. Hwand
Wr.alda thêr mild is, kêrath him fona gyriga. Fåsta
het vs rêden ånd buppa tha dura fon alle burgum is t in
stên ut wryten : bist årg bâtsjochtig sêide Fåsta, bihod
thån jvwe nêsta, bithjod thån jvwe nêsta, help thån juwe
nesta, så skilun hja t thi witherdva. Is i thina rêd navt
god noch, ik nêt får thi nên bêtera. Skâmrâd wårth then
mån ånd hi drupte stolkes hinne.

how the water ran down the pendent leaves; so she made
a roof of leaves fastened with sticks, but the wind blew
the rain under it. She observed that the stem would
afford protection. She then built a wall of sods, first on
one side, and then all round. The wind grew stronger
and blew away the roof, but she made no complaint of
Wr-alda. She made a roof of rushes, and put stones
upon it. Having found how hard it is to toil alone, she
showed her children how and why she had done it. They
acted and thought as she did. This is the way in which
we became possessed of houses and porches, a street, and
lime-trees to protect us from the rays of the sun. At
last we have built a citadel, and all the rest. If your
house is not strong enough, then you must try and make
another. My house was strong enough, he said, but the
flood and the wind destroyed it. Where did your house
stand? Troost asked. On the bank of the Rhine, he
answered. Did it not stand on a knoll? Troost asked.
No, said the man; my house stood alone on the bank. I
built it alone, but I could not alone make a hillock. I
knew it, Troost answered; the maidens told me. All
your life you have avoided your neighbours, fearing that
you might have to give or do something for them; but
one cannot get on in the world in that way, for Wr-alda,
who is kind, turns away from the niggardly. Fâsta has
advised us, and it is engraved in stone over all our
doors. If you are selfish, distrustful towards your
neighbours, teach your neighbours, help your neighbours, and they will return the same to you. If this
advice is not good enough for you, I can give you no
better. The man blushed for shame, and slunk away.

Nw wil ik selva skriwa êrost fon over min Burch
and than over hwat ik hav muge sjan.

Min burch lêid an-t north-ende thêre Liudgârda. Thju
tore heth sex syda. Thrya thrittich fêt is hju hâch. Flât
fon boppa. En lyth huske thêr vppa, hwâna mån tha
stâra bisjath. An aider syd thêre tore stât en hus, long
thrya hondred, brêd thrya sjugun fêt, êlika hâch bihalva
thju hrof, thêr rondlik is. Altham fon hyrbakken stên,
ånd fon buta ne send nênen ôthera. Om tha burch is en
hringdik, thêrom en grâft diap thrya sjugun fêt, wyd thrya
twilif fêt. Siath hwa fonêre tore del, sa siath hi thju
dânte fon et Jol. Vppa grvnd twisk tha sûdlika hûsa
thêre, send allerlêja krûda fon hêinde ånd fêr, thêrof
moton tha fâmna tha krefta lêra. Twisk tha nortlika
hûsa is allêna fjeld. Tha thrju nortlika hûsa send fol
kêren ånd ôther bihof. Twa sûdar send to fâra tha
fâmkes vmbe to skola ånd to hêma. Thet sûdlikoste hus
is thêre Burchfâm his hêm. Inna tore hangt thju foddik.
Tha wagar thêre tore send mith kestlika stêna smukad.
In vppa thêre sûderwach is thêne Tex wrytten. An
tha fêre syde thêra finth mån thju formlêre; anna winstere syde tha êwa. Tha ora sêka finth mån vppa ôra
thrja. Tojenst tha dik by-t hus thêr fâm stêt thju
owne ånd thju molmâk thrvch fjuwer bufla kroden.
Buta vsa burchwal is-t hêm, thêr vppa tha burchhêra
ånda wêrar hême. Thju riugdik thêra is en stonde grât,
nên stjurar, men svnna stonde, hwêrfon twya twilif
vppen etmelde kvma. In vpper binnasyde fona dik
is eu flât, fif fêt vndera krûn. Thêr vppa send thrya
hondred krânboga, todekt mith wod ånd lêther. Bihalva
tha hûsa thêra inhêmar send thêr binna alingne tha

Now I WILL WRITE MYSELF, FIRST ABOUT MY CITADEL,
AND THEN ABOUT WHAT I HAVE BEEN ABLE TO SEE.

My city lies near the north end of the Liudgaarde.
The tower has six sides, and is ninety feet high, flat-
roofed, with a small house upon it out of which they look
at the stars. On either side of the tower is a house three
hundred feet long, and twenty-one feet broad, and twenty-
one feet high, besides the roof, which is round. All this
is built of hard-baked bricks, and outside there is nothing
else. The citadel is surrounded by a dyke, with a moat
thirty-six feet broad and twenty-one feet deep.. If one
looks down from the tower, he sees the form of the Juul.
In the ground among the houses on the south side all
kinds of native and foreign herbs grow, of which the
maidens must study the qualities. Among the houses
on the north side there are only fields. The three houses
on the north are full of corn and other necessaries; the
two houses on the south are for the maidens to live in
and keep school. The most southern house is the dwell-
ing of the Burgtmaagd. In the tower hangs the lamp.
The walls of the tower are decorated with precious stones.
On the south wall the Tex is inscribed. On the right side
of this are the formulæ, and on the other side the laws;
the other things are found upon the three other sides.
Against the dyke, near the house of the Burgtmaagd,
stand the oven and the mill, worked by four oxen. Outside the citadel wall is the place where the Burgtheeren
and the soldiers live. The fortification outside is an hour
long—not a seaman's hour, but an hour of the sun,
of which twenty-four go to a day. Inside it is a
plain five feet below the top. On it are three hundred
crossbows covered with wood and leather.

Besides the houses of the inhabitants, there are along

dik jeta thrya twilif nêdhûsa to fâra tha omhêmar. Thet
fjeld thjanath to kâmp ånd to wêde. Anna sûdsyde fon
tha bûtenste hringdik is thju Liudgârde omtûnad thrvch
thet grâte Lindawald. Hjara dânte is thrju hernich, thet
brêde buta, til thju svnne thêr in sia mêi. Hwand thêr
send fêlo fêrlandeska thrêja ånd blommen thrvch tha
stjurar mith brocht. Alsa thju dânte vsar burch is, send
alle ôthera; thach vs-is is thju grâteste; men thi fon Texland is tha aldergrâteste. Thju tore fon Fryasburch is alsa
hâch thât hju tha wolka torent, nêi thêre tore is al et
ôthera.

By vs vppa burch ist alsa dêlad. Sjugun jonge fâmna
wâkath by thêre foddik. Aider wâk thrja stonda. In ha
ôre tid moton hja huswârk dva, lêra ånd slêpa. Send hja
sjugun jêr wâkande wêsen, alsa send hja fry. Thân
mügon hja emong tha månniska gâ, vp-ra sêd to letane
ånd rêd to jêvane. Is hwa thrju jêr fâm wêst, sâ mêi hju
alto met mith tha alda fâmna mith gâ.

Thi skrywer mot tha fâmkes lêra lêsa, skrywa ånd
rêkenja. Tha grysa jeftha grêva moton lêra hjam rjucht
ånd plicht, sêdkunda, krûdkunda, hêlkunda, skêdnesa,
tellinga ånd sanga, bijunka allerlêja thinga thêr hjam
nêdlik send vmbe rêd to jêva. Thju Burchfâm mot lêra
hjam ho hja thêrmith to wârk gâ mota by thâ månniska.
Êr en Burchfâm hjra stêd innimt, mot hju thrvch thet
lând fâra en fvl jêr. Thrê grêva burchhêra ånd thrja
alda fâmna gan mith hiri mitha. Alsa is-t âk my
gvngon. Min fârt is alingen thêre Rêne wêst, thjus
kâd opward, alingen thêre ôre syde ofward. Ho hâger
ik upkêm, to ârmer likte mi tha månniska. Wral
inna Rêne hêde mån utstekka makad. Thet sôn thât
thêr ain kêm, wr mith wêter wr skêpfachta gâten
vmbe gold to winnande. Men tha mångêrta ne drogon thêr nêne golden krone fon. Êr wêron thêr

the inside of the dyke thirty-six refuge-houses for the people who live in the neighbourhood. The field serves for a camp and for a meadow. On the south side of the outer fortification is the Liudgaarde, enclosed by the great wood of lime-trees. Its shape is three-cornered, with the widest part outside, so that the sun may shine in it, for there are a great number of foreign trees and flowers brought by the seafarers. All the other citadels are the same shape as ours, only not so large; but the largest of all is that of Texland. The tower of the Fryaburgt is so high that it rends the sky, and all the rest is in proportion to the tower. In our citadel this is the arrangement: Seven young maidens attend to the lamp; each watch is three hours. In the rest of their time they do housework, learn, and sleep. When they have watched for seven years, they are free; then they may go among the people, to look after their morals and to give advice. When they have been three years maidens, they may sometimes accompany the older ones.

The writer must teach the girls to read, to write, and to reckon. The elders, or "Greva," must teach them justice and duty, morals, botany, and medicine, history, traditions, and singing, besides all that may be necessary for them to give advice. The Burgtmaagd must teach them how to set to work when they go among the people. Before a Burgtmaagd can take office, she must travel through the country a whole year. Three grey-headed Burgtheeren and three old maidens must go with her. This was the way that I did. My journey was along the Rhine—on this side up, and on the other side down. The higher I went, the poorer the people seemed to be. Everywhere about the Rhine the people dug holes, and the sand that was got out was poured with water over fleeces to get the gold, but the girls did not wear golden crowns of it. Formerly they were mâr wêst, men sont wi Skênland iniste, send hja nêi tha berga gvngon. Thêr delvath hja yserirtha, thêr hja yser of mâkja. Boppa thêre Rêne twisk thet berchta, thêr hâv ik Mârsâta sjan. Tha Mârsâta thât send mânniska thêr invppa mâra hêma. Hjara husa send vp pâlum buwad. Thât is vret wilde kwik ânda bose mânniska. Thêr send wolva, bâra ând swârte grislika lawa.* And hja send tha swetsart† jeftha pâlingar fonda hêinde Krêkalandar, thêra Kâlta folgar ând tha vrwildere Twiskar, alle gyrich nêi râv ând but. Tha Mârsâta helpath hjara selva mith fiska ând jûga. Tha huda wrdat thrvch tha wiva tomâkad ând birhet mith skors fon berkum. Tha litha huda saft lik fâmnafilt. Thju burchfâm et Fryasburch‡ sêide vs thât hja gode ênfalde mânniska weron. Thach hêd ik hja êr navt sprêken hêred, ik skolde mênath hâve thât hja nên Fryas wêre, men wilda, sâ bryst sâgon hja ut. Hjara fachta ând kruda wrdon thrvch tha Rênhêmar vrwandelath ând thrvch tha stjurar buta brocht. Alingen thêre Rêne wêr et alên, til Lydasburch.§   Thêr was en grâte flyt.‖ Invppa thisra flyt wêron âk mânniska, thêr husa vp pâla hêde. Men thât nêr nên Fryas folk, men thât wêron swarte ând bruna mânniska, thêr thjanath hêde to rojar vmbe tha butafârar to honk to helpane. Hja moston thêr bilywa til thju thju flâte wither wêi brûda.

To tha lersta kêmon wi to-t Alderga. By-t suderhâva-hâved stêt thju Wâraburch, en stênhus, thêrin send aller-lêja skulpa, hulka, wêpne ând klathar wârad, fon fêre landum, thrvch tha stjurar mith brocht. En fjardêl dâna is-t Alderga. En grâte flyt omborad mith lothum, husa ând gârdum ella riklik sjarad. Invpper flyt lêi en grâte flâte rêd, mith fônon fon allerlêja farwa. Et Fryas dêi hon-gon tha skilda omma tha borda to. Svme blikton

---

* Leeuweu in Europa, Herodotus, VII. 125.

† Swetsar, Switsers.   ‡ Fryasburch, Freiburg.

§ Lydasburch, Leiden, de burcht.   ‖ Flyt, jeftha mârs, de Mare.

more numerous, but since we lost Schoonland they have gone up to the mountains. There they dig ore and make iron. Above the Rhine among the mountains I have seen Marsaten. The Marsaten are people who live on the lakes. Their houses are built upon piles, for protection from the wild beasts and wicked people. There are wolves, bears, and horrible lions. Then come the Swiss, the nearest to the frontiers of the distant Italians, the followers of Kalta and the savage Twiskar, all greedy for robbery and booty. The Marsaten gain their livelihood by fishing and hunting. The skins are sewn together by the women, and prepared with birch bark. The small skins are as soft as a woman's skin. The Burgtmaagd at Fryasburgt (Freiburg) told us that they were good, simple people; but if I had not heard her speak of them first, I should have thought that they were not Frya's people, they looked so impudent. Their wool and herbs are bought by the Rhine people, and taken to foreign countries by the ship captains. Along the other side of the Rhine it was just the same as at Lydasburcht (Leiden). There was a great river or lake, and upon this lake also there were people living upon piles. But they were not Frya's people; they were black and brown men who had been employed as rowers to bring home the men who had been making foreign voyages, and they had to stay there till the fleet went back.

At last we came to Alderga. At the head of the south harbour lies the Waraburgt, built of stone, in which all kinds of clothes, weapons, shells, and horns are kept, which were brought by the sea-people from distant lands. A quarter of an hour's distance from there is Alderga, a great river surrounded by houses, sheds, and gardens, all richly decorated. In the river lay a great fleet ready, with banners of all sorts of colours. On Frya's day the shields were hung on board likewise. Some shone

---

* Lions in Europe, see Herodotus, vii. 125.
† Swetsar are Swiss.   ‡ Fryasburch is Freiburg.
§ Lydasburch is Leyden, the city.   ‖ *Flyt, jeftha mâre*, is a lake or sea.

lik svnna. Tha skilda thêr witking ånd thêra skolta bi
tha nachtum wêron mith gold vmborad.   Abefta thêre
flyt was en gråft gråven, to hlåpande dåna alingen thêre
burch Forâna* ånd forth mith en ênga mudat in sê. To
fåra thêre flåte wêre thit tha utgvng ånd et Fly tha in-
gvng. A bêde syda thêre gråft send skêne husa mith hel
blikanda farwa målad. Tha gårdne send mit altid grêne
hågvm omtunad. Ik håv thêr wiva sian, thêr filtne
tohnekna drogon as t skriffilt wêre. Lik to Stavere wêron
tha mångêrtne mith golden kronum vppira holum ånd
mith hringum‡ om årma ånd fêt sjarad. Sudward fon
Forâna lêid Alkmårum. Alkmårum is en måre jefta flyt,
thêrin lêid en êland, vppa thåt êland moton tha swarte
ånd bruna månniska hwila êvin as to Lydahisburch. Thju
Burchfåm fon Forâna sêide my, thåt tha burchhêra dêistik
to-rå gvngon vmb ra to lêrande, hwat åfte frydom sy, ånd
ho tha månniska an thêre minne agon to lêvane vmbe
sêjen to winnande fon Wr.aldas gåst. Was thêr hwa
thêr hêra wilde ånd bigripa machte, sa wårth er halden,
alont er fvl lêrad wêre. Thåt wrde dên vmbe tha fêrhêmande folka wis to måkane, ånd vmbe vral åtha to winnande. Êr hêd ik anda Såxanamarka to thêr burch
Månnagårda forda§ wêst. Thach thêr hêd ik mår skå-
melhêd sjan, as-k hyr rikdom spêrde. Hju andere: så
hwersa thêr an da Såxanamarka en frêjar kvmath en
mangêrte to bi frêjande, alsa frêjath tha mångêrtne thêr,
kanst thin hus fry wêra tojenst tha bannane Twisklandar,
håst nach nêne fålad, ho fêlo bufle håst al fånsen ånd
ho fêlo båra ånd wolva huda håst ål vppa thêre mårk
brocht? Dåna ist kvmen thåt tha Saxmanna thju buw
anda wiva vrlêten håve. Thåt fon hvndred to sêmine nên
êne lêsa mêi ner skriwa ne kån. Dåna is-t kvmen,
thåt nimman nên sprêk vppa sin skild neth, men
blåt en mislikande dånte fon en diar, thåt er fålad

---

* Forana, Vroonen.   † Engamuda, Egmond.
‡ Diod. Sic. V. 27, van de Galliers.   § Mannagårdaforda, Munster.

like the sun. The shields of the sea-king and the admiral
were bordered with gold. From the river a canal was dug
going past the citadel Forana (Vroonen), with a narrow
outlet to the sea. This was the egress of the fleet; the
Fly was the ingress. On both sides of the river are fine
houses built, painted in bright colours. The gardens are
all surrounded by green hedges. I saw there women
wearing felt tunics, as if it were writing felt.[1] Just as
at Staveren, the girls wore golden crowns on their heads,
and rings on their arms and ankles. To the south of
Forana lies Alkmarum. Alkmarum is a lake or river in
which there is an island. On this island the black and
brown people must remain, the same as at Lydasburgt.
The Burgtmaagd of Forana told me that the burgtheeren
go every day to teach them what real freedom is, and how
it behoves men to live in order to obtain the blessing of
Wr-alda's spirit. If there was any one who was willing
to listen and could comprehend, he was kept there till he
was fully taught. That was done in order to instruct the
distant people, and to make friends everywhere. I had
been before in the Saxenmarken, at the Mannagardaforde
castle (Munster). There I saw more poverty than I could
discover wealth here. She answered: So whenever at the
Saxenmarken a young man courts a young girl, the girls
ask: Can you keep your house free from the banished
Twisklanders? Have you ever killed any of them?
How many cattle have you already caught, and how
many bear and wolfskins have you brought to market?
And from this it comes that the Saxons have left the
cultivation of the soil to the women, that not one in a
hundred can read or write; from this it comes, too,
that no one has a motto on his shield, but only a
misshapen form of some animal that he has killed;

---

[1] *Felt*, very thin and compressed, with a smooth surface.

* Forana is Vroonen.   † Engamuda is Egmond.

‡ Diodorus Siculus, v. 27, on the Gauls.   § Mannagârdaforda is Munster.

heth. And ândlik, dâna is-t kvmen, thât hja sêr wichandlik ewrden send, men to met êvin dvm send as et kwik,
thât hja fânsa, ând êvin erm as tha Twisklândar, hwêr
mith hja, orloge. To fâra Fryas folk is irtha ând sê eskêpen. Al vsa rinstrâma runath vppa sê to. Thât Lydas
folk ând thât Findas folk skil ekkorum vrdelgja, ând wy
moton tha lêthoga landa bifolka. In-t fon ând omme fâra
lêid vs held. Wilst nw thât tha boppalânder dêl hâve an
vsa rikdom ând wisdom, sâ skil ik thi en rêd jêva. Lêt
et tha mangêrtne to wênhêd wrde hjara frêjar to frêjande,
êr hja ja segsa : hwêr hâst al in wralda ommefâren, hwad
kânst thin bern tella wra fêra landa ând wra fêrhêmanda
folka? Dvath hja alsa, sâ skilun tha wickandlika knâpa
to vs kvma. Hja skilun wiser wârtha ând rikkâr ând wi
ne skilun nên bihof longer navt nâve an thât wla thjud.
Tha jongste thêr fâmna fon thêra thêr by mi wêron, kêm
uta Saxsanamarka wêi. As wi nw to hongk kêmon, heth
hju orlovi frêjad vmbe nêi hjra hus to gâne. Afternêi is
hju thêr Burchfâm wrden, ând dâna is-t kvmen thât er
hjudêga sâ felo Saxmânna by tha stjurar fâre.

ENDE FON THET APOLLONIA BOK.

and lastly, from this comes also that they are very warlike, but sometimes as stupid as the beasts that they
catch, and as poor as the Twisklanders with whom they
go to war. The earth and the sea were made for Frya's
people. All our rivers run into the sea. The Lydas
people and the Findas people will exterminate each other,
and we must people the empty countries. In movement
and sailing is our prosperity. If you wish the highlanders
to share our riches and wisdom, I will give you a piece of
advice. Let the girls, when they are asked to marry,
before they say yes, ask their lovers : What parts of the
world have you travelled in ? What can you tell your
children about distant lands and distant people ? If they
do this, then the young warriors will come to us ; they
will become wiser and richer, and we shall have no occasion to deal with those nasty people. The youngest of
the maids who were with me came from the Saxenmarken.
When we came back she asked leave to go home. Afterwards she became Burgtmaagd there, and that is the reason
why in these days so many of our sailors are Saxons.

END OF APOLLONIA'S BOOK.

THA SKRIFTA FON FRETHORIK AND WILJOW.

MIN nôm is Frêthorik to nomath oera Linda, thât wil segsa ovir tha Linda. To Ljudwardja bin ik to Asga kêren. Ljudwardja is en ny thorp, binna thene ringdik fon thêr burch Ljudgarda, hwêrfon tha nôma an vnêr kvmen is. Vnder mina tida is er fül bêred. Fül hêd ik thêr vr skrêven, men âfternêi send mi âk fêlo thinga meld. Fon ên ând ôther wil ik en skêdnese âfter thit bok skrywa, tha goda mânniska to-n êre tha ârga to vnêre.

In min jüged hêrd ik grêdwird alomme, ârge tid kêm, ârge tid was kvmen, Frya hêd vs lêton, hjra wâkfâmkes, hêde hju abefta halden, hwand drochten likande bylda wêron binna vsa lândpâla fvnden.

Ik brônde fon nysgyr vmbe thi bylda to bisjan. In vsa bûrt strompele en ôld fâmke to tha husa uta in, immer to kêthande vr ârge tid. Ik gryde hja ling syde. Hju strik mi omme kin to. Nw wrd ik drist ând frêje jef hju mi ârge tid ând tha bylda rêis wisa wilde. Hju lakte godlik ând brocht mi vpper burch. En grêve mân frêje my jef ik al lêsa ând skrywa kv. Nê sêid ik. Thân most êrost to ga ând lêra, sêid-er owers ne mêi-t jow navt wysen wrde. Dystik gvng ik bi tha skriwer lêra. Acht jêr lêtter hêrd ik, vsa burchfâm hêde hordom bidryven ând svme burchhêra hêdon vrrêd plêgad mith tha Magy, ând fêlo mânniska wêron vp hjara syde. Vral kêm twispalt. Thêr wêron bern, thêr vpstandon ajen hjara eldrum. Inna gluppa

THE WRITINGS OF FRÊTHORIK AND WILJOW.

My name is Frêthorik, surnamed oera Linda, which means over the Linden. In Ljudwardia I was chosen as Asga. Ljudwardia is a new village within the fortification of the Ljudgaarda, of which the name has fallen into disrepute. In my time much has happened. I had written a good deal about it, but afterwards much more was related to me. I will write an account of both one and the other after this book, to the honour of the good people and to the disgrace of the bad.

In my youth I heard complaints on all sides. The bad time was coming; the bad time did come—Frya had forsaken us. She withheld from us all her watch-maidens, because monstrous idolatrous images had been found within our landmarks. I burnt with curiosity to see those images. In our neighbourhood a little old woman tottered in and out of the houses, always calling out about the bad times. I came to her; she stroked my chin; then I became bold, and asked her if she would show me the bad times and the images. She laughed good-naturedly, and took me to the citadel. An old man asked me if I could read and write. No, I said. Then you must first go and learn, he replied, otherwise it may not be shown to you. I went daily to the writer and learnt. Eight years afterwards I heard that our Burgtmaagd had been unchaste, and that some of the burgtheeren had committed treason with the Magy, and many people took their part. Everywhere disputes arose. There were children rebelling against their parents ; good

wrdon tha froda mânniska morth.   Thet alde fâmke, thêr
ella bâr mâkade, wârth dâd fvnden in en grupe.   Min tât,
thêr rjuchter wẹre, wilde hja wrêken hâ.   Nachtis wârth
er in sin hus vrmorth.   Thrju jêr lêtter wêr thene Mâgy
bâs svnder strid.   Tha Saxmânna wêron frome ånd frod
bilywen.   Nêi tham fljuchton alle gode mânniska.   Min
mâm bistvrv-et.   Nw dêd ik lik tha ôthera.   Thi Mâgy
bogade vppa sinra snôdhêd.   Men Irtha skold im thâna,
thât hja nên Mâgy ner afgoda to lêta ne mochte to thêre
hêlge skêta, hwêrut hju Frya bêrade.   Êvin sa thet wilde
hors sina mânna sked, nêi thât thet sina ridder gersfal-
lich mâkad heth, êvin sâ skodde Irtha hjara walda ånd
berga.   Rinstrâma wrdon ovira fjelda sprêd.   Sê kokade.
Berga spydon nêi tha wolkum, ånd hwad hja spyth hêde,
swikton tha wolka wither vp jrtha.   By-t anfang there
Arnemônath nigade jrtha northward, hju sêg del, ôl lêgor
ånd lêgor.   Anna Wolfamônath lêidon tha Dênemarka
fon Fryas lând vnder-ne sê bidobben.   Tha walda thêr
bylda in wêron, wrdon vphyvath ånd thêr windum spel.
Thet jêr âfter kêm frost inna Herdemônath ånd lêid ôld
Fryas lând vnder en plônke skul.   In Sellamônath
kêm stornewind ut et northa wêi, mith forande berga
fon ise ånd stênum.   Tha spring kâm, hyf jrtha hjra
selva vp.   Ise smolt wêi.   Ebbe kêm ånd tha walda
mith byldum drêvon nêi sê.   Inner Winna jeftha Min-
namônath gvng aider thurvar wither hêm fâra.   Ik kêm
mith en fâm to thêre burch Ljudgârda.   Ho drove sach
et ut.   Tha walda thêra Lindawrda wêron mêst wêi.   Thêr
tha Ljudgârde wêst hêde, was sê.   Sin hef fêtere thene
hringdik.   Ise hêde tha tore wêi brocht ånd tha husa lêide
in thrvch ekkôrum.   Anna helde fonna dik fond ik in sten.

people were secretly murdered. The little old woman who had brought everything to light was found dead in a ditch. My father, who was a judge, would have her avenged. He was murdered in the night in his own house. Three years after that the Magy was master without any resistance. The Saxmen had remained religious and upright. All the good people fled to them. My mother died of it. Now I did like the others. The Magy prided himself upon his cunning, but Irtha made him know that she would not tolerate any Magy or idol on the holy bosom that had borne Frya. As a wild horse tosses his mane after he has thrown his rider, so Irtha shook her forests and her mountains. Rivers flowed over the land; the sea raged; mountains spouted fire to the clouds, and what they vomited forth the clouds flung upon the earth. At the beginning of the Arnemaand (harvest month) the earth bowed towards the north, and sank down lower and lower. In the Welvenmaand (winter month) the low lands of Fryasland were buried under the sea. The woods in which the images were, were torn up and scattered by the wind. The following year the frost came in the Hardemaand (Louwmaand, January), and laid Fryasland concealed under a sheet of ice. In Sellemaand (Sprokkelmaand, February) there were storms of wind from the north, driving mountains of ice and stones. When the spring-tides came the earth raised herself up, the ice melted; with the ebb the forests with the images drifted out to sea. In the Winne, or Minne-maand (Bloeimaand, May), every one who dared went home. I came with a maiden to the citadel Liudgaarde. How sad it looked there. The forests of the Lindaoorden were almost all gone. Where Liudgaarde used to be was sea. The waves swept over the fortifications. Ice had destroyed the tower, and the houses lay heaped over each other. On the slope of the dyke I found a stone

vsa skriver hêd er sin nôm inwryten, thât wêre my en
bâken. Sâ-t mith vsa burch gvngen was, was-t mith
mitha ôra gvngon. Inna hâga lânda wêron hja thrvch
jrtha, inna dêna landa thrvch wêter vrdên. Allêna Fryasburch to Texland wârth vnedêrad fvnden. Men al et lând
thet northward lêid hêde, wêre vnder sê. Noch nis-t navt
boppa brocht. An thâs kâd fon-t Flymâre wêron nêi
meld wrde thrichtich salta mâra kvmen, vnstonden thrvch
tha walda, thêr mith grvnd ând al vrdrêven wêron. To
Westflyland fiftich. Thi grâft thêr fon-t Alderga thweres
to het land thrvchlâpen hêde, was vrsôndath ând vrdên.
Tha stjurar ând ôr fârande folk, thêr to honk wêron, hêde
hjara selva mith mâga ând sibba vppira skepum hret.
Men thât swarte folk fon Lydasburch ând Alikmarum
hêde alên dên. Thawil tha·swarta sûdward dryvon, hêdon
hja fêlo mângêrtne hret, ând nêidam nimman ne kêm to
aska tham, hildon hja tham to hjara wiva. Tha mânniska
thêr to bek kêmon, gvngon alle binna tha hringdika thêra
burgum hêma, thrvchdam et thêr buta al slyp ând brok-
lând wêre. Tha gamla husa wrde byên klust. Fona bop-
palândum kâpade mân ky ând skêp, ând inna tha grâte
husa thêr to fâra tha fâmna sêton hêde, wrde nw lêken ând
filt mâkad, vmbe thes lêvens willa. Thât skêd 1888* jer
nêi thât Atlând svnken was.

In 282 jer † nêdon wi nên Êremoder navt hât, and nw ella
tomet vrlêren skinde, gvng mân êne kjasa. Thet hlot falde
vp Gosa to nômath·Makonta. Hju wêre Burchfâm et Fryasburch to Texlând. Hel fon hawed ând klâr fon sin, êlle
god, ând thrvchdam hira burch allêna spârad was, sach
alrik thêrut hira hropang. Tjan jêr lêttere kêmon tha
stjurar fon Forana ând fon Lydas burch. Hja wildon tha
swarta mânniska mith wif ând bern to thet lând utdryva.
Thêrwr wildon hja thêre Moder is rêd biwinna. Men Gosa

on which the writer had inscribed his name. That was a
sign to me. The same thing had happened to other
citadels as to ours. In the upper lands they had been
destroyed by the earth, in the lower lands by the water.
Fryasburgt, at Texland, was the only one found uninjured,
but all the land to the north was sunk under the sea,
and has never been recovered. At the mouth of the
Flymeer, as we were told, thirty salt swamps were found,
consisting of the forest and the ground that had been
swept away. At Westflyland there were fifty. The
canal which had run across the land from Alderga was
filled up with sand and destroyed. The seafaring people
and other travellers who were at home had saved themselves, their goods, and their relations upon their ships.
But the black people at Lydasburgt and Alkmarum had
done the same; and as they went south they saved many
girls, and as no one came to claim them, they took them
for their wives. The people who came back all lived
within the lines of the citadel, as outside there was nothing but mud and marsh. The old houses were all
smashed together. People bought cattle and sheep from
the upper lands, and in the great houses where formerly
the maidens were established cloth and felt were made for
a livelihood. This happened 1888 years after the submersion of Atland.

For 282 years we had not had an Eeremoeder, and now,
when everything seemed lost, they set about choosing one.
The lot fell upon Gosa, surnamed Makonta. She was
Burgtmaagd at Fryasburgt, in Texland. She had a clear
head and strong sense, and was very good; and as her
citadel was the only one that had been spared, every one
saw in that her call. Ten years after that the seafarers
came from Forana and Lydasburgt. They wished to drive
the black men, with their wives and children, out
of the country. They wished to obtain the opinion
of the mother upon the subject. She asked them:

---

* 2193 – 1888 is 305 before Christ.
† Since 587 before Christ. See pages 110 and 112.

fréje, kånst ên ånd ôr to bek fora nêi hjra låndum, thån
åchste spod to måkjande, owers ne skilun hja hjara måga
navt wither ne finda.　Nê sêide hja.　Thå sêide Gosa:
Hja håvon thin salt provad ånd thin bråd êten.　Hjara
lif ånd lêva håvon hja vnder jow hod stålad.　I moste jow.
anje hirta bisêka.　Men ik wil thi en rêd jeva.　Hald
hjam alond jow wåldich biste vm ra wither honk to fora.
Men hald hjam bi jow burgum thêr bûta.　Wåk ovir hjara
sêd ånd lêr hjam as jef hja Fryas svna wêre.　Hjra wiva
send hyr tha steriksta.　As rêk skil hjara blod vrfljuchta,
til er tha lesta navt owers as Fryas blod in hjara åfterkv-.
mande skil bilywa.　Så send hja hyr bilêwen.　Nw winst
ik wel thåt mina åfterkvmande thêr vp letta, ho fêr Gosa
wêrhêd sprek.　Thå vsa lånda wither to bigana wêr, kêmon
thêr banda erma Saxmanna ånd wiva nêi tha vvrdum fon
Stavere ånd thåt Alderga, vmbe golden ånd ôra sjarhêd to
sêkane fon ut tha wasige bodeme.　Thach tha stjurar nildon hja navt to lêta.　Tha gvngon hja tha lêthoga thorpa
bihêma to West Flyland, vmbe ra lif to bihaldane.

NW WIL IK SKRIWA HO THA GÊRTMANNA AND FÊLO
HÊLÊNJA FOLGAR TOBEK KÊMON.

Twa jêr nêi thåt Gosa Moder wrde,* kêm er en flåte to
thet Flymara in fala.　Thet folk hropte ho.n.sêen.　Hja foron
til Stavere, thêr hropton hja jeta rêis.　Tha fôna wêron an
top ånd thes nachtes skåton hja barnpila† anda loft.　Thå
dêirêd wêre rojadon svme mith ên snåke to thêre hava in.
Hja hropton wither ho.n.sêen.　Tha hja landa hipte-n jong
kerdel wal vp.　In sina handa hêdi-n skild, thêrvp was bråd
ånd salt lêid.　Afterdam kêm en grêva, hi sêide wi kvmath

---

* 303. v. Chr.
† Barnpila. De *falarica* by Livius XXI. 8.

Can you send them all back to their country ? ' If so, then lose no time, or they will find no relatives alive. No, they said. Gosa replied : They have eaten your bread and salt; they have placed themselves entirely under your protection. You must consult your own hearts. But I will give you one piece of advice. Keep them till you are able to send them back, but keep them outside your citadels. Watch over their morals, and educate them as if they were Frya's sons. Their women are the strongest here. Their blood will disappear like smoke, till at last nothing but Frya's blood will remain in their descendants. So they remained here. Now, I should wish that my descendants should observe in how far Gosa spoke the truth. When our country began to recover, there came troops of poor Saxon men and women to the neighbourhoods of Staveren and Alderga, to search for gold and other treasures in the swampy lands. But the sea-people would not permit it, so they went and settled in the empty village of the West Flyland in order to preserve their lives.

Now I will relate how the Geertman and many followers of Hellenia came back.

Two years after Gosa had become the mother (303 B.C.) there arrived a fleet at Flymeer. The people shouted " Ho-n-sêen " (What a blessing). They sailed to Staveren, where they shouted again. Their flags were hoisted, and at night they shot lighted arrows into the air. At daylight some of them rowed into the harbour in a boat, shouting again, " Ho-n-sêen." When they landed a young fellow jumped upon the rampart. In his hand he held a shield on which bread and salt were laid. After him came a grey-headed man, who said we come from

---

* 303 before Christ.
† *Barnpila*, De falarica, Livy, xxi. 8.

fona fere Krêkalandum wêi, vmb vsa sêd to warjande, nw
winstath wi i skolde alsa mild wêsa vs alsa fül lånd to
jêvane thåt wi thêrvp müge hêma. Hi telade-n êle skêdnese thêr ik åfter bêtre skryva wil. Tha grêva niston navt
hwat to dvande, hja sandon bodon allerwêikes; åk ta my.
Ik gvng to ånd sêide : nw wi-n Moder håve agon wi hjra
rêd to frêjande. Ik selva gvng mitha. Thju Moder, thêr
ella wiste, sêide, lêt hja kvme, så mügon hja vs lånd helpa
bihalda : men lêt hjam navt up êne stêd ne bilyva, til thju
hja navt waldich ne wrde ovir vs. Wi dêdon as hju sêid
hêde. That wêre êl nêi hjra hêi. Fryso reste mith sinå
ljudum to Stavere, that hja wither to êne sêstêde måkade,
sa god hja machte. Wichhirte gvng mith sinum ljudum
astward nêi there Êmude. Svme thêra Johnjar, thêr
mênde thåt hja font Alderga folk sproten wêre, gvngen
thêr hinne. En lyth dêl thêr wånde thåt hjara êthla fon tha
sjugon êlanda wei kêmon, gvngon hinne ånd setton hjara
selva binna tha hringdik fon thêre burch Walhallagåra del.
Ljudgert thene skolte bi nachte fon Wichhirte wårth min
åthe åfternêi min frjund. Fon ut sin dêibok håv ik thju
skêdnese thêr hir åfter skil folgja.

Nei thåt wi 12 mel 100 ånd twia 12 jêr bi tha fif wêtrum
sêten hêde, thahwila vsa sêkåmpar alle sêa bifåren hêde
thêr to findane, kêm Alexandre (*) tham kêning mith en
weldich hêr fon boppa allingen thêr stråm vsa thorpa bifåra.
Nimman ne måcht in wither worda. Thach wi stjurar thêr
by tha sê såton, wi skêpt vs mith al vsa tilbêre hava in
ånd brûda hinna. Tha Alexandre fornom thåt im så ne
gråte flåte vntfåra was, wårth er wodinlik, to swêrande hi
skolde alle thorpa an logha offerja jef wi navt to bek kvma
nilde. Wichhirte lêide siak to bedde. Thå Alexandre thåt
fornom heth er wacht alont er bêter wêre. Afternêi kêm
er to him sêr kindlyk snakkande, thach hi thrjvchde lik

---

the distant Greek land to preserve our customs. Now we wish you to be kind enough to give us as much land as will enable us to live. He told a long story, which I will hereafter relate more fully. The old man did not know what to do. They sent messengers all round, also to me. I went, and said now that we have a mother it behoves us to ask her advice. I went with them myself. The mother, who already knew it all, said: Let them come, they will help us to keep our lands, but do not let them remain in one place, that they may not become too powerful over us. We did as she said, which was quite to their liking. Fryso remained with his people at Staveren, which they made again into a port as well as they could. Wichhirte went with his people eastwards to the Emude. Some of the descendants of Jon who imagined that they sprang from the Alderga people went there. A small number, who fancied that their forefathers had come from the seven islands, went there and set themselves down within the enclosure of the citadel of Walhallagara. Liudgert, the admiral of Wichhirt, was my comrade, and afterwards my friend. Out of his diary I have taken the following history.

After we had been settled 12 times 100 and twice 12 years in the Five Waters (Punjab), whilst our naval warriors were navigating all the seas they could find, came Alexander* the King, with a powerful army descending the river towards our villages. No one could withstand him; but we sea-people, who lived by the sea, put all our possessions on board ships and took our departure. When Alexander heard that such a large fleet had escaped him, he became furious, and swore that he would burn all the villages if we did not come back. Wichhirte was ill in bed. When Alexander heard that, he waited till he was better. After that he came to him, speaking very kindly—but he deceived,

---

* Alexander at the Indus, 327 before Christ.
† 327 + 1224 is 1551 before Christ.

hi êr dên hêde. Wichhirte andere thêr åfter, o alder-
gråteste thêra kêuingar. Wi stjurar kvmath allerwêikes,
wi håven fon jow gråte dêdun hêred. Thêrvmbe send wi
fvl êrbidenese to fara jowa wêpne, tha jet mar vr thina
witskip. Men wi ôthera wy send frybern Fryas bern. Wy
ne mügon nêne slåfona navt ne wrde. Jef ik wilde, tha
ôra skolde rêder sterva willa, hwand alsa ist thrvch vsa
êwa bifôlen. Alexandre sêide: ik wil thin lånd navt
ne måkja to min bût, ner thin folk to mina slåfona. Ik
wil blåt thåt ste my thjanja skolste vmb lån. Thêrvr wil
ik swêra by vs bêdar godum, that nimman vr my wrogja
skil. Tha Alexandre åfternei bråd ånd salt mith im
dêlade, heth Wichhirte that wiste dêl kåsen. Hi lêt
tha skêpa hala thrvch sin svne. Tha thi alle tobek wêron,
heth Alexandre thi alle hêred. Thêr mitha wilde hi sin
folk nêi tha helge Gônga fåra, thêr hi to land navt hêde
müge nåka. Nw gvng er to ånd kås altham ut sin folk
ånd ut sina salt-atha thêr wenath wêron vvr-ne sê to
fårane. Wichhirte was wither siak wrden, thêrvmbe
gvng ik allêna mitha ånd Nearchus fon thes keningis
wêga. Thi tocht hlip svnder fardêl to-n-ende, uthåvede
tha Johnjar immerthe an vnmin wêron with tha Phonisjar,
alsa Nêarchus thêr selva nên bås ovir bilywe ne kv.
Intwiska hêde tham kêning navt stile nêst. Hi hêde sina
salt-atha båma kapja lêta ånd to planka måkja. Thrvch
help vsar timberljud hêder thêr of skêpa måkad. Nw wilder
selva sêkêning wertha, ånd mith êl sin hêr thju Gonga
vpfåra. Thach tha salt-atha thêr fon thet bergland kêmon,
wêron ang to fara sê. As hja hêradon thåt hja mith
moste, stakon hja tha timberhlotha ane brônd. Thêr thrvch
wrde vs êle thorp anda aska lêid. Thet forma wånde wy
thåt Alexandre thåt bifalen hêde ånd jahwêder stand rêd
vmb sê to kjasane. Men Alexander wêre wôdin, hi wilde
tha salt-atha thrvch sin ajn folk ombrensa lêta. Men Nêar-

as he had done before. Wichhirte answered : Oh greatest
of kings, we sailors go everywhere ; we have heard of your
great deeds, therefore we are full of respect for your arms,
and still more for your wisdom ; but we who are free-born
Fryas children, we may not become your slaves ; and even
if I would, the others would sooner die, for so it is commanded in our laws. Alexander said : I do not desire to
take your land or make slaves of your people, I only wish
to hire your services. That I will swear by both our Gods,
so that no one may be dissatisfied. When Alexander
shared bread and salt with him, Wichhirte had chosen the
wisest part. He let his son fetch the ships. When they
were all come back Alexander hired them all. By means
of them he wished to transport his people to the holy
Ganges, which he had not been able to reach. Then he
chose among all his people and soldiers those who were
accustomed to the sea. Wichhirte had fallen sick again,
therefore I went alone with Nearchus, sent by the king.
The voyage came to an end without any advantage, because the Joniers and the Phœnicians were always quarrelling, so that Nearchus himself could not keep them in
order. In the meantime, the king had not sat still. He
had let his soldiers cut down trees and make planks, with
which, with the help of our carpenters, he had built ships.
Now he would himself become a sea-king, and sail with
his whole army up the Ganges ; but the soldiers who
came from the mountainous countries were afraid of the
sea. When they heard that they must sail, they set fire
to the timber yards, and so our whole village was laid
in ashes. At first we thought that this had been done
by Alexander's orders, and we were all ready to cast ourselves into the sea : but Alexander was furious, and wished
his own people to kill the soldiers. However, Nearchus,

chus tham navt allêna sin êroste forst men ak sin frjund
wêre, rêde him owers to dvande. Nw bêrad er as wen der
lavade thet vnluk et dên hêde. Tha hi ne thvrade sin
tocht navt vrfata. Nw wild er to bek kêra, thach êr hi
thât dêde, lêt hi thet forma bisêka hwa-r skeldich wêron.
Dry-r thât wiste lêt er altham svnder wêpne bilywa, vmb
en ny thorp to mâkjande. Fon sin ajn folk lêt er wepned
vmbe tha ôra to tâmma, ând vmbe êne burch to bvwande.
Wy moston wiv ând bern mith nimma. Kêmon wi anda
muda thêre Êuphrat, sa machton wi thêr en stêd kiasa
jeftha omkêra, vs lân skold vs êvin blyd to dêlath wrde.
An tha nya skêpa, thêr tha brônd vntkvma wêron, let-er
Johniar ând Krêkalandar gâ. Hi selva gvng mith sin ôra
folk allingen thêre kâd thrvch tha dorra wostêna, thât is
thrvch et land thât Irtha vphêid hêde uta sê, tha hju thju
strête after vsa êthela vphêide as hja inna Râde sê kêmon.

Tha wy to ny Gêrtmanja kêmon (ny Gêrtmanja is en
hâva thêr wi selva makad hede, vmbe thêr to wêterja)
mêton wi Alexandre mith sin hêr. Nêarchus gvng wal
vp ând bêide thrja dêga. Tha gvng et wither forth. Tha
wi bi thêre Êuphrat kêmon, gvng Nêarchus mith sina salt-
alta ând fêlo fon sin folk wal vp. Tha hi kêm hring
wither. Hi sêide, thi kêning lêt jow bidda, i skille jet en
lithge tocht to sinra wille dvan, alont et ende fona Râde
sê. Thêrnêi skil jawehder sâ fül gold krêja as er bêra mêi.
Tha wi thêr kêmon, lêt er vs wysa hwêr thju strête êr wêst
hêde. Thêr nêi wylader ên ând thritich dêga, alan ut
sjande vvra wostêne.

Tho tha lesta kêm er en hloth mânniska mith forande twa hondred êlephanta thvsend kêmlun tolêden
mith wodin balkum, râpum ând allerlêja ark vmbe vsa
flâte nêi tha Middelsê to tyande. Thât bisâwd-vs, ând likt

who was not only his chief officer, but also his friend, advised him not to do so. So he pretended to believe that it had happened by accident, and said no more about it. He wished now to return, but before going he made an inquiry who really were the guilty ones. As soon as he ascertained it, he had them all disarmed, and made them build a new village. His own people he kept under arms to overawe the others, and to build a citadel. We were to take the women and children with us. When we arrived at the mouth of the Euphrates, we might either choose a place to settle there or come back. Our pay would be guaranteed to us the same in either case. Upon the new ships which had been saved from the fire he embarked the Joniers and the Greeks. He himself went with the rest of his people along the coast, through the barren wilderness; that is, through the land that Irtha had heaved up out of the sea when she had raised up the strait as soon as our forefathers had passed into the Red Sea.

When we arrived at New Gertmania (New Gertmania is the port that we had made in order to take in water), we met Alexander with his army. Nearchus went ashore, and stayed three days. Then we proceeded further on. When we came to the Euphrates, Nearchus went ashore with the soldiers and a large body of people; but he soon returned, and said, The King requests you, for his sake, to go a voyage up the Red Sea; after that each shall receive as much gold as he can carry. When we arrived there, he showed us where the strait had formerly been. There he spent thirty-one days, always looking steadily towards the desert.

At last there arrived a great troop of people, bringing with them 200 elephants, 1000 camels, a quantity of timber, ropes, and all kinds of implements necessary to drag our fleet to the Mediterranean Sea. This astounded us, and seemed

o

vs bal to, men Nêarchus teld vs, sin kêning wilde tha
ôthera kêninggar tâna that i weldiger wêre, sa tha kêninggar fon Thyris êr wêsen hêde. Wi skoldon men mith
helpa, sêkur skolde vs thât nên skâda navt dva. Wi
moston wel swika, ånd Nêarchus wiste ella sâ pront to
birjuchte thât wi inna Middelsê lêide êr thrja mônatha
forby wêron. Tha Alexandre fornom ho-t mith sinra
onwerp ofkvmen was, wårth er sa vrmêten thât er tha
drage strête utdiapa wilde Irtha to-n spot. Men Wr.alda
lêt sine sêle lås, thêrvmbe vrdronk er inna win ånd in sina
ovirmodichhêd, êr thât er bijinna kvste. After sin dåd
wrde thet rik dêlad thrvch sina forsta. Hja skolde alrek
en dêl to fara sina svnum wårja, thach hja wêron vnmênis.
Elk wilde sin dêl bihalda ånd selva formåra. Tha kêm
orloch ånd wi ne kvste navt omme kêra. Nêarchus wilde
nw, wi skolde vs del setta an Phonisi his kåd, men thât
nilde nimman navt ne dva. Wi sêide, rêder willath wi
wåga nêi Fryasland to gâna. Tha brocht-er vs nei thêre
nya hâva fon Athenia, hwêr alle åfte Fryas bern formels
hin têin wêron. Forth gvngon wi salt-åtha liftochta ånd
wêpne fåra. Among tha fêlo forsta hêde Nêarchus en
frjund mith nôme Antigonus. Thisse strêdon bêde vmb
ên dol, så hja sêidon as follistar to fåra-t kêninglike
slachte ånd forth vmbe alle Krêkalanda hjara alda frydom
wither to jêvane. Antigonus hêde among fêlo ôtherum
ênnen svn, thi hête Demêtrius, åfter tonômad thene
stêda winner. Thisse gvng ênis vpper stêde Salâmis of.
Nêi thât er thêr en stât mêi strêden hêde most er
mith thêre flåte strida fon Ptholemeus. Ptholemeus, alsa
hête thene forst thêr welda ovir Êgiptaland. Dêmêtrius
wn thêre kêse, tha navt thrvch sina salt-åtha, men thrvch
dam wy him helpen hêde. Thit hêde wi dên thrvch
athskip to fåra Nêarchus, hwand wi him far bastard
blod bikånde thrvch sin friska hûd ånd blåwa âgon mith

most extraordinary; but Nearchus told us that his king wished to show to the other kings that he was more powerful than any kings of Tyre had ever been. We were only to assist, and that surely could do us no harm. We were obliged to yield, and Nearchus knew so well how to regulate everything, that before three months had elapsed our ships lay in the Mediterranean Sea. When Alexander ascertained how his project had succeeded, he became so audacious that he wished to dig out the dried-up strait in defiance of Irtha; but Wr-alda deserted his soul, so that he destroyed himself by wine and rashness before he could begin it. After his death his kingdom was divided among his princes. They were each to have preserved a share for his sons, but that was not their intention. Each wished to keep his own share, and to get more. Then war arose, and we could not return. Nearchus wished us to settle on the coast of Phœnicia, but that no one would do. We said we would rather risk the attempt to return to Fryasland. Then he brought us to the new port of Athens, where all the true children of Frya had formerly gone. We went, soldiers with our goods and weapons. Among the many princes Nearchus had a friend named Antigonus. These two had only one object in view, as they told us—to help the royal race, and to restore freedom to all the Greek lands. Antigonus had, among many others, one son named Demetrius, afterwards called the " City Winner." He went once to the town of Salamis, and after he had been some time fighting there, he had an engagement with the fleet of Ptolemy. Ptolemy was the name of the prince who reigned over Egypt. Demetrius won the battle, not by his own soldiers, but because we helped him. We had done this out of friendship for Nearchus, because we knew that he was of bastard birth by his white skin, blue eyes, and

wit hêr.   After nêi gvng Dêmêtrius lâs vp Hrodus* thêr
hinne brochton wi sina salt-âtha ånd liftochta wr.   Thâ
wi tha leste rêis to Hrodus kêmon, was orloch vrtyan.
Dêmêtrius was nêi Athenia fåren.   Tha vs kêning thåt
vnderstande, lêd-er vs tobek.   Tha wi anda håve kêmon,
wêre êl et thorp in row bidobben.   Friso thêr kêning wêr
ovir-a flåte, hêde en svn ånd eu toghater tûs, så bjustre
fres, as jef hja pås ut Fryasland wêi kvmen wêren, ånd så
wonderskên as nimman mocht hügja.   Thjv hrop thêrvr
gvng vvr alle Krêkalanda ånd kêm in tha åra fon Dêmêtrius.   Dêmêtrius wêre vvl ånd vnsêdlik, ånd hi thogte
thåt-im ella fry stvnde.   Hi lêt thju toghater avbêr skåkja.
Thju moder ne thvrade hjra joi† navt wachtja, joi nomath
tha stjurar wiva hira måna, thåt is blideskip, ak segsath
hja swêthirte.   Tha stjurar hêton hjra wiva tråst, ånd fro
jefta frow thåt is frü åk frolik, thåt is êlik an frü.   Thrvchdam hju hjra man navt wachtja thurade, gvng hju mith
hjra svne nêi Dêmêtrius ånd bad, hi skolde hja hjra toghater wither jêva.   Men as Dêmêtrius hira svn sa, lêt-er
tham nêi sinra hove fora, ånd dêde alên mith him, as-er
mith tham his suster dên hêde.   Anda moder sand hi en
buda gold, thach hju stirt-et in sê.   As hju thûs kêm, warth
hju wansinnich, allerwêikes run hju vvra strête : nåst min
kindar navt sjan, o wach, lêt mi to jow skul sêka, wand
min joi wil mi dêja for tha-k sina kindar wêi brocht håv.
Tha Dêmêtrius fornom, thåt Friso to honk wêre, sand-i en
bodja to him segsande, thåt hi sina bern to him nomen hêde
wmbe ra to fora to-n håge ståt vmbe to lånja him to fåra
sina thjanesta.   Men Friso thêr stolte ånd herdfochtich wêre,
sand en bodja mith en brêve nêi sinum bern tha, thêrin
månde hi hjam, hja skolde Dêmêtrius to willa wêsa, vrmithis
tham hjara luk jêrde.   Thach thene bodja hêde jeta-n ora
brêve mith fenin, thêrmêi bifål-er hja skolde that innimma,

---

* 305 voor Chr.
† Joi †en tråst.   Te Scheveningen hoort men nog : joei en troos.   Joi,
Fransch *joye*.

fair hair. Afterwards, Demetrius attacked Rhodes, and we transported thither his soldiers and provisions. When we made our last voyage to Rhodes, the war was finished. Demetrius had sailed to Athens. When we came into the harbour, the whole village was in deep mourning. Friso, who was king over the fleet, had a son and a daughter so remarkably fair, as if they had just come out of Fryasland, and more beautiful than any one could picture to himself. The fame of this went all over Greece, and came to the ears of Demetrius. Demetrius was vile and immoral, and thought he could do as he pleased. He carried off the daughter. The mother did not dare await the return of her *joi* (the sailors wives call their husbands *joi* or *zoethart* (sweetheart). The men call their wives *troost* (comfort) and *fro* or *frow*, that is, *vreuyde* (delight) and frolic; that is the same as *vreugde*.

As she dared not wait for her husband's return, she went with her son to Demetrius, and implored him to send back her daughter; but when Demetrius saw the son he had him taken to his palace, and did to him as he had done to his sister. He sent a bag of gold to the mother, which she flung into the sea. When she came home she was out of her mind, and ran about the streets calling out: Have you seen my children. Woe is me! let me find a place to hide in, for my husband will kill me because I have lost his children.

When Demetrius heard that Friso had come home, he sent messengers to him to say that he had taken his children to raise them to high rank, and to reward him for his services. But Friso was proud and passionate, and sent a messenger with a letter to his children, in which he recommended them to accept the will of Demetrius, as he wished to promote their happiness; but the messenger had another letter with poison, which he ordered them to take:

---

* 305 before Christ.

† *Joi en trâst*. At Scheveningen you still hear "Joei en troos." *Joi* is the French *joye*.

hwand sêid-er-vnwillinglik is thin lif bivvllad; thât ne
skil jow navt to rêkned ni wrde, thach sâhwersa jow jowe
sêle bivvlath sa ne skil jow nimmerthe to Walhâlla ne
kvma, jow sêle skil thân ovir irtha ommewâra, svnder â
thet ljucht sja to mugande, lik tha flâramusa ând nachtula
skilstv alra dystik in thina hola skula, thes nachtis
utkvma, then vp vsa grâva grâja ând hûla, thahwila Frya
hjra haved fon jow ofwenda mot. Tha bern dêde lik-ra
bifâlen warth. Dêmêtrius lêt ra likka in sê werpa ând to
tha mânniska wrde sêid, thât hja fljucht wêron. Nw
wilde Friso mith alleman nêi Fryasland fâra, thêr-i êr
wêst hêde, men tha mêst nilde thât navt ne dva. Nw
gvng Friso to ând skât thet thorp mith-a kêninglika
fârrêdskûrum anda brônd. Hjud ne kv ni thvrade
ninman ne bilywa, ând alle wêron blyde, that hja
bûta wêre, bihalva wif ând bern hêdon wi ella abefta
lêten, thach wi wêron to lêden mith liftochtum ând
orluchtuch.

Friso nêde nach nên fretho. Tha wi by tha alda hâve
kêmon gvnger mith sina drista ljudum to ând skât vnwarlinga tha brônd inna skêpa, thêr-i mith sina pilum bigâna
kv. After sex dêgum sâgon wi tha orlochflâte fon Dêmêtrius
vp vs to kvma. Friso bifâl vs, wi moston tha lithste skêpa
âfterhâde in êne brêde line, tha stora mith wif ând bern
fârut. Forth bâd-er wi skoldon tha krânboga fon for nimma
ând anda âftestêwen fâstigja, hwand sêid-er, wi achon al
fljuchtande to fjuchtane. Nimman ne mêi him formêta vmb
en enkeldera fyand to forfolgjande, alsa sêid-er is min
bislut. Tha hwila wi thêrmitha al dvande wêron, kêm
wind vs vppa kop, to thêra lâfa ând thêra wiva skrik,
thrvchdam wi nêne slâvona navt nêde as thêra thêr vs
bi aju willa folgan wêre. Wi ne machton hja thus navt
thruch roja ni vntkvma. Men Wr. alda wiste wel, hwêrvmb-er

But, said he, your bodies have been defiled against your
will. That you are not to blame for; but if your souls are
not pure, you will never come into Walhalla. Your spirits
will haunt the earth in darkness. Like the bats and owls,
you will hide yourselves in the daytime in holes, and in
the night will come and shriek and cry about our graves,
while Frya must turn her head away from you. The children did as their father had commanded. The messenger
had their bodies thrown into the sea, and it was reported
that they had fled. Now Friso wished to go with all his
people to Frya's land, where he had been formerly, but
most of them would not go. So Friso set fire to the village and all the royal storehouses; then no one could
remain there, and all were glad to be out of it. We left
everything behind us except wives and children, but we
had an ample stock of provisions and warlike implements.

Friso was not yet satisfied. When we came to the old
harbour, he went off with his stout soldiers and threw fire
into all the ships that he could reach with his arrows.
Six days later we saw the war-fleet of Demetrius coming
down upon us. Friso ordered us to keep back the small
ships in a broad line, and to put the large ships with the
women and children in front. Further, he ordered
us to take the crossbows that were in the fore part
and fix them on the sterns of the ships, because, said
he, we must fight a retreating battle. No man must
presume to pursue a single enemy—that is my order.
While we were busy about this, all at once the wind came
ahead, to the great alarm of the cowards and the women,
because we had no slaves except those who had volun-
tarily followed us. Therefore we could not escape the
enemy by rowing. But Wr-alda knew well why he

så dêde, ånd Friso thêr-et fata, lêt tha bårnpila ring inna
krånboga lidsa. To lik båd-er thåt nimman skiata ne
machte, êr hy skåten hêde. Forth sêid-er thåt wi alle nêi
thåt midloste skip skiata moste, is thåt dol god biracht
sêid-er, så skilun tha ôra him to helpane kvma ånd thån
mot alrik skiata sa-r alderbesta mêi. As wi nw arhalf
ketting fon-ra of wêre, bigoston tha Phonisiar to skiata.
Men Friso n-andere navt bi fåra tha êroste pil del falde a
sex fadema fon sin skip. Nw skåt-er. Tha ôra folgade,
thet likte en fjurrêin ånd thrvchdam vsa pila mith wind
mêi gvngon, bilêvon hja alle an brônd, ånd nåkade selva
tha thridde låge. Allera månnelik gyradon ånd jûwgade.
Men tha krêta vsar witherlågum wêron sa herde, thet-et
vs thet hirte binêpen warth. As Friso mênde thåt et to
koste, lêt-er ofhalde ånd wi spode hinne. Thach nêi that
wi twa dêga forth pilath hêde, kêm thêr en ôre flåte ant
sjocht, fon thrittich skêpun, thêr vs stêdis in wnne. Friso
lêt vs wither rêd makja. Men tha ôthera saudon en lichte
snåka fvl rojar forut, tha bodon thêra bådon ut alera nôma
jef hja mith fåra machte. Hja wêron Johniar, thrvch
Dêmêtrius wêron hja wåldantlik nêi there alda håve skikad.
Thêr hêdon hja fon thêre kêse hêrad ånd nw hêdon hja
thet stolta swêrd antjan, ånd wêron vs folgad. Friso thêr
fül mitha Jôhnjar faren hêde sêide jå, men Wichhirte vsa
kêning sêide nê, Tha Johnjar send afgoda thjanjar sêid-er,
ik selva håv hêrad, ho hja thi an hropte. Friso sêide thet
kvmath thrvch tha wandel mith tha åfta Krêkalandar.
Thåt håv ik.våken selva dên. Thach ben ik alsa herde
Fryas as tha finste fon jow. Friso wêre thene mån thêr
va to Fryasland wisa moste. Thus gvngon tha Johnjar
mith. Ak likt-et nei Wr.aldas hêi, hwand êr thrja mô-
nathe om hlåpen wêron, gvngon wi allingen Britannja,
ånd thrja dêga lôter machton wi ho.n.sêen hropa.

did this; and Friso, who understood it, immediately had
the fire-arrows placed on the crossbows. At the same
time he gave the order that no one should shoot before
he did, and that we should all aim at the centre ship. If
we succeeded in this, he said, the others would all go to
its assistance, and then everybody might shoot as he best
was able. When we were at a cable and a half distance
from them the Phœnicians began to shoot, but Friso did
not reply till the first arrow fell six fathoms from his
ship. Then he fired, and the rest followed. It was like
a shower of fire; and as our arrows went with the wind,
they all remained alight and reached the third line.
Everybody shouted and cheered, but the screams of our
opponents were so loud that our hearts shrank. When
Friso thought that it was sufficient he called us off, and
we sped away; but after two days' slow sailing another
fleet of thirty ships came in sight and gained upon us.
Friso cleared for action again, but the others sent forward
a small rowing-boat with messengers, who asked permission to sail with us, as they were Joniers. They had
been compelled by Demetrius to go to the old haven;
there they had heard of the battle, and girding on their
stout swords, had followed us. Friso, who had sailed a
good deal with the Joniers, said Yes; but Wichirte, our
king, said No. The Joniers, said he, are worshippers of
heathen gods; I myself have heard them call upon them.
That comes from their intercourse with the real Greeks,
Friso said. I have often done it myself, and yet I am as
pious a Fryas man as any of you. Friso was the man to
take us to Friesland, therefore the Joniers went with us.
It seems that this was pleasing to Wr-alda, for before
three months were past we coasted along Britain, and
three days later we could shout huzza.

THIT SKRIFT IS MIJ OWER NORTLAND JEFTHA SKÊNLAND
JÊVEN.

Vndera tida thât vs land del sêg, wêre ik to Skênland.
Thêr gvng et alsa to. Thêr wêron grâte mâra, thêr fon
tha bodeme lik en blêse vt setta, then spliton hja vt-ên.
Uta rêta kêm stof as-t gliande yser wêre. Thêr wêron
berga thêr tha krunna of swikte. Thesse truldon nêther
ånd brochton walda ånd thorpa wêi. Ik self så thât en
berch fon tha ôra of torent wrde. Linrjucht sêg-er del.
As ik afternêi sjan gvng, was thêr en mâre kvmen. Tha
irtha bêterad was, kêm er en hêrtoga fon Lindasburch wêi,
mit sin folk ånd en fâm, tbju fâm kêthe allomme : Thene
Mâgy is skeldich an al-eth lêt thât wi lêden håve. Hja
tågon immer forth en thet hêr wårth al grâter. Thene
Mâgy fluchte hinne, mån fand sin lik, hi hêde siu self
vrdên. Tha wrdon tha Finna vrdrêven nêi ênre stêd, thêr
machton hja lêva. Thêr wêron fon basterde blode. Thissa
machton biliwa, thach fêlo gvngon mith tha Finna mêi.
Thi hêrtoga warth to kêniug kêren. Tha kårka thêr êl
bilêven wêron wrde vrdên. Sont komath tha gode North-
ljud våken to Texland vmb there Moder-is rêd. Thâ wi
ne mügath hjam for nêne rjuchta Fryas mar ne halde.
Inna Dênamarka ist sêkur as bi vs gvngon. Tha stjurar,
tham hjara self thêr stoltelika sêkåmpar bêton, send vppira
skêpa gvngon, ånd åfternêi sind lija to bek gvngon.

Held!   .

Hwersa thene Kroder en tid forth kroden heth,
thån skilun tha åfterkomanda wåna thât tha lêka ånd
brêka, thêr tha Brokmanna mith brocht håve, åjen
were an hjara êthla. Thêr vr wil ik wåka ånd thus så
fül vr hjåra plêga skriva as ik sjan hå. Vr tha Gêrt-

THIS WRITING HAS BEEN GIVEN TO ME ABOUT NORTHLAND
AND SCHOONLAND (SCANDINAVIA).

When our land was submerged I was in Schoonland.
It was very bad there. There were great lakes which
rose from the earth like bubbles, then burst asunder, and
from the rents flowed a stuff like red-hot iron. The tops
of high mountains fell and destroyed whole forests and
villages. I myself saw one mountain torn from another
and fall straight down. When I afterwards went to see
the place there was a lake there. When the earth was
composed there came a duke of Lindasburgt with his
people, and one maiden who cried everywhere, Magy is
the cause of all the misery that we have suffered. They
continued their progress, and their hosts increased. The
Magy fled, and his corpse was found where he had killed
himself. Then the Finns were driven to one place where
they might live. There were some of mixed blood who
were allowed to stay, but most of them went with the
Finns. The duke was chosen as king. The temples
which had remained whole were destroyed. Since that
time the good Northmen come often to Texland for the
advice of the mother; still we cannot consider them real
Frisians. In Denmark it has certainly happened as with
us. The sea-people, who call themselves famous sea-
warriors, went on board their ships, and afterwards went
back again.

Heil!

Whenever the Carrier has completed a period, then posterity shall understand that the faults and misdeeds that
the Brokmannen have brought with them belonged to their
forefathers; therefore I will watch, and will describe as much
of their manners as I have seen. The Geertmannen I can

manna kån ik rêd hinne stappa. Ik nåv navt fül mithra
omme gvngen. Tha så fêr ik sjan hå send hja thåt mast
bi tål ånd sêd bilêwen. Thåt ne mêi ik navt segsa fon
tha ôthera. Thêr fon.a Krêkalånda wêi kvme, send kwåd
ther tål ånd vppira sêd ne mêi mån êl navt boga. Fêlo
håvath brûna ågon ånd hêr. Hja send nidich ånd drist
ånd ång thrvch overbilåwichhêd. Hwêrsa hja sprêka, så
nômath hja the worda får vppa thêr lerst kvma mosta.
Ajen ald segath hja åd, åjen salt såd, må fori mån, sel
fori skil, sode fori skolde, to fül vmb to nomande. Ak
forath hja mêst vrdvaliske ånd bikirte nôma, hwêran mån
nên sin an hefta ne mêi. Tha Johniar sprêkath bêtre,
thach hja swygath thi h ånd hwêri navt nêsa mot, wårth
er ûtekêth. Hwersa imman en blyd måkath åfter ênnen
vrstvrven ånd thet likt, så låwath hja, thåt thene gåst
thes vrsturvene thêr inne fårath. Thêrvr håvath hja alle
bylda vrburgen fon Frya, Fåsta, Mêdêa, Thjanja, Hellênja
ånd fêlo ôthera. Hwerth thêr en bern ebern, så kvmath
tha sibba et sêmne ånd biddath an Frya thåt hju hjara
fåmkes mêi kvma lêta thåt bern to sêenande. Håvon hja
bêden sa ne mêi nimman him rora ni hêra lêta. Kvmt
et bern to gråjande ånd halt thit en stvnde an, alsa is
thåt en kwåd têken ånd man is an formoda, thåt thju måm
hordom dên heth. Thêrvr håv ik al årge thinga sjan.
Kvmt et bern to slêpande, så is thåt en têken, thåt tha
fåmkes vr-et kvmen send. Lakt et inna slêp, så håvon
tha fåmkes thåt bern luk to sêit. Olon låwath hja an
bosa gåsta, hexna, kolla, aldermankes ånd elfun, as jef
hja fon tha Finna weï kêmen. Hyrmitha wil ik enda
ånd nw mên ik tha-k går skrêven hå, as ên minra êthla.
Frêthorik.

Frêthorik min gåd is 63 jêr wrden. Sont 100 ånd
8 jêr is hi thene êroste fon sin folk, thêr frêdsum

readily pass by. I have not had much to do with them, but as far as I have seen they have mostly retained their language and customs. I cannot say that of the others. Those who descend from the Greeks speak a bad language, and have not much to boast of in their manners. Many have brown eyes and hair. They are envious and impudent, and cowardly from superstition. When they speak, they put the words first that ought to come last. For old they say at; for salt, sât; and for man, ma—too many to mention. They also use abbreviations of names, which have no meaning. The Joniers speak better, but they drop the H, and put it where it ought not to be. When they make a statue of a dead person they believe that the spirit of the departed enters into it; therefore they have hidden their statues of Frya, Fâsta, Medea, Thiania, Hellenia, and many others. When a child is born, all the relatives come together and pray to Frya to send her servants to bless the child. When they have prayed, they must neither move nor speak. If the child begins to cry, and continues some time, it is a bad sign, and they suspect that the mother has committed adultery. I have seen very bad things come from that. If the child sleeps, that is a good sign—Frya's servants are come. If it laughs in its sleep, the servants have promised it happiness. Moreover, they believe in bad spirits, witches, sorcerers, dwarfs, and elves, as if they descended from the Finns. Herewith I will finish, and I think I have written more than any of my forefathers. Frethorik.

Frethorik, my husband, lived to the age of 63. Since 108 years he is the first of his race who died a

sturven is, alle ôthera send vndera slêga swikt, thêrvr thât
alle kâmpade with ajn ând fêrhêmande vmb rjucht ând
plicht.

Min nôm is Wil-jo, ik bin tha fâm thêr mith him fona
Saxanamarka to honk for. Thrvch tâl ând ommegang kêm
et ut, thât wi alle bêde fon Adela his folk wêron, thâ kêm
ljafde ând âfternêi send wi man ând wif wrden. Hi heth
mi fyf bern lêten, two suna ând thrju toghatera. Konerêd
alsa hêt min forma, Hâchgâna min ôthera, mine aldeste
toghater hêth Adela, thju ôthera Frulik ând tha jongeste
Nocht. Thâ-k nêi tha Saxanamarka for, hâv ik thrju boka
hret. Thet bok thêra sanga, thêra tellinga, ând thet
Hêlênja bok. Ik skrif thit til thju mân navt thânka ne
mêi thât hja fon Apollânja send; ik hâv thêr fül lêt vr had
ând wil thus âk thju êra hâ. Ak hâv ik mâr den, tha
Gosa-Makonta fallen is, hwames godhêd ând klârsjanhêd
to en sprêkword is wrden, thâ ben ik allêna nêi Texland
gvngen vmbe tha skrifta vr to skrivane, thêr hju âfter
lêten heth, ând thâ tha lerste wille fonden is fon Frâna
ând tha nêilêtne skrifta fon Adela jefta Hellênja, hâv ik
thât jetta rêis den. Thit send tha skrifta Hellênjas. Ik
set hjam fâr vppa vmbe thât hja tha aldesta send.

ALLE AFTA FRYAS HELD.

In êra tida niston tha Slâvona folkar nawet fon
fryhêd. Lik oxa wrdon hja vnder et juk brocht. In
irthas wand wrdon hja jâgath vmbe mêtal to delvane ând
ut-a herde bergum moston hja hûsa hâwa to forst ând
presterums hêm. Bi al hwat hja dêdon, thêr nas
nawet to fâra hjara selva, men ella moste thjanja vmbe
tha forsta ând prestera jeta riker ând weldiger to mâkjane hjara selva to sâdene. Vnder thesse arbêd wrdon hja

peaceable death; all the others died by violence, because they all fought with their own people, and with foreigners for right and duty.

My name is Wiljo. I am the maiden who came home with him from Saxsenmarken. In the course of conversation it came out that we were both of Adela's race—thus our affection commenced, and we became man and wife. He left me with five children, two sons and three daughters. Konreed was my eldest son, Hachgana my second. My eldest daughter is called Adela, my second Frulik, and the youngest Nocht. When I went to Saxsenmarken I preserved three books—the book of songs, the book of narratives, and the Hellenia book.

I write this in order that people may not think they were by Apollonia. I have had a good deal of annoyance about this, and therefore now wish to have the honour of it. I also did more. When Gosa Makonta died, whose goodness and clear-sightedness have become a proverb, I went alone to Texland to copy the writings that she had left; and when the last will of Frana was found, and the writings left by Adela or Hellenia, I did that again. These are the writings of Hellenia. I have put them first because they are the oldest.

HAIL TO ALL TRUE FRISIANS.

In the olden times, the Slavonic race knew nothing of liberty. They were brought under the yoke like oxen. They were driven into the bowels of the earth to dig metals, and had to build houses of stone as dwelling-places for princes and priests. Of all that they did nothing came to themselves, everything must serve to enrich and make more powerful the priests and the princes, and to satisfy them. Under this treatment they grew grêv ånd stråm êr hja jêrich wêron, ånd sturvon svnder nochta afshên irtha tham overflodlik fvl jêf to båta al hjara bern. Men vsa britna kêmon ånd vsa bânnalinga thrvch tha Twisklånda vr in hjara marka fårä ånd vsa stjurar kemon in hjara håvna. Fon hjam hêradon hja kålta vr êlika frydom ånd rjucht ånd overa êwa, hwer bûta nimman omme ne mêi. Altham wrde vpsugon thrvch tha drova månniska lik dåwa thrvch tha dorra fjelde. As hju fvl wêron bijonnon tha alderdrista månniska to klippane mith hjara kêdne, alsa-t tha forsta wê dêde. Tha forste send stolte ånd wichandlik, thêrvmbe is thêr åk noch düged in hjara hirta, hja birêdon et sêmine ånd javon awet fon hjara overflodalikhêd. Men tha låfa skin fråna prestara ne machton thåt navt ne lyda, emong hjara forsinde godum hêdon hja åk wrangwråda drochtne eskêpen. Pest kêm inovera lånda. Nw sêidon hja, tha drochtna send tornich overa overhêrichhêd thêra bosa. Tha wrdon tha alderdrista månniska mith hjara kêdne wirgad. Irtha heth hjara blod dronken, mith thåt blod fode hju früchda ånd nochta, ånd alle tham thêr of êton wrdon wis.

16 wåra 100 jêr lêden* is Atland svnken, ånd to thêra tidum bêrade thêr awat hwêr vppa nimman rêkned nêde. In-t hirte fon Findas lånd vppet berchta lêid en del, thêr is kêthen Kasamyr,† thet is sjeldsum. Thêr werth en bern e-bern, sin måm wêre thju toghater enis kêning ånd sin tåt wêre-n håvedprester. Vmb skôm to vnkvma mosten hja hjara åjen blod vnkvma. Thêrvmbe wårth er bûta thêre stêde brocht bi årma månniska. In twiska was-t im navt forhêlad ne wrden, thêr vmbe dêd er ella vmbe wisdom to gêtane ånd gårane. Sin forstån wêre så gråt thåt er ella forstånde hwat er så ånd hêrade. Thåt folk skowdc him mit êrbêdenese and tha prestera wr don ang vr sina frêga. Thå-r jêrich wrde gvnger nêi sinum

---

* 2193 – 1600 = 593 v. Chr.   † Kasamyr, Kashmir.

gray and old before their time, and died without any enjoyment; although the earth produces abundantly for the good of all her children. But our runaways and exiles came through Twiskland to their boundaries, and our sailors came to their harbours. From them they heard of liberty, of justice, and laws, without which men cannot exist. This was all absorbed by the unhappy people like dew into an arid soil. When they fully understood this, the most courageous among them began to clank their chains, which grieved the princes. The princes are proud and warlike; there is therefore some virtue in their hearts. They consulted together and bestowed some of their superfluity; but the cowardly hypocritical priests could not suffer this. Among their false gods they had invented also wicked cruel monsters. Pestilence broke out in the country; and they said that the gods were angry with the domineering of the wicked. Then the boldest of the people were strangled in their chains. The earth drank their blood, and that blood produced corn and fruits that inspired with wisdom those who ate them.

Sixteen hundred years ago (she writes, 593 B.C.), Atland was submerged; and at that time something happened which nobody had reckoned upon. In the heart of Findasland, upon a mountain, lies a plain called Kasamyr (Cashmere) that is "extraordinary." There was a child born whose mother was the daughter of a king, and whose father was a high-priest. In order to hide the shame they were obliged to renounce their own blood. Therefore it was taken out of the town to poor people. As the boy grew up, nothing was concealed from him, so he did all in his power to acquire wisdom. His intellect was so great that he understood everything that he saw or heard. The people regarded him with respect, and the priests were afraid of his questions. When he was of full age he went to his

---

* 2193 – 1600 is 593 years before Christ.   † *Kasamyr* is Kashmere.

P

aldrum. Hja moston herda thinga hêra, vmb-im kwit to
werthane javon hja him vrflod fon kestlika stênum ; men
hja ne thvradon him navt avbêr bikânnâ as hjara âjne
blod. Mith drovenese in vrdelven overa falxe skôm sinra
aldrnm gvnger ommedwâla. Al forth fârande mête hi
en Fryas stjurar thêr as slâv thjanade, fon tham lêrd-i vsa
sêd ând plêgum. Hi kâpade him fry, ând to ther dâd
send hja frjunda bilêwen. Alomme hwêr er forth hinne
tâch, lêrd-i an tha ljuda thât hja nêne rika ner prestera
tolêta moston, thât hja hjara selva hode moston âjen falxe
skôm, ther allerwêikes kvad dvat an tha ljavde. Irtha
sêid-er skânkath hjara jêva nêi mêta men hjara hûd
klâwat, thât mân thêrin âch to delvane to êrane ând to
sêjane, sâ mân thêrof skêra wil. Thach sêid-er nimman
hovat thit to dvande fori ennen ôthera hit ne sy, thât et
bi mêne wille jef ut ljavade skêd. Hi lêrde thât nimman
in hjara wand machte frota vmbe gold her silver ner kestlika stêna, hwêr nid an klywath ând ljavde fon fljuchth.
Vmbe jow manghêrta ând wiva to sjarane, sêid-er, jêvath
hjara rin strâma ênoch. Nimman sêid-er is weldich alle
mânniska mêtrik ând êlika luk to jân. Tha thât it alra
mânniska plicht vmbe tha mânniska alsa mêtrik to mâkjane ând sa fêlo nocht to jân, as to binâka is. Nêne witskip sêid-er ne mêi mân minachtja, thach êlika dêla is tha
grâteste witskip, thêr tid vs lêra mêi. Thêrvmbe thât hjv
argenese fon irtha wêrath ând ljavde feth.

Sin forme nôm wêre Jes-us,* thach tha prestera thêr-im
sêralik hâton hêton him Fo thât is falx, thât folk hête him
Kris-en thât is herder, ând sin Fryaske frjund hêta him
Bûda, vmbe that hi in sin hâvad en skât fon wisdom hêde
ând in sin hirt en skât fon ljavde.

To tha lersta most-er fluchta vr tha wrêka thêra prestera,
men vral hwêr er kêm was sine lêre him fârut gvngen

---

* Jes-us, evenmin te verwarren met Jezus, als Krisen (Krishna) met
Christus.

parents. They had to listen to some hard language; and
to get rid of him they gave him a quantity of jewels, but
they dared not openly acknowledge him. Overcome with
sorrow at the false shame of his parents, he wandered
about. While travelling he fell in with a Frisian sailor
who was serving as a slave, and who taught him our
manners and customs. He bought the freedom of the
slave, and they remained friends till death. Wherever
he went he taught the people not to tolerate rich men or
priests, and that they must guard themselves against false
shame, which everywhere did harm to love and charity.
The earth, he said, bestowed her treasures on those who
scratch her skin; so all are obliged to dig, and plough,
and sow if they wish to reap, but no one is obliged to do
anything for another unless it be out of goodwill. He
taught that men should not seek in her bowels for gold,
or silver, or precious stones, which occasion envy and
destroy love. To embellish your wives and daughters, he
said, the river offers her pure stream. No man is able to
make everybody equally rich and happy, but it is the duty
of all men to make each other as equally rich and as happy
as possible. Men should not despise any knowledge; but
justice is the greatest knowledge that time can teach,
because she wards off offences and promotes love.

His first name was Jessos, but the priests, who hated
him, called him Fo, that is, false; the people called him
Krishna, that is, shepherd; and his Frisian friend called
him Buddha (purse), because he had in his head a treasure of wisdom, and in his heart a treasure of love.

At last he was obliged to flee from the wrath of
the priests; but wherever he went his teaching had
preceded him, whilst his enemies followed him like

---

* *Jes-us*—not to be confounded with Jesus any more than Krisen (Krishna)
with Christ.

ånd vral hwêr-er gvng folgadon him sina lêtha lik sine skåde nêi. Thâ Jes-vs alsa twilif jêr om fåren hêde, sturv-er, men sina frjunda wâradon sine lêre ånd kêthon hwêr-et åron fvnde.

Hwat mênst nw thât tha prestera dêdon, thât mot ik jo melde, åk mot-i thêr sêralik acht vp jån, forth mot-i over hjara bidryv ånd renka wåka mith alle kråftum, thêr Wr.alda in jo lêid heth. Thahwila Jes-us lêre vr irtha for, gvngon tha falxe prestera nêi-t lånd sinra berta sin dåd avbêra, hja sêidon thât hja fon sinum frjundum wêron, hja bêradon gråte rowa, torennande hjara klåthar to flardum ånd to skêrande hjara hola kål. Inna hôla thêra berga gvngon hja hêma, thach thêrin hêdon hja hjara skåt brocht, thêr binna måkadon hja blydon åfter Jes-us, thessa blydon jåvon hja antha vnårg thånkanda ljuda, to longa lersta sêidon hja thât Jes-us en drochten wêre, thât-i thât selva an hjam bilêden hêde, ånd thât alle thêr an him ånd an sina lêra låwa wilde, nêimels in sin kêningkrik kvme skolde, hwêr frü is ånd nochta send. Vrmites hja wiston thât Jes-us åjen tha rika to fjelda tågen hêde, så kêthon hja allerwêikes, that årmode hå ånd ênfald så thju düre wêre vmbe in sin rik to kvmane, thât thêra thêr hyr vp irtha thât måste lêden hêde, nêimels tha måsta nochta håva skolde. Thahwila hja wiston thât Jes-us lêrad hêde thât mån sina tochta welda ånd bistjura moste, så lêrdon hja thât mån alle sina tochta dêja moste, ånd thât tha fvlkvminhêd thêra månniska thêrin bistande thât er êvin vnforstoren wrde så thât kalde stên. Vmbe thât folk nw wis to måkjande thât hja alsa dêdon, alsa bêradon hja årmode overa strêta ånd vmb forth to biwisane thât hja al hjara tochta dåd hêde, nåmon hja nêne wiwa. Thach sahwêrsa en toghater en misstap hêde, så wårth hja that ring forjån, tha wrakka sêidon hja most mån helpa and vmbe sin åjn his shadow. When Jessos had thus travelled for twelve years he died; but his friends preserved his teaching, and spread it wherever they found listeners.

What do you think the priests did then? That I must tell you, and you must give your best attention to it. Moreover, you must keep guard against their acts and their tricks with all the strength that Wr-alda has given you. While the doctrine of Jessos was thus spreading over the earth, the false priests went to the land of his birth to make his death known. They said they were his friends, and they pretended to show great sorrow by tearing their clothes and shaving their heads. They went to live in caves in the mountains, but in them they had hid all their treasures, and they made in them images of Jessos. They gave these statues to simple people, and at last they said that Jessos was a god, that he had declared this himself to them, and that all those who followed his doctrine should enter his kingdom hereafter, where all was joy and happiness. Because they knew that he was opposed to the rich, they announced everywhere that poverty, suffering, and humility were the door by which to enter into his kingdom, and that those who had suffered the most on earth should enjoy the greatest happiness there. Although they knew that Jessos had taught that men should regulate and control their passions, they taught that men should stifle their passions, and that the perfection of humanity consisted in being as unfeeling as the cold stones. In order to make the people believe that they did as they preached, they pretended to outward poverty; and that they had overcome all sensual feelings, they took no wives. But if any young girl had made a false step, it was quickly forgiven; the weak, they said, were to be assisted, and to save sêle to bihaldane most mån fül anda cherke jån. Thus todvande hêde hja wiv ånd bern svnder hûshalden ånd wrdon hja rik svnder werka, men that folk wårth fül årmer ånd mår êlåndich as å to fåra. Thas lêre hwêrbi tha prestera nên ôre witskip hova as drochtlik rêda, fråna skin ånd vnrjuchta plêga, brêd hiri selva ut fon-t asta to-t westa ånd skil åk vr vsa landa kvma.

Men astha prestera skilun wåna, thåt hja allet ljucht fon Frya ånd fon Jes-us lêre vtdåvath håva, så skilum thêr in alle vvrda månniska vpstonda, tham wêrhêd in stilnise among ekkorum wårath ånd to fåra tha prestera forborgen håve. Thissa skilun wêsa ut forsta blod, fon presterum blod, fon Slåvonum blod, ånd fon Fryas blod. Tham skilun hjara foddikum ånd thåt ljucht bûta bringa, så thåt allera månnalik wêrhêd mêi sjan; hja skilun wê hropa overa dêda thêra prestera ånd forsta. Tha forsta thêr wêrhêd minna ånd rjucht tham skilun fon tha prestera wika, blod skil stråma, men thêrut skil-et folk nye kråfta gåra. Findas folk skil sina findingrikhêd to mêna nitha wenda, thåt Lydas folk sina kråfta ånd wi vsa wisdom. Tha skilun tha falxa prestera wêi fågath wertha fon irtha. Wr.alda his gåst skil alomme ånd allerwêikes êrath ånd bihropa wertha. Tha êwa thêr Wr.alda bi-t anfang in vs mod lêide, skilun allêna hêrad wertha, thêr ne skilun nêne ôra måstera, noch forsta, ner båsa navt nêsa, as thêra thêr bi mêna wille kêren send. Thån skil Frya juwgja ånd Irtha skil hira jêva allêna skånka an tha werkande månnisk. Altham skil anfanga fjuwer thusand jêr nêi Atland svnken is ånd thusand jêr lêter skil thêr longer nên prester ner tvang vp irtha sa.

Dela tonômath Hellênja, wåk!

their souls men must give largely to the Church. Acting
in this way, they had wives and children without households, and were rich without working; but the people
grew poorer and more miserable than they had ever been
before. This doctrine, which requires the priests to possess no further knowledge than to speak deceitfully, and
to pretend to be pious while acting unjustly, spreads from
east to west, and will come to our land also.

But when the priests fancy that they have entirely extinguished the light of Frya and Jessos, then shall all
classes of men rise up who have quietly preserved the
truth among themselves, and have hidden it from the
priests. They shall be of princely blood of priests, Slavonic,
and Frya's blood. They will make their light visible, so
that all men shall see the truth; they shall cry woe to the
acts of the princes and the priests. The princes who love
the truth and justice shall separate themselves from the
priests ; blood shall flow, but from it the people will gather
new strength. Finda's folk shall contribute their industry
to the common good, Linda's folk their strength, and we
our wisdom. Then the false priests shall be swept away
from the earth. Wr-alda's spirit shall be invoked everywhere and always ; the laws that Wr-alda in the beginning
instilled into our consciences shall alone be listened to.
There shall be neither princes, nor masters, nor rulers,
except those chosen by the general voice. Then Frya
shall rejoice, and the earth will only bestow her gifts on
those who work. All this shall begin 4000 years after the
submersion of Atland, and 1000 years later there shall
exist no longer either priest or oppression.

Dela, surnamed Hellenia, watch !

Så lùda Frânas ûtroste wille. Alle welle Fryas held.
An tha nôme Wr.aldas, fon Frya, ånd thêre fryhêd grête
ik jo, ånd bidde jo, sahwersa ik falla machte êr ik en folgster nômath hêde, så bifêl ik jo Tüntja thêr Burchfâm is to
thêre burch Mêdêasblik, til hjud dêgum is hja tha besta.
Thet heth Gôsa nêi lêten. Alle månniska held. Ik
nåv nêne êremoder binomad thrvchdam ik nêne niste, ånd
et is jo bêter nêne Moder to håvande as êne hwêr vp-i jo
navt forlêta ne mêi. Arge tid is forbi fåren, men thêr
kvmt en ôthere. Irtha heth hja navt ne bårad ånd
Wr.alda heth hja navt ne skêren. Hju kvmt ut et åsta
ut-a bosma thêra prestera wêi. Så fêlo lêd skil hju broda,
thåt Irtha-t blod algådvr navt drinka ne kån fon hira vrs-
lêjana bernum. Thjustrenesse skil hju in overne gåst
thêra månniska sprêda, lik tongar-is wolka oviret svnne-
ljucht. Alom ånd allerwêikes skil lest ånd drochten
bidryf with fryhêd kåmpa ånd rjucht. Rjucht ånd fryhêd
skilun swika ånd wi mith tham. Men thesse winst skil
hjara vrlias wrochta. Fon thrju worda skilun vsa åfterkvmande an hjara ljuda ånd slåvona tha bithjutnesse lêra.
Hja send mêna ljavde, fryhêd ånd rjucht. Thåt forma
skilun hja glora, åfternêi with thjustrenesse kåmpa al
ont et hel ånd klår in hjawlikes hirt ånd holle wårth.
Thån skil tvang fon irtha fågad wertha, lik tongarswolka
thrvch stornewind, ånd alle drochten bidryv ne skil thêr
åjen nawet navt ne formüga. Gôsa.

Thus runs Frana's last will: All noble Frisians, Heil! In the name of Wr-alda, of Frya, and of Freedom, I greet you ; and pray you if I die before I have named a successor, then I recommend to you Teuntja, who is Burgtmaagd in the citadel of Medeasblik ; till now she is the best.

This Gosa has left behind her: Hail to all men ! I have named no Eeremoeder, because I know none, and because it is better for you to have no mother than to have one you cannot trust. One bad time is passed by, but there is still another coming. Irtha has not given it birth, and Wr-alda has not decreed it. It comes from the East, out of the bosom of the priests. It will breed so much mischief that Irtha will not be able to drink the blood of her slain children. It will spread darkness over the minds of men like storm-clouds over the sunlight. Everywhere craft and deception shall contend with freedom and justice. Freedom and justice shall be overcome, and we with them. But this success will work out its own loss. Our descendants shall teach their people and their slaves the meaning of three words ; they are *universal love, freedom,* and *justice.* At first they shall shine, then struggle with darkness, until every man's head and heart has become bright and clear. Then shall oppression be driven from the earth, like the thunder-clouds by the storm-wind, and all deceit will cease to have any more power. Gosa.

THET SKRIFT FON KONERÊD.

Min êthla hâvon in âfter thit bok skrêven. Thit wil ik boppa ella dva, vmbe thât er in min stât nên burch ovir is, hwêrin tha bêrtnesa vp skrêven wrde lik to fâra. Min nôme is Konerêd, min tât-his nôme was Frêthorik, min mem his nôme Wiljow. After tât his dâd ben ik to sina folgar kêren, ånd tha-k fiftich jêr tålde kås men mij to vrste grêvetmån. Min tât heth skrêven ho tha Linda-wrda ånd tha Ljudgårdne vrdilgen send. Lindahêm is jeta wêi, tha Linda-wrda far en dêl, tha northlikka Ljudgårdne send thrvch thene salta sê bidelven. That brûwsende bef slikt an tha hringdik thêre burch. Lik tât melth heth, så send tha hâvalåsa månniska to gvngen ånd hâvon hûskes bvwad binna tha hringdik thêra burch. Thêrvmbe is thât ronddêl nw Ljvdwerd hêten. Tha stjurar segath Ljvwrd, men thât is wansprêke. Bi mina jüged was-t ôre lånd, thât bûta tha hringdik lêid, al pol ånd brok. Men Fryas folk is diger ånd flitich, hja wrdon mod ner wirg, thrvchdam hjara dol to tha besta lêide. Thrvch slåta to delvane ånd kådika to måkjane fon tha grvnd thêr ût-a slåta kêm, alsa hâvon wi wither en gode hêm bûta tha hringdik, thêr thju dånte het fon en hof, thrê pêla åstwarth, thrê pêla sûdwarth ånd thrê pêla wêstwarth mêten. Hjud dêgum send wi to dvande å-pêla to hêjande, vmb êne hâve to winnande ånd mith ên vmb-vsa hringdik to biskirmande. Jef et werk rêd sy, så skilun wi stjurar utlvka. Bi min jüged stand-et hyr bljûstre om-to, men hjud send tha hûskes

THE WRITING OF KONERÊD.

My forefathers have written this book in succession. I
will do this, the more because there exists no longer in
my state any citadel on which events are inscribed as used
to be the case. My name is Konerêd (Koenraad). My
father's name was Frethorik, my mother's name was Wiljow. After my father's death I was chosen as his successor. When I was fifty years old I was chosen for chief
Grevetman. My father has written how the Lindaoorden
and Liudgaarden were destroyed. Lindahem is still lost,
the Lindaoorden partially, and the north Lindgaarden are
still concealed by the salt sea. The foaming sea washes
the ramparts of the castle. As my father has mentioned,
the people, being deprived of their harbour, went away and
built houses inside the ramparts of the citadel; therefore
that bastion is called Lindwerd. The sea-people say Lin-
werd, but that is nonsense. In my youth there was a
portion of land lying outside the rampart all mud and
marsh; but Frya's people were neither tired nor exhausted
when they had a good object in view. By digging ditches,
and making dams of the earth that came out of the
ditches, we recovered a good space of land outside the
rampart, which had the form of a hoof three poles eastward, three southwards, and three westwards. At present we are engaged in ramming piles into the ground to
make a harbour to protect our rampart. When the work
is finished we shall attract mariners. In my youth it
looked very queer, but now there stands a row of houses.

al hûsa thêr an rêja stân. And lek ånd brek thêr mith
ermode hir in glupt wêron, send thrvch flit a-buta drêven.
Fon hir ut mêi allera månnalik lêra, thåt Wr.alda vsa
Alfoder, al sina skepsela fot, mits thåt hja mod halde ånd
månlik ôtherum helpa wille.

Nv wil ik vr Friso skriva.

Friso thêr al weldich wêre thrvch sin ljud, wårth åk to
vrste grêve kêren thrvch Staverens ommelandar. Hi spot
mith vsa wisa fon lånd-wêr ånd sêkåmpa, thêrvmbe heth-
er en skol stift hwêr in tha knåpa fjuchta lêra nêi Krêkalandar wysa. Thån ik låv thåt i thåt dên heth vmb thåt
jongk-folk an sin snôr to bindane. Ik håv min brother
thêr åk hin skikt, tha-s nv thjan jêr lêden. Hwand tocht
ik nv wi nêne Moder lônger navt nåve, vmbe tha ênen
åjen tha ôre to bi skirmande, åch ik dubbel to wåkane
thåt hi vs nên måster ne wårth.

Gosa neth vs nêne folgstere nômeth, thêr vr nil ik nên
ordêl ne fella, men thêr send jeta alda årg thenkande månniska, thêr mêne thåt hju-t thêr-vr mith Friso ênis wrden
is. Thå Gosa fallen was, thå wildon tha ljud fon alle
wrda êne ôthere Moder kjasa. Men Friso thêr to dvande
wêre vmb-en rik to fara him selva to måkjane, Friso ne
gêrde nên rêd ner bodo fon Texland. As tha bodon thêra
Landsåtum to him kêmon, sprek-i ånde kêth. Gosa
sêid-er was fêrsjande wêst ånd wiser as alle grêva êtsêmne
ånd thach nêde hju nêu ljucht nêr klårhêd in thjuse sêke
ne fvnden, thêrvmbe nêde hju nene mod håu vmb êne
folgstere to kjasane, ånd vmb êne folgstere to kjasane thêr
tvyvelik wêre, thêr heth hju bald in sjan, thêrvmbe heth hju
in hjara ûtroste wille skrêven, thåt is jow bêtre nêne Moder
to håvande as êne hwêr vpp-i jo selva navt forlêta ne mêi.
Friso hêde fûl sjan, bi orloch was er vpbrocht, ånd fon

Leaks and deficiencies produced by poverty have been remedied by industry. From this men may learn that Wr-alda, our universal father, protects all his creatures, if they preserve their courage and help each other.

Now I will write about Friso.

Friso, who was already powerful by his troops, was chosen chief Grevetman of the districts round Staveren. He laughed at our mode of defending our land and our sea-fights; therefore he established a school where the boys might learn to fight in the Greek manner, but I believe that he did it to attach the young people to himself. I sent my brother there ten years ago, because I thought, now that we have not got any mother, it behoves me to be doubly watchful, in order that he may not become our master.

Gosa has given us no successors. I will not give any opinion about that; but there are still old suspicious people who think that she and Friso had an understanding about it. When Gosa died, the people from all parts wished to choose another mother; but Friso, who was busy establishing a kingdom for himself, did not desire to have any advice or messenger from Texland. When the messengers of the Landsaten came to him, he said that Gosa had been far-seeing and wiser than all the counts together, and yet she had been unable to see any light or way out of this affair; therefore she had not had the courage to choose a successor, and to choose a doubtful one she thought would be very bad; therefore she wrote in her last will, It is better to have no mother than to have one on whom you cannot rely. Friso had seen a great deal. He had been brought up in the wars, and he had just learned and gathered as much of the tricks and

tha hrenkum ånd lestum thêra Golum ånd forstum hêder
krek sa fül lêred ånd geth, as-er nêdich hêde vmbe tha
ôra grêva to wêiande hwêr hi hjam wilde.   Sjan hir ho-r
thêrmith to gvngen is.

Friso hêde hir-ne ôther wif nimth, thju toghater fon
Wil-frêthe, bi sin lêve was-er vrste Grêva to Staveren
wêst.   Thêr bi hêder twên svna wnnen ånd twa toghatera.
Thrvch sin bilêid is Kornêlja sin jongste toghater mith
min brother mant.   Kornêlja is wan Fryas and mot Korn-
hêlja skrêven wrde.   Wêmod sin aldeste heth er an Kavch
bonden.   Kavch thêr åk bi him to skole gvng is thi svnv
fon Wichhirte thene Gêrtmanna kåning.   Men Kavch is
åk wan Fryas ånd mot Kåp wêsa.   Men kvade tåle håvon
hja mar mithbrocht as gode sêda.

Nw mot ik mith mine skêdnese a-befta kêra.

Aftre gråte flod hwêr vr min tåt skrêven heth, wêron
fêlo Juttar ånd Lêtne mith ebbe uta Balda jefta kvade
sê * fored.   Bi Kåt his gat drêvon hja in hjara kåna mith
yse vppa tha Dênemarka fåst ånd thêr vp send hja sitten
bilêwen.   Thêr nêron narne nên månniska an-t sjocht.
Thêrvmbe håvon hja thåt lånd int, nêi hjara nôme håvon
hja thåt land Juttarland hêten.   Afternêi kêmon wel fêlo
Denemarker to bek fon tha håga landum, men thissa setton
hjara selva sûdliker del.   And as tha stjurar to bek kêmon
thêr navt vrgvngen navt nêron, gvng thi êna mith tha
ôthera nei tha sê jefta êlandum.†   Thrvch thisse skikking
mochton tha Juttar thåt land halda, hwêr-vppa Wr.alda
ra wêjad hêde.   Tha Sêlandar stjurar tham hjara selva
mith blåte fisk navt helpa ner nêra nilde, ånd thêr en årge
grins hêde an tha Gola, tham gvngon dåna tha Phonisjar
skêpa biråwa.   An tha sûdwester herne fon Skênland, thêr
lêid Lindasburcht tonômath Lindasnôse, thrvch vsa Apol
stift, alsa in thit bok ‡ biskrêwen ståt.   Alle kådhêmar ånd

---

cunning ways of the Gauls and the princes as he required, to lead the other counts wherever he wished. See here how he went to work about that.

Friso had taken here another wife, a daughter of Wil-frêthe, who in his lifetime had been chief count of Staveren. By her he had two sons and two daughters. By his wish Kornelia, his youngest daughter, was married to my brother. Kornelia is not good Frisian; her name ought to be written Korn-helia. Weemoed, his eldest daughter, he married to Kauch. Kauch, who went to school to him, is the son of Wichhirte, the king of the Geertmen. But Kauch is likewise not good Frisian, and ought to be Kaap (Koop). So they have learned more bad language than good manners.

Now I must return to my story.

After the great flood of which my father wrote an account, there came many Jutlanders and Letlanders out of the Baltic, or bad sea. They were driven down the Kat-tegat in their boats by the ice as far as the coast of Den-mark, and there they remained. There was not a creature to be seen; so they took possession of the land, and named it after themselves, Jutland. Afterwards many of the Denmarkers returned from the higher lands, but they settled more to the south; and when the mariners re-turned who had not been lost, they all went together to Zeeland. By this arrangement the Jutlanders retained the land to which Wr-alda had conducted them. The Zeeland skippers, who were not satisfied to live upon fish, and who hated the Gauls, took to robbing the Phœnician ships. In the south-west point of Scandi-navia there lies Lindasburgt, called Lindasnôse, built by one Apol, as is written in the book. All the people

---

* *Balda jefta kvade sê* is the Baltic. *Juttarland* is Jutland.
† *Zeeland* is the Danish Islands.   ‡ See page 124.

ommelandar dåna.wêron eft Fryas bilêven, men thrvch tha
lnst thêre wrêke åjen tha Golum ånd åjen tha Kåltana folgar gvngon hja mitha Sêlandar såma dvan, men that såma
dva neth nen stek navt ne halden. Hwand tha Sêlandar
hêde felo mislika plêga ånd wenhêde ovir nommen fon tha
vvla Mågjarum, Fryas folk to-n spot. Forth gvng ek to
fara him selva råwa, thach jef et to pase kêm thån standon
hja månlik ôtherum trvlik by. Thach to tha lesta bijon-
don tha Sêlandar brek to krêjande an goda skêpa. Hjara
skipmåkar weron omkvmen ånd hjara walda wêron mith
grvnd ånd al fon-t land of fåged. Nw kêmon thêr vnwar-
lingen thry skêpa by tha ringdik fon vsa burch mêra.
Thrvch tha inbrêka vsra landum wêron hja vrdvaled ånd
tha Flymvda misfaren. Thi kåpmon thêr mith gvngen
was, wilde fon vs nya skêpa hå, thêrto hêdon hja mithbrocht allerlêja kestlika wêra, thêr hja råwed hêdon fon
tha Kåltanarlandnm ånd fon tha Phonisjar * skêpum.
Nêidam wy selva nêne skêpa navt n-êde, jêf ik hjam
flingka horsa ånd fjvwer wêpende rinbodon mith nei Friso.
Hwand to Ståveren ånd allingen thåt Aldergå thêr wrdon
tha besta wêrskêpa maked fon herde êken wod thêr nimmerthe nên rot an ne kvmth. Thahwila tha sêkampar
by my byde, wêron svme Juttar nêi Texland fåren ånd dånå
wêron hja nêi Friso wêsen. Tha Sêlandar hêdon felo fon
hjara storeste knåpum råwed, thi moston vppa hjara benka
roja, ånd fon hjara storeste toghtera vmb thêr by bern to
têjande. Tha stora Juttar ne mochton et navt to wêrane,
thrvchdam hja nêne gode wêpne navt nêde. Thå hja
hjara lêth telad hêde ånd thêrvr fêlo wordon wixlad
wêron, frêje Friso to tha lesta jef hja nêne gode have
in hjara gå navt n-êde. O-jes, anderon hja, êne besta
ên, êne thrvch Wr.alda skêpen. Hju is net krek lik jow
bjarkrûk thêr, hira hals is eng, thå in hira bålg kåu-
nath wel thvsanda gråte kåna lidsa, men wi nåvath
nêna burch ner burchwêpne, vmbe tha råwskêpa thêr ut

---

* Phonisiar, hier Puniers, Carthagers.

who live on the coasts, and in the neighbouring districts, had remained true Frisians; but by their desire for vengeance upon the Gauls, and the followers of Kaltona, they joined the Zeelanders. But that connection did not hold together, because the Zeelanders had adopted many evil manners and customs of the wicked Magyars, in opposition to Frya's people. Afterwards, everybody went stealing on his own account; but when it suited them they held all together. At last the Zeelanders began to be in want of good ships. Their shipbuilders had died, and their forests as well as their land had been washed out to sea. Now there arrived unexpectedly three ships, which anchored off the ringdyk of our citadel. By the disruption of our land they had lost themselves, and had missed Flymond. The merchant who was with them wished to buy new ships from us, and for that purpose had brought all kinds of valuables, which they had stolen from the Celtic country and Phœnician ships. As we had no ships, I gave them active horses and four armed couriers to Friso; because at Stavere, along the Alberga, the best ships of war were built of hard oak which never rots. While these sea rovers remained with us, some of the Jutmen had gone to Texland, and thence to Friso. The Zeelanders had stolen many of their strongest boys to row their ships, and many of their finest daughters to have children by. The great Jutlanders could not prevent it, as they were not properly armed. When they had related all their misfortunes, and a good deal of conversation had taken place, Friso asked them at last if they had no good harbours in their country. Oh, yes, they answered; a beautiful one, created by Wr-alda. It is like a bottle, the neck narrow, but in the belly a thousand large boats may lie; but we have no citadel and no defences to keep out

---

* *Phonisjar* are Punics or Carthaginians.

to haldane. Thån mosten jow gvnst måkja sêide Friso. God rêden anderon tha Juttar, men wi n-åvath nêne ambachtisljud ner bvwark, wi alle send fiskar ånd juttar. Tha ora send vrdrvnken jefta nêi tha håga landum fljucht. Midlar hwila hja thus kålta, kêmon mina bodon mitha Sêlåndar hêra et sina hove. Hir most nw letta ho Friso alle to bidobbe wiste to nocht fon bêde partja ånd to båte fon sin åjn dol. Tha Sêlandar sêider to, hja skoldon jêrlikes fiftech skêpa håve, nêi fåsta mêtum ånd nêi fåsta jeldum, to hrêd mith ysere kêdne ånd kråubogum ånd mith fvlle tjuch alsa far wêrskêpa hof ånd nêdlik sy, men tha Juttar skoldon hja thån mith frêthe lêta, ånd all-et folk thåt to Fryasbern hêred. Jå hi wilde mar dva, hi wilde al vsa sêkåmpar utnêda thåt hja skolde mith fjuchta ånd råwa. Thå tha Sêlandar wêi brit wêron, thå lêt-er fjuwertich alda skêpa to laja mith burchwêpne, wod, hirbaken stên, timberljud, mirtselêra ånd smêda vmbe thêr mith burga to bvwande. Witto, that is witte sin svn, sand hi mith vmb to to sjanande. Hwat thêr al får fallen is, n-is my navt ni meld, men sa fül is my bår wrden, an byde sida thêre haves mvde is êne withburch bvwed, thêr in is folk lêid that Friso uta Saxanamarka tåch. Witto heth Sjuchthirte bifrêjad ånd to sin wiv nomen. Wilhem alsa hête hira tat, hi was vreste Aldermån thêra Juttar, that is vrste Grêvetman jefta Grêve. Wilhem is kirt after sturven ånd Witto is in sin stêd koreu.

Ho Friso forther dêde.

Fon sin êrosta wif hêder twên sviaringa bihalda, thêr sêr klok wêron. Hetto, that is hête, thene jongste skikt er as

the pirate ships. Then you should make them, said Friso.
That is very good advice, said the Jutlanders; but we
have no workmen and no building materials; we are all
fishermen and trawlers. The others are drowned or fled
to the higher lands. While they were talking in this
way, my messengers arrived at the court with the Zeeland
gentlemen. Here you must observe how Friso understood
deceiving everybody, to the satisfaction of both parties,
and to the accomplishment of his own ends. To the Zeelanders he promised that they should have yearly fifty
ships of a fixed size for a fixed price, fitted with iron
chains and crossbows, and full rigging as is necessary and
useful for men-of-war, but that they should leave in peace
the Jutlanders and all the people of Frya's race. But he
wished to do more; he wanted to engage all our sea
rovers to go with him upon his fighting expedition. When
the Zeelanders had gone, he loaded forty old ships with
weapons for wall defences, wood, bricks, carpenters,
masons, and smiths, in order to build citadels. Witto,
or Witte, his son, he sent to superintend. I have never
been well informed of what happened; but this much is
clear to me, that on each side of the harbour a strong
citadel has been built, and garrisoned by people brought
by Friso out of Saksenmarken. Witto courted Siuchthirte
and married her. Wilhem, her father, was chief Alderman
of the Jutmen—that is, chief Grevetman or Count. Wilhem died shortly afterwards, and Witto was chosen in his
place.

WHAT FRISO DID FURTHER.

Of his first wife he still had two brothers-in-law,
who were very daring. Hetto—that is, heat—the
youngest, he sent as messenger to Kattaburgt, which

senda boda nêi Kattaburch thåt djap inna Saxanamarka
lêid. Hi hêde fon Friso mith krêjen sjugon horsa buta
sin åjn, to lêden mith kestlika sêkum, thrvch tha sêkåmpar råwed. Bi jahweder hors wêron twên jonga sêkåmpar
ånd twên jonga hrutar mith rika klådarum klåth ånd jeld
in hiara bûdar. Êvin as er Hetto nêi Kattaburch skikte,
skikter Brnno, thåt is brûne, thene ôthera svjaring nêi
Mannagårda wrda, Mannagårda wrda is får in thit bok*
Mannagårda forda skrêven, men thåt is misdên. Alle
rikdoma thêr hja mith hede wrdon nêi omstand wêi skånkt
an tha forsta and forstene ånd an tha utforkêrne mangêrtne.
Kêmon thå sine knapa vppa thêre mêid vmbe thêr mith et
jongkfolk to dônsjane, sa lêton hja kvra mith krûdkok
kvma ånd bårgum jeftha tonnum fon tha besta bjar. After
thissa bodon lêt-er immer jongkfolk over tha Saxanarmarka
fåra, thêr alle jeld inna budar hêde ånd alle mêida jeftha
skånkadja mith brochton, ånd vppa thêre mêid têradon
hja alon vnkvmmerlik wêi. Jef-t nv bêrde thåt tha
Saxana knåpa thêr nydich nêi utsågon, thån lakton hja
godlik ånd sêidon, aste thvrath thene mêna fyand to bi-
kåmpane, så kånst thin brêid jet fül riker mêida jån ånd
jet forstelik têra. Al bêda sviaringa fon Friso send bos-
tigjad mith toghaterum thêra romriksta forstum, ånd
åfkernêi kêmon tha Saxanar knåpa ånd mangêrtne by
êlle keddum nêi thåt Flymar del.

Tha burchfåmna ånd tha alda fåmna thêr jeta fon hjar
êre gråthêd wiste, nygadon navt vr nêi Frisos bedriv, thêrvmbe ne kêthon hja nên god fon him. Men Friso snôder
as hja lêt-ra snåka. Men tha jonga fåmna spônd-er mith
goldne fingrum an sina sêk. Hja sêidon alomme wy
nåvath longer nên Moder mår, men thåt kvmth dåna thåt
wit jêroch send. Jvd past vs ne kåning, til thju wi vsa landa
wither winna, thêr tha Modera vrlêren håve thrvch hjara

---

* Zie bl. 11.

lies far in the Saxsenmarken. Friso gave him to take
seven horses, besides his own, laden with precious things
stolen by the sea-rovers. With each horse there were
two young sea-rovers and two young horsemen, clad in
rich garments, and with money in their purses. In the
same way as he sent Hetto to Kattaburgt, he sent Bruno
—that is, brown—the other brother-in-law, to Mannagarda
oord. Mannagarda oord was written Mannagarda ford in
the earlier part of this book, but that is wrong. All the
riches that they took with them were given away, according to circumstances, to princes, princesses, and chosen
young girls. When his young men went to the tavern to
dance with the young people there, they ordered baskets
of spice, gingerbread, and tuns of the best beer. After
these messengers he let his young people constantly go
over to the Saxsenmarken, always with money in their
purses and presents to give away, and they spent money
carelessly in the taverns. When the Saxsen youths looked
with envy at this they smiled, and said, If you dare go
and fight the common enemy you would be able to give
much richer presents to your brides, and live much more
princely. Both the brothers-in-law of Friso had married
daughters of the chief princes, and afterwards the Saxsen
youths and girls came in whole troops to the Flymeer.

The burgtmaidens and old maidens who still remembered
their greatness did not hold with Friso's object, and therefore they said no good of him; but Friso, more cunning
than they, let them chatter, but the younger maidens he
led to his side with golden fingers. They said everywhere,
For a long time we have had no mother, but that comes
from our being fit to take care of ourselves. At present it
suits us best to have a king to win back our lands that
we have lost through the imprudence of our mothers.

---

* See page 11.

vudigerhêd. Forth kêthon hja, alrek Fryasbern is frydom
jêven, sin stem hêra to lêtane bi fara thêr bisloten wârth
bi t kjasa ênre forste, men ast alsa wyd kvma machte thât
i jo wither ne kâning kjasa, sâ wil ik âk min mêne segse.
Nêi al hwat ik skoja mêi, sâ is Friso thêr to thrvch
Wr.alda kêren, hwand hi heth im wonderlik hir hinne
wêiad. Friso wêt tha hrenka thêra Golum, hwam his
tâle hi sprêkt, hi kân thus âjen hjara lestum wâka. Thân
is thêr jeta awet to skojande, hok Grêva skolde mân to
kâning kjasa svnder that tha ôra thêr nidich vr wêron.
Aldulkera tâlum wârth thrvch tha jonga fâmnn kethen,
men tha alde fâmma afskên fê an tal, tapadon hjara rêdne
ut en ôthera bârg. Hja kêthon allerwêikes ând to alla
mannalik : Friso kêthon hja dvath sâ tha spinna dvan,
thes nachtis spôuth-i netta nêi alle sidum ând thes dêis
vrskalkth-i thêr sina vnâftertochtlika frjunda in. Friso
sêith that-er nêne prestera ner poppa forsta lyde ne mêi,
men ik seg, hi ne mêi nimman lyda as him selva. Thêrvmbe nil hi navt ne dâja thât thju burch Stavia wither vp
hêjath warth. Thêrvmbe wil hi nêne Moder wêr hâ. Jud
is Friso jow rêd jêvar, men morne wil hi jow kâning wertha,
til thju hi over jo alle rjuchta mei. Inna bosm thes folk-
is antstondon nw twa partyja. Tha alda ând ârma wildon
wither êne Moder hâ, men thât jongkfolk, thât fvl strêd-
lust wêre wilde ne tât jeftha kâning hâ. Tha êrosta
hêton hjara selva moder his svna ând tha ôthera hêton
hjara selva tât his svna, men tha Moder his svna ne wrde
wrde navt ni meld, hwand thrvchdam thêr fêlo skêpa
mâked wrde, was thêr ovirflod to fâra skipmâkar, smêda,
sylmâkar, rêpmâkar ând to fâra alle ôra ambachtisljud.
Thêr to boppa brochton tha sêkâmpar allerlêja syrhêda
mith. Thêr fon hêdon tha wiva nocht, tha fâmna nocht,
tha mangêrtne nocht, ând thêrof hêdon al hjara mêgum
nocht, ând al hjara frjundum ând âthum.

Further they said, Every child of Frya has permission to
let his voice be heard before the choice of a prince is de-
cided; but if it comes to that, that you choose a king,
then also we will have our say. From all that we can see,
Wr-alda has appointed Frisó for it, for he has brought
him here in a wonderful way. Friso knows the tricks of
the Gauls, whose language he speaks; he can therefore
watch against their craftiness. Then there is something
else to keep the eye upon. What count could be chosen
as king without the others being jealous of him? All such
nonsense the young maidens talked; but the old maidens,
though few in number, tapped their advice out of another
cask. They said always and to every one: Friso does like
the spiders. At night he spreads his webs in all directions, and in the day he catches in them all his unsuspect-
ing friends. Friso says he cannot suffer any priests or
foreign princes, but we say that he cannot suffer anybody
but himself; therefore he will not allow the citadel of
Stavia to be rebuilt; therefore he will not have the
mother again. To-day Friso is your counsellor, to-morrow
he will be your king, in order to have full power over you.
Among the people there now existed two parties. The
old and the poor wished to have the mother again, but the
young and the warlike wished for a father and a king. The
first called themselves mother's sons, the others father's
sons, but the mother's sons did not count for much; because there were many ships to build, there was a good
time for all kinds of workmen. Moreover, the sea-rovers
brought all sorts of treasures, with which the maidens
were pleased, the girls were pleased, and their relations
and friends.

Tha Friso bi fjuwertich jêr et Stâveren hushalden hêde
sturf-er.* Thrvch sin bijelda hêde-r fêlo stâta wither to
manlik ôtherum brocht, thach jef wi thêr thrvch bêter wrde
thvr ik navt bijechta. Fon alle Grêva thêr bifâra him wê-
rou n-as thêr nimman sâ bifâmed lik Friso wêst. Tha sâ
as-k êr sêide, tha jonge fâmna kêthon sina love, thahwila
tha alda fâmna ella dêdon vmb-im to achtjane ând hâtlik
to mâkjane bi alle mânniska. Nw ne machton tha alda
fâmna him thêr mitha wel navt ne stôra in sina bijeldinga,
men hja hâvon mith hjara bâra thach alsa fül utrjucht
thât-er sturven is svnder thât er kâning wêre.

NW WIL IK SKRIWA VR ADEL SIN SVNV.

Friso thêr vsa skidnese lêred hêde ut-et bok thêra Adel-
linga, hêde ella dên vmbe hjara frjundskip to winnande.
Sin êroste svnv thêr hi hir won by Swêthirte sin wif,
heth-er bi stonda Adel hêten. And afskên hi kâmpade mith
alle sin weld, vmbe nêne burga to forstâlane ner wither
vp to bvwande, thach sand hi Adel nêi thêre burch et
Texland til thju hi diger bi diger kvd wertha machta,
mith ella hwat to vsa êwa, tâle ând sedum hêreth. Tha
Adel twintich jêr tâlde lêt Friso him to sin âjn skol kvma,
ând as er thêr utlêred was, lêt-er him thrvch ovir alle
stâta fâra. Adel was-ne minlika skalk, bi sin fâra heth-
er fêlo âtha wnnen. Dâna is-t kvmen thât et folk him
Atha-rik hêten heth, awet hwat him âfternêi sa wel to
pase kêm, hwand as sin tât fallen was, bilêv-er in sin stêd
svnder that er vr-et kjasa ên er ôthera Grêva sprêka kêm.

Thahwila Adel to Texland inna lêre wêre, was thêr tefta
en êlle ljawe fâm in vpper burch. Hju kêm fon ut tha Saxanamarkum wêi, fon ut-êre stâtha thêr is kêthen Svôbaland
thêr thrvch wârth hju to Texland Svôbene† hêten, afskêu

---

* 263 v. Chr.   † Hamconius, p. 8. Suobinna.

When Friso had been nearly forty years at Staveren he died. Owing to him many of the states had been joined together again, but that we were the better for it I am not prepared to certify. Of all the counts that preceded him there was none so renowned as Friso; for, as I said before, the young maidens spoke in his praise, while the old maidens did all in their power to make him hateful to everybody. Although the old women could not prevent his meddling, they made so much fuss that he died without becoming king.

Now I will write about his son Adel.

Friso, who had learned our history from the book of the Adelingen, had done everything in his power to win their friendship. His eldest son, whom he had by his wife Swethirte, he named Adel; and although he strove with all his might to prevent the building or restoring any citadels, he sent Adel to the citadel of Texland in order to make himself better acquainted with our laws, language, and customs. When Adel was twenty years old Friso brought him into his own school, and when he had fully educated him he sent him to travel through all the states. Adel was an amiable young man, and in his travels he made many friends, so the people called him Atharik—that is, rich in friends—which was very useful to him afterwards, for when his father died he took his place without a question of any other count being chosen.

While Adel was studying at Texland there was a lovely maiden at the citadel. She came from Saxenmarken, from the state of Suobaland, therefore she was called at Texland Suobene, although her name

---

* 263 before Christ.   † Hamconius, page 8.   Suobinna.

hjra nôme Ifkja wêre. Adel hêde hja ljaf krêjen ånd hju
hêde Adel ljaf, men sin tåt bêd-im hi skolde jet wachtja.
Adel was hêrich, men alsa ring sin tåt fallen was ånd hi
sêten, sand hi bistonda bodon nei Berth-holda hira tåt
hin, as-er sine toghter to wif håva machte. Bertholda
wêr-ne forste fon vnforbastere sêd, hi hêde Ifkja nêi
Texland inna lêre svnden inner håpe that hja ênis to
burchfåm kêre wrde skolde in sine åjn land. Thach hi
hêde hjara bêder gêrte kånna lêred, thêrvmbe gvng-er to
ånd jef hjam sina sêjen. Ifkja wêr-ne kante Fryas.
Far sa fêre ik hja håv kånna lêred, heth hju alôn wrocht
ånd wrot til thju Fryasbern wither kvma machte vndera
selva êwa ånd vnder ênen bôn. Vmbe tha månniska
vppa hira syd to krêjande, was hju mith hira frjudelf
fon of hira tåt thrvch alle Saxanamarka fåren and forth
nêi Gêrtmånnja. Gêrtmannja alsa hêdon tha Gêrtmanna hjara ståt hêten, thêr hja thrvch Gosa hira bijeldinga krêjen hêde. Dåna gvngen hja nei tha Dênemarka.
Fon tha Dênemarka gvngon hja skip nei Texland. Fon
Texland gvngon hja nêi Westflyland en sa allingen tha sê
nêi Walhallagåra hin. Fon Walhallagåra brûdon hja
allingen thêra sûder Hrênum al ont hja mith gråta frêse
boppa thêre Rêne bi tha Marsåta kêmon* hwêrfon vsa
Apollånja skrêven heth. Tho hja thêr en stût wêst hêde,
gvngon hja wither nêi tha delta.† As hja nw en tid lông
nêi tha delta offåren wêron al ont hja inna strêk fon thêre
alda burch Aken‡ kêmon, sind thêr vnwarlinga fjuwer
skalka morth and naked uteklåt. Hja wêron en lith åfter
an kvmen. Min brother thêr vral by was hêde hja often
vrbêden, thach hja nêde navt ne hêred. Tha bônar
thêr thåt dên hêde wêron Twisklåndar thêr juddêga
drist wêi ovira Hrêna kvma to morda and to råwande.
Tha Twislåndar thåt sind bannane ånd wêi britne Fryas-

---

* Zie bl. 150.　　　　　　　　　‡ Aken, Aken.
† Delte nog in N. Holland in gebruik, laagte.

was Ifkja. Adel fell in love with her, and she with him,
but his father wished him to wait a little. Adel did
as he wished; but as soon as he was dead, sent messengers to Berthold, her father, to ask her in marriage.
Berthold was a prince of high-principled feelings. He
had sent his daughter to Texland in the hope that she
might be chosen Burgtmaagd in her country, but when
he knew of their mutual affection he bestowed his blessing upon them. Ifkja was a clever Frisian. As far as I
have been able to learn, she always toiled and worked to
bring the Frya's people back under the same laws and
customs. To bring the people to her side, she travelled
with her husband through all Saxenmarken, and also to
Geertmannia—as the Geertmen had named the country
which they had obtained by means of Gosa. Thence they
went to Denmark, and from Denmark by sea to Texland.
From Texland they went to Westflyland, and so along the
coast to Walhallagara; thence they followed the Zuiderryn
(the Waal), till, with great apprehension, they arrived
beyond the Rhine at the Marsaten of whom our Apollonia
has written. When they had stayed there a little time,
they returned to the lowlands. When they had been
some time descending towards the lowlands, and had
reached about the old citadel of Aken, four of their servants were suddenly murdered and stripped. They had
loitered a little behind. My brother, who was always on
the alert, had forbidden them to do so, but they did not
listen to him. The murderers that had committed this
crime were Twisklanders, who had at that time audaciously
crossed the Rhine to murder and to steal. The Twisklanders are banished and fugitive children of Frya,

---

* See page 150.
† *Delta*, still in use in North Holland for swampy land.

bern, men hjara wiva håvath hja fon tha Tartarum râwet.
Tha Tartara is en brûn Findas folk, althus hêten thrvchdam hja alle folka to strida uttarta. Hja send al hrutar
ånd râwar. Thêr fon send tha Twisklåndar alsa blod
thorstich wrden. Tha Twisklåndar tham thju årgnise dên
hêde, hêton hjara selva Frya jeftha Franka. Ther wêron
sêide min brother râda bruna ånd wita mong. Thêre thêr
råd jeftha brun wêron biton hjara hêre mith sjalkwêter *
wit. Nêidam hjara ônthlita thêr brun by wêr, alsa wrdon
hja thesto lêdliker thêr thrvch. Êvin as Apollånja bisko-
jadon hja åfternêi Lydasburch ånd et Aldergå. Dåna
tågon hju in over Ståverens wrde by hjara ljuda rond.
Alsa minlik hêdon hja hjara selva anståled that tha månniska ra allerwêikes halda wilde. Thrê mônatha forther
sand Adel bodon nêi alle åthum thêr hi biwnnen hêde ånd
lêt tham bidda, hja skoldon inna Minna mônath lichta
ljuda to him senda.†

---

* Diod Sic. V. 28.
† Hier heeft de afschrijver Hiddo oera Linda een blad te veel omgeslagen,
en daardoor twee bladzijden overgeslagen.

but their wives they have stolen from the Tartars. The Tartars are a brown tribe of Finda's people, who are thus named because they make war on everybody. They are all horsemen and robbers. This is what makes the Twisklanders so bloodthirsty. The Twisklanders who had done the wicked deed called themselves Frijen or Franken. There were among them, my brother said, red, brown, and white men. The red and brown made their hair white with lime-water—but as their faces remained brown, they were only the more ugly. In the same way as Apollonia, they visited Lydasburgt and the Alderga. Afterwards they made a tour of all the neighbourhood of Stavera. They behaved with so much amiability, that everywhere the people wished to keep them. Three months later, Adel sent messengers to all the friends that he had made, requesting them to send to him their " wise men " in the month of May.†

---

* Diodorus Siculus, V. 28.

  † Here the copyist, Hiddo oera Linda, has turned over a leaf too much, and has thus omitted two pages.

sin wif sêid er thêr fâm wêst hêde to Texlând, hêde dâna
en ovirskrift krêjen. To Texland warthat jeta fêlo skrifta
fvnden, thêr navt in-t bok thêra Adelinga vrskrêven send.
Fon thissa skriftum hêde Gosa ên bi hira utroste wille
lêid, thêr thrvch tha aldeste fâm Albêthe avbêr mâkt
wertha most, alsa ringen Friso fallen was.

HYR IS THAT SKRIFT MITH GOSAS RÊD.

Tha Wr.alda bern jêf an tha modera fon thât mânnis-
kelik slachte, thâ lêid er êne tâle in aller tonga ând vp
aller lippa. Thjus mêide hêde Wr.alda an tha mânniska
jêven, til thju hja mânlik ôthera thêrmith machte kânbêr
mâkja, hwat mân formyde mot ând hwat mân bijagja mot
vmbe sêlighêd to findane ând sêlighêd to haldane in al
êvghêd. Wr.alda is wis ând god ând al fârsjande. Nêidam er nw wist, thât luk ând sêlighêd fon irtha flya mot,
jef boshêd düged bidroga mêi, alsa heth er an thju tâl êne
rjuchtfêrdige âjendomlikhêd fâst bonden. Thjus âjendomlikhêd is thêr an lêgen, thât mân thêr mith nên lêjen sêge,
ner bidroglika worda sprêka ne mêi svnder stem lêth
noch svnder skâmrâd, thrvch hvam mân tha bosa fon
hirte bistonda vrkânna mêi. Nêidam vsa tâle thus
to luk ând to sêlighêd wêjath, ând thus mith wâkt
âjen tha bosa nygonga, thêrvmbe is hju mith alle rjucht
godis tâle hêten, ând alle tha jêna hwam hja an êre
halda hâvath thêr gôme fon. Tha hwat is bêrth. Alsa
ring thêr mong vsa halfsusterum ând halfbrotharum
bidrogar vpkêmon, tham hjara selva fori godis skalkum
utjavon, also ring is thât owers wrden. Tha bidroglika prestera ând tha wraugwrêja forsta thêr immer sêmin hêladon,
wildon nêi wilkêr lêva ând buta god-is êwa dvan. In hjara

his wife, he said, who had been maagd of Texland, had received a copy of it. In Texland many writings are still found which are not copied in the book of the Adelingen. One of these writings had been placed by Gosa with her last will, which was to be opened by the oldest maiden, Albetha, as soon as Friso was dead.

HERE IS THE WRITING WITH GOSA'S ADVICE.

When Wr-alda gave children to the mothers of mankind, he gave one language to every tongue and to all lips. This gift Wr-alda had bestowed upon men in order that by its means they might make known to each other what must be avoided and what must be followed to find salvation, and to hold salvation to all eternity. Wr-alda is wise and good, and all-foreseeing. As he knew that happiness and holiness would flee from the earth when wickedness could overcome virtue, he has attached to the language an equitable property. This property consists in this, that men can neither lie nor use deceitful words without stammering or blushing, by which means the innately bad are easily known.

As thus our language opens the way to happiness and blessedness, and thus helps to guard against evil inclinations, it is rightly named the language of the gods, and all those by whom it is held in honour derive honour from it. But what has happened? As soon as among our half brothers and sisters deceivers arose, who gave themselves out as servants of the good, it soon became otherwise. The deceitful priests and the malignant princes, who always clung together, wished to live according to their own inclinations, without regard to the laws of right. In their wickedness they went

tsjodishêd send hja to gvngen ånd håvon ôthera tåla forsvnnen, til thju hja hêmlik machte sprêka in åjenwårtha
fon alrek ôtherum, vr alle bosa thinga ånd vr alle vnwêrth-
lika thinga svnder thåt stemlêth hjam vrrêda mocht nach
skåmråd hjara gelåt vrderva. Men hwat is thêrut bern.
Êvin blyd as-t sêd thêra goda krûdum fon vnder ne grvnd
ut vntkêmth, thåt avbêr sêjed is thrvch goda ljuda by helle
dêi, êven blyd brength tyd tha skådlika krûda an-t ljucht,
thêr sêjed send thrvch bosa ljuda in-t forborgne ånd by
thjustrenesse.

Tha lodderiga mangertne ånd tha vnmånlika knåpa thêr
mitha vvla presterum ånd forstnm horadon vntlvkadon tha
nya tåla an hjara bola, thêrwisa send hja forth kvmen
êmong tha folkrum, til thju hja god-is tåle glåd vrjetten
håve. Wilst nw wêta hwat thêr of wrden is? Nv stemlêth ner gelåt hjara bosa tochta navt longer mar vrrêdon,
nv is düged fon ut hjara midden wêken, wisdom is folgth
ånd frydom is mith gvngen, êndracht is sok råkt ånd twispalt heth sin stêd innommen, ljafde is fljucht ånd hordom
sith mith nyd an têfel, ånd thêr êr rjuchtfêrdichhêd welde,
welth uv thåt swêrd. Alle send slåvona wrden, tha ljuda
fon hjara hêra, fon nyd, bosa lusta ånd bigyrlikhêd. Hêde
hja nvmår êne tåle forsvnnen, müglik was-t thån jet en
lith god gvngen. Men hja håvon alsa fêlo tåla utfonden
as thêr ståta send. Thêrthrvch mêi thåt êne folk thåt ôre
folk êvin min forstån as thju kv thene hvnd ånd thi wolf
thåt skêp. Thit mügath tha stjurar bitjuga. Thach dånå
is-t nv wêi kvmen, thåt alle slåvona folkar månlik ôthara
lik ôra månniska biskoja ånd thåt hja to straffe hjarar
vndigerhêd ånd fon hjara vrmêtenhêd, månlik ôthera alsa
long biorloge ånd bikampa moton til thju alle vrdilgad
send.

so far as to invent other languages, so that they might speak secretly in anybody's presence of their wicked and unworthy affairs without betraying themselves by stammering, and without showing a blush upon their countenances. But what has that produced? Just as the seed of good herbs which has been sown by good men in the open day springs up from the ground, so time brings to light the evil seed which has been sown by wicked men in secret and in darkness.

The wanton girls and effeminate youths who consorted with the immoral priests and princes, taught the new language to their companions, and thus spread it among the people till God's language was clean forgotten. Would you know what came of all this? how that stammering and blushing no longer betrayed their evil doings;—virtue passed away, wisdom and liberty followed; unity was lost, and quarrelling took its place; love flew away, and unchastity and envy met round their tables; and where previously justice reigned, now it is the sword. All are slaves—the subjects of their masters, envy, bad passions and covetousness. If they had only invented one language things might possibly have still gone on well; but they invented as many languages as there are states, so that one people can no more understand another people than a cow a dog, or a wolf a sheep. The mariners can bear witness to this. From all this it results that all the slave people look upon each other as strangers; and that as a punishment of their inconsiderateness and presumption, they must quarrel and fight till they are all destroyed.

R

HYR IS NV MIN RÊD.

Bist thv alsa gyrich that thu irtha allêna erva wilste,
alsa achst thv nimmer mâre nên ôre tâle ovir thina wêra
ni kvma to lêtane as god-is tâle, ånd thån achst thv to
njodane, til thju thin åjn tâle fry fon uthêmeda klinka
bilyweth. Wilst thv thåt er svme fon Lydas bern ånd
fon Findas bern resta, så dvath stv êvin alsa. Thju tâle
thêra Ast Skênlandar is thrvch tha wla Mâgjara vrbrûd;
thju tâle thêra Kaltana folgar is thrvch tha smûgrige
Gole vrderveu. Nv send wi alsa mild wêst vmbe tha
witherkvmande Hellêna folgar wither in vs midden to nêmande, men ik skrom ånd ben sêrelik ange, thåt hja vs
mild-sa vrjelda skilun mith vrbrûding vsra rêne tâle.

Fül håvon wi witherfåren, men fon alle burgum, thêr
thrvch arge tyd vrhomlath send ånd vrdiligad, heth Irtha
Fryasburch vnforleth bihalden; åk mêi ik thêr by melda
thåt Fryas jeftha god-is tâle hir evin vnforleth bihalden is.

Hyr to Texland most mån thus skola stifta, fon alle
stâtum thêr et mitha alda sêdum halda, most-et jongk
folk hyr hinne senden wrde, åfterdam mochton thêra
utlêred wêre tha ôra helpa thêr to honk vrbêide. Willath
tha ôra folkar ysre wêron fon thi sella ênd thêrvr mith
thi sprêka ånd thinga, så moton hja to god-istâle wither
kêra. Lêrath hja god-istâle så skilun tha worda fry-så
ånd rjucht-hå to hjara inkvma, in hjara brêin skilet thån
bijina to glimmande ånd to glorande til thju ella to-ne
logha warth. Thissa logha skil alle balda forsta vrtêra
ånd alle skinfråna ånd smûgriga prestera.

Tha hêinde ånd fêrhêmande sendabodon hêdon nocht fon
vr thåt skrift, thach thêr ne kêmon nêne skola. Thå stifte
Adel selva skola, åfter him dêdon tha ôra forsta lik hy. Jêr-
likis gvngon Adel ånd Ifkja tha skola skoja. Fandon hja
thån êmong tha inhêmar ånd uthêmar seliga thêr ekkorum

HERE IS MY COUNSEL.

If you wish that you alone should inherit the earth, you must never allow any language but God's language to pass your lips, and take care that your own language remains free from outlandish sounds. If you wish that some of Lyda's children and some of Finda's children remain, you must do the same. The language of the East Schoonlanders has been perverted by the vile Magyars, and the language of the followers of Kaltana has been spoiled by the dirty Gauls. Now, we have been weak enough to admit among us the returned followers of Hellenia, but I anxiously fear that they will reward our weakness by debasing our pure language.

Many things have happened to us, but among all the citadels that have been disturbed and destroyed in the bad time, Irtha has preserved Fryasburgt uninjured; and I may remark that Frya's or God's language has always remained here untainted.

Here in Texland, therefore, schools should be established; and from all the states that have kept to the old customs the young people should be sent here, and afterwards those whose education is complete can help those who remain at home. If foreigners come to buy ironwares from you, and want to talk and bargain, they must come back to God's language. If they learn God's language, then the words, " to be free " and "to have justice," will come to them, and glimmer and glitter in their brains to a perfect light, and that flame will destroy all bad princes and hypocritical dirty priests.

The native and foreign messengers were pleased with that writing, but no schools came from it. Then Adel established schools himself. Every year Adel and Ifkja went to inspect the schools. If they found a friendly feeling

frjundskip bâradon, så lêton bêde grâte blidskip blika.
Hêdon svme seliga ekkorum frjundskip sworen, alsa lêton
hja alra mannalik to manlik ôrum kvma, mith grâte stât
lêton hja thân hjara nôma in en bok skriva, thrvch hjam
thât bok thêra frjundskip hêten, âfter dam warth fêrst
halden. Al thissa plêga wrde dên vmbe tha asvndergana
twyga fon Fryas stam wither et sêmene to snôrane. Men
tha famna thêr Adel ând Ifkja nydich wêron, sêidon that
hja-t niwerth ôre vr dêdon as vmb en gode hrop, ând vmb
bi grâdum to weldana in ovir ênis ôther man his stât.
By min tât sinra skriftum hâv ik ênen brêf funden, skrê-
vin thrvch Ljudgêrth thene Gêrtmân,* bihalva svmlika
sêka thêr min tât allêna jelde, jêf ik hyr thât ôthera to
thât besta.

Pang-ab, thât is fyf wâtera ând hwêr neffen wi wech
kvme, is-ne runstrâmé fon afsvnderlika skênhêd, ând
fif wâtera hêten vmb thet fjuwer ôra runstrâma thrvch
sine mvnd in sê floja. Êl fere âstwarth is noch ne
grâte runstrâme thêr hêlige jeftha frâna Gong-ga hêten.
Twisk thysum runstrâmne is-t lônd thêra Hindos. Bêda
runstrama runath fon tha hâga bergum nêi tha delta
del. Tha berga hwanâ se del strâme sind alsa hâch thet
se to tha himel lâja. Thêrvmbe wârth-et berchta Himel-
lâja berchta hêten. Vnder tha Hindos ând ôthera ut-a
lôndum sind welka ljuda mank thêr an stilnise by mal-
korum kvma. Se gelâvath thet se vnforbastere bern
Findas sind. Se gelâvath thet Finda fon ut-et Him-
mellâja berchta bern is, hvanâ se mith hjara bern nêi
tha delta jeftha lêgte togen is. Welke vnder tham gelâvath thet se mith hjra bern vppet skum thêr hêlige
Gongga del gonggen is. Thêrvmbe skolde thi runstrâme
hêlige Gongga hêta. Mâr tha prestera thêr ut en ôr lônd
wech kvma lêton thi ljuda vpspêra ând vrbarna, thêrvmbe

---

* Zie bl. 164.

existing between the natives and foreigners, they were extremely pleased. If there were any who had sworn friendship together, they assembled the people, and with great ceremony let them inscribe their names in a book which was called the Book of Friendship, and afterwards a festival was held. All these customs were kept up in order to bring together the separate branches of Frya's race; but the maidens who were opposed to Adel and Ifkja said that they did it for no other reason than to make a name for themselves, and to bring all the other states under their subjection.

Among my father's papers I found a letter from Liudgert the Geertman. Omitting some passages which only concern my father, I proceed to relate the rest.

Punjab, that is five rivers, and by which we travel, is a river of extraordinary beauty, and is called Five Rivers, because four other streams flow into the sea by its mouth. Far away to the eastward is another large river, the Holy or Sacred Ganges. Between these two rivers is the land of the Hindoos. Both rivers run from the high mountains to the plains. The mountains in which their sources lie are so high that they reach the heavens (laia), and therefore these mountains are called Himmellaia. Among the Hindoos and others out of these countries there are people who meet together secretly. They believe that they are pure children of Finda, and that Finda was born in the Himmellaia mountains, whence she went with her children to the lowlands. Some of them believe that she, with her children, floated down upon the foam of the Ganges, and that that is the reason why the river is called the Sacred Ganges. But the priests, who came from another country, traced out these people and had them burnt, so that they

---

* See page 164.

ne thurvath se far hjara sêk nit ôpentlik ut ni kvma. In
thet lônd sind ôlle prestera tjok ånd rik. In hjara chårka
werthat ôllerlêja drochtenlika byldon fvnden, thêr vnder
sind fêlo golden mank. Biwesta Pangab thêr sind tha
Yra jeftha wranga, tha Gedrostne jeftha britne, ånd tha
Orjetten jeftha vrjetne. Ol thisa nôma sind-ar thrvch tha
·nydige prestera jêven, thrvchdam hja fon ar fljuchte, vmb
sêda ånd gelâv, bi hjara kvmste hêdon vsa êthla hjara
selva åk an tha åstlika ower fon Pangab del set, men vmb
thêra prestera wille sind se åk nêi thêr wester ower fåren.
Thêrthrvch håvon wi tha Yra ånd tha ôthera kenna lêrth.
Tha Yra ne sind nêne yra mår gôda minska thêr nêna
byldon to lêta nach ônbidda, åk willath se nêna chårka
nach prestar doga, ånd êvin als wi-t fråna ljucht fon Fåsta
vpholda, êvin så holdon se ôllerwechs fjur in hjara hûsa
vp. Kvmth môn efter êl westlik, ôlså kvmth môn by tha
Gedrostne. Fon tha Gedrostne. Thisa sind mith ôra
folkrum bastered ånd sprêkath ôlle afsvnderlika tåla.
Thisa minska sind wêrentlik yra bonar, thêr ammer mith
hjara horsa vp overa fjelda dwåla, thêr ammer jågja ånd
råwa ånd thêr hjara selva als salt-åtha forhêra an tha
omhêmmande forsta, ther wille hwam se alles nither håwa
hwat se birêka müge.

Thet lônd twisk Pangab ånd ther Gongga is like
flet as Fryaslônd an tha sê, afwixlath mith fjeldum ånd
waldum, fruchtbår an alle dêlum, mår thet mach nit
vrletta that thêr bi hwila thûsanda by thûsanda thrvch
honger biswike. Thisa hongernêde mach thêrvmbe nit
an Wr.alda nach an Irtha wyten nit wertha, mår allêna
an tha forsta and prestera. Tha Hindos sind ivin blode
ånd forfêred from hjara forstum, als tha hindne from
tha wolva sind. Thêrvmbe håvon tha Yra ånd ôra ra
Hindos hêten, thêt hindne bitjoth. Mår fon hjara blodhêd
wårth afgrislika misbruk måkth. Kvmat thêr fêrhêmande
kåpljud vmb kêren to kåpjande, alsa warth alles to jeldum

do not dare to declare openly their creed. In this country all the priests are fat and rich. In their churches there are all kinds of monstrous images, many of them of gold. To the west of the Punjab are the Yren (Iraniers), or morose (Drangianen), the Gedrosten (Gedrosiers), or runaways, and the Urgetten, or forgotten. These names are given by the priests out of spite, because they fled from their customs and religion. On their arrival our forefathers likewise established themselves to the east of the Punjab, but on account of the priests they likewise went to the west. In that way we learned to know the Yren and other people. The Yren are not savages, but good people, who neither pray to nor tolerate images; neither will they suffer priests or churches; but as we adhere to the light of Fasta, so they everywhere maintain fire in their houses. Coming still further westward, we arrive at the Gedrosten. Regarding the Gedrosten : They have been mixed with other people, and speak a variety of languages. These people are really savage murderers, who always wander about the country on horseback hunting and robbing, and hire themselves as soldiers to the surrounding princes, at whose command they destroy whatever they can reach.

The country between the Punjab and the Ganges is as flat as Friesland near the sea, and consists of forests and fields, fertile in every part, but this does not prevent the people from dying by thousands of hunger. The famines, however, must not be attributed to Wr-alda or Irtha, but to the princes and priests. The Hindoos are timid and submissive before their princes, like hinds before wolves. Therefore the Yren and others have called them Hindoos, which means hinds. But their timidity is frightfully abused. If strangers come to purchase corn, everything is turned måkth. Thrvch tha prestera ni warth et nit wêrth, hwand thisa noch snoder ånd jyriger als alle forsta to samene, wytath êl god, thet al-et jeld endlik in hjara bûdar kvmth. Buta ånd bihalva thet tha ljuda thêr fül fon hjara forsta lyda, moton hja åk noch fül fon thet fenynige ånd wilde kwik lyda. Thêr send store elefante thêr by êle keddum hlåpa, thêr bihwyla êle fjelda kêren vrtrappe ånd êle thorpa. Thêr sind bonte ånd swarte katta, tigrum hêten, thêr så gråt als gråte kalvar sind, thêr minsk ånd djar vrslynue. Bûta fêlo ôra wriggum sind thêr snåka fon af tha gråte êner wyrme ål to tha gråte êner båm. Tha gråteste kennath en êle kv vrslynna, går tha lythste sind noch frêsliker als tham. Se holdon hjara selva twisk blom ånd fruchta skul vmb tha minska to bigåna tham thêr of plokja wille. Is môn thêr fon byten, så mot môn stårva, hwand åjen hjara fenyn heth Irtha nêna krûda jêven, ôlsånåka tha minska hjara selva håvon skildich måkt an afgodie. Forth sind thêr ôllerlêja slacht fon håchdiska nyndiska ånd adiska, ôl thisa diska sind yvin als tha snåka fon of ne wyrme til-ne båmstame gråt, nêi that hja gråt jof frêslik sind, sind hjara nôma, thêr ik alle nit noma ni ken, tha aldergråtesta ådiska sind algåtter hêten, thrvchdam se yvin grûsich bitte an thet rotte kwik, that mith-a stråma fon boppa nêi tha delta dryweth as an thet lêvande kwik, that se bigåna müge. An tha westsyde fon Pangab, wånå wi wech kvme ånd hwer ik bern ben, thêr blojath ånd waxath tha selva frûchta ånd nochta as an tha åstsyde. To fåra wrdon er åk tha selva wrigga fonden, går vsa êthla havon alle krylwalda vrbårnath ånd alsånåka åfter et wilde kwik jåged, that ther fê går resta. Kvmtk man êl westlik fon Pangab, then finth man neffen fette etta åk into money, and this is not prevented by the priests, because they, being more crafty and rapacious than all the princes put together, know very well that all the money will come into their pockets. Besides what the people suffer from their princes, they suffer a great deal from poisonous and wild beasts. There are great elephants that sometimes go about in whole flocks and trample down cornfields and whole villages. There are great black and white cats which are called tigers. They are as large as calves, and they devour both men and beasts. Besides other creeping animals there are snakes from the size of a worm to the size of a tree. The largest can swallow a cow, but the smallest are the most deadly. They conceal themselves among the fruits and flowers, and surprise the people who come to gather them. Any one who is bitten by them is sure to die, as Irtha has given no antidote to their poison, because the people have so given themselves up to idolatry. There are, besides, all sorts of lizards, tortoises, and crocodiles. All these reptiles, like the snakes, vary from the size of a worm to the trunk of a tree. According to their size and fierceness, they have names which I cannot recollect, but the largest are called alligators, because they eat as greedily the putrid cattle that float down the stream as they do living animals that they seize. On the west of the Punjab where we come from, and where I was born, the same fruits and crops grow as on the east side. Formerly there existed also the same crawling animals, but our forefathers burnt all the underwood, and so diligently hunted all the wild animals, that there are scarcely any left. To the extreme west of the Punjab there is found rich clay land

dorra gêstlanda thêr vnendlik skina, bihwila ofwixlath
mith ljaflika strêka, hwêran thet åg forbonden bilywet.
Vnder tha fruchta fon min land sind fêlo slachta mank,
thêr ik hyr nit fvnden håv. Vnder allerlêja kêren is er
åk golden mank, åk goldgêle aple, hwêrfon welke så swêt
as hûning sind, ånd welka sa wrang as êk. By vs werthat
nochta fonden lik bern-håveda så gråt, thêr sit tays ånd
melok in, werthat se ald så måkt man ther ôlja fon, fon
tha bastum måkt mån tåw ånd fon tha kernum måkt mån
chelka ånd ôr geråd. Hyr inna walda håv ik krup ånd
ståkbêja sjan. By vs sind bêibåma als jow lindabåma,
hwêrfon tha bêja fül swêter ånd thêrwåra gråter as ståkbêja sind. Hwersa tha dêga vppa sin olderlôngste sind
ånd thju svnne fon top skinth, then skinth se linrjucht
vppa jow hole del. Is mån then mith sin skip êl fêr
sûdlik faren, ånd mån thes meddêis mith sin gelåt nêi-t
åsten kêred, så skinth svnne åjen thine winstere syde lik
se ôwers åjen thine fêre syde dvath. Hyrmitha wil ik
enda, mår after min skrywe skil-et thi licht nog falla,
vmb tha lêgenaftiga teltjas to müge skiftane fon tha wara
tellinga.—Jow Ljudgêrt.

THET SKRIFT FON BÊDEN.

Mine nôm is Bêden, Hachgåna his svn. Konerêd min
êm is nimmer bostigjath ånd alsa bernlås sturven. My
heth mån in sin stêd koren. Adel thene thredde kåning
fon thjuse nôme heth thju kêse godkêrth, mites ik him as
mina måstre bikenna wilde. Buta thåt fvlle erv minre êm
heth-er mi en êle plek grvnd jêven thåt an mina erva
pålade, vnder fårwêrde that ik thêrvp skolde månniska
stålla ther sina ljuda nimmerthe skolde.*

---

* Hier ontbreken in het H. S. twintig bladzijden (misschien meer), waarin
Beeden geschreven heeft ovir dien koning Adel III. (Bij onze kronijk schrijvers Ubbo genoemd.)

as well as barren heaths, which seem endless, occasionally varied lovely spots on which the eye rests enchanted. Among the fruits there are many that I have not found here. Among the various kinds of corn some is as yellow as gold. There are also golden apples, of which some are as sweet as honey and others as sour as vinegar. In our country there are nuts as large as a child's head. They contain cheese and milk. When they are old oil is made from them. Of the husks ropes are made, and of the shells cups and other household utensils are made. I have found in the woods here bramble and holly berries. In my country we have trees bearing berries, as large as your lime-trees, the berries of which are much sweeter and three times as large as your gooseberries. When the days are at the longest, and the sun is in the zenith, a man's body has no shadow. If you sail very far to the south and look to the east at midday, the sun shines on your left side as it does in other countries on the right side. With this I will finish. It will be easy for you, by means of what I have written, to distinguish between false accounts and true descriptions.—Your Luidgert.

THE WRITING OF BEEDEN.

My name is Beeden, son of Hachgana. My uncle, not having married, left no children. I was elected in his place. Adel, the third king of that name, approved of the choice, provided I should acknowledge him as master. In addition to the entire inheritance of my uncle, he gave me some land which joined my inheritance, on condition that I would settle people there who should never his people*

---

* Here there are wanting in the manuscript twenty pages (perhaps more), in which Beeden has written about the King, Adel the Third, called Ubbo by the writers of our chronicles.

thêrvmbe wil ik thet hir-ne sted forjune.

BRÊF FON RIKA THJU ALDFAM, VPSEID TO STAVEREN BY-T JOLFÊRSTE.

Jy alle hwam his êthla mith Friso hir kêmon, min êrbydnesse to jo. Alsa jy mêne, send jy vnskeldich an afgodie. Thêr nil ik jvd navt vr sprêka, men jvd wil ik jo vppen brek wysa, thât fê bêtre sy. Jy wêtath jeftha jy nêtath navt, ho Wr.alda thusand glornôma heth, thach thât wêtath jy alle thât hy warth Alfêder hêten, ut êrsêke thât alles in ut him warth ånd waxth to fêding sinra skepsela. T-is wêr, thât Irtha warth bihwyla âk Alfêdstre hêten, thrvchdam hju alle früchd ånd nochta bêrth, hwermitha månnisk ånd djar hjara selva fêde. Thach ne skolde hju nêne früchd ner nocht navt ne bêra, bydam Wr.alda hja nêne krefta ne jêf. Ak wiva ther hjara bern måma lêta an hjara brosta, werthat fêdstra hêten. Thâ ne jêf Wr.alda thêr nên melok in, sa ne skoldon tha bern thêr nêne bâte by finda. Sâ thât by slot fon reknong Wr.alda allêna fêder bilywet. Thât Irtha bihwyla warth Alfêdstre heten, ånd êne måm fêdstre, kån jeta thrvch-ne wende, men thât-ne mån him lêt fêder hête vmbe thât er tât sy, thât strid with-åjen alle rêdnum. Thâ ik wêt wânât thjus dwêshêd wêi kvmth. Hark hyr, se kvmth fon vsa lêtha, ånd såhwersa thi folgath werthe, så skilun jy thêrthrvch slâvona wertha to smert fon Frya ånd jowe hâgmod to.ne straf. Ik skil jo melda ho-t by tha slâvona folkar to gvngen is, thêr åfter mêi jy lêra. Tha poppa kåningar tham nêi wilkêr lêva, stêkath Wr.alda nêi thêre krône, utn yd that Wr.alda Alfêder hêt, sa wildon hja fêdrum thêra folkar hêta. Nw wêt allera mannalik thât-ne kêning navt ovir-ne waxdom therefore I will allow it a place here.

LETTER OF RIKA THE OUDMAAGD, READ AT STAVEREN AT THE JUUL FEAST.

My greeting to all of you whose forefathers came here with Friso. According to what you say, you are not guilty of idolatry. I will not speak about that now, but will at once mention a failing which is very little better. You know, or you do not know, how many titles Wr-alda has; but you all know that he is named universal provider, because that everything comes and proceeds from him for the sustenance of his creatures. It is true that Irtha is named sometimes the feeder of all, because she brings forth all the fruits and grains on which men and beasts are fed; but she would not bear any fruit or grain unless Wr-alda gave her the power. Women who nourish their children at their breasts are called nurses, but if Wr-alda did not give them milk the children would find no advantage; so that, in short, Wr-alda really is the nourisher. That Irtha should be called the universal nourisher, and that a mother should be called a feeder, one can understand, figuratively speaking; but that a father should be called a feeder, because he is a father, goes against all reason. Now I know whence all this folly comes. Listen to me. It comes from our enemies; and if this is followed up you will become slaves, to the sorrow of Frya and to the punishment of your pride. I will tell you what happened to the slave people; from that you may take warning. The foreign kings, who follow their own will, place Wr-alda below the crown. From envy that Wr-alda is called the universal father, they wish also to be called fathers of the people. Now, everybody knows that kings do not regulate

ne welth, ånd thåt im sin fêding thrvch thåt folk brocht
warth, men thach wildon hja fvlherdja by hjara formêten-
hêd. Til thju hja to-ra dol kvma machte, alsa håvon hja
thet forma navt fvldên wêst mith tha frya jefta, men håvon
hja thåt folk êne tins vplêid. Fori thene skåt, tham
thêrof kêm, hêradon hja vrlandiska salt-åtha, tham hja
in-om hjara hova lêidon. Forth namon hja alsa fêlo wiva,
as-ra luste, ånd tha lithiga forsta ånd hêra dêdon al-ên.
As twist ånd tvyspalt åfternêi inna hûshaldne glupte ånd
thêr-vr klåchta kêmon, thå håvon hja sêid, ja-hweder mån
is thêne fêder fon sin hûshalden, thêrvmbe skil-er thêr åk
bås ånd rjuchter ovir wêsa. Thå kêm wilkêr ånd êvin as
tham mitha månnum in ovir tha hûshaldne welde, gvng
er mit tha kåningar in ovir hjara ståt ånd folkar dvan.
Thå tha kåningar et alsa wyd brocht hêdon, thåt hja fêde-
rum thêra folkar hête, thå gvngon hja to ånd lêton byldon
åfter hjara dåntne måkja, thissa byldon lêton hja inna tha
cherka stalla nêst tha byldon thêra drochtne ånd thi jena
tham thêr navt far bûgja nilde, warth ombrocht jeftha an
kêdne dên. Jow êthla ånd tha Twisklandar håvon mitha
poppa forsta ommegvngen, dåna håvon hja thjuse dwêshêd
lêred. Tha navt allêna thåt svme jower mån hjara selva
skeldich måkja an glornôma råw, åk mot ik my vr fêlo
jower wiva biklågja. Werthat by jo mån fvnden, tham
mith Wr.alda an ên lin wille, thêr werthat by jo wiva
fynden, thêr et mêi Frya wille. Vmbe thåt hja bern
bêred håve, lêtath hja hjara selva modar hêta. Tha hja
vrjettath, that Frya bern bêrde svnder jengong ênis mån.
Jå navt allêna thåt hja Frya ånd tha êremodar fon hjara
glor-rika nôma biråwa wille, hwêran hja navt nåka
ne müge, hja dvath alên mitha glornôma fon hjara nêsta.
Thêr send wiva thêr hjarar selva lêtath frovva hêta,

the productiveness of the earth; and that they have their
sustenance by means of the people, but still they will persist
in their arrogance. In order to attain their object they were
not satisfied from the beginning with free gifts, but imposed
a tax upon the people. With the tax thus raised they hired
foreign soldiers, whom they retained about their courts.
Afterwards they took as many wives as they pleased, and
the smaller princes and gentry did the same. When, in
consequence, quarrels and disputes arose in the households,
and complaints were made about it, they said every man is
the father (feeder) of his household, therefore he shall be
master and judge over it. Thus arose arbitrariness, and as
the men ruled over their households the kings would do
over their people. When the kings had accomplished that,
they should be called fathers of the people, they had statues
of themselves made, and erected in the churches beside
the statues of the idols, and those who would not bow
down to them were either killed or put in chains. Your
forefathers and the Twisklanders had intercourse with the
kings, and learned these follies from them. But it is not
only that some of your men have been guilty of stealing
titles, I have also much to complain of against your wives.
If there are men among you who wish to put themselves
on a level with Wr-alda, there are also women who wish
to consider themselves equals of Frya. Because they have
borne children, they call themselves mothers; but they
forget that Frya bore children without having intercourse
with a man. Yes, they not only have desired to rob Frya
and the Eeremoeders of their honourable title (with whom
they cannot put themselves upon an equality), but they do
the same with the honourable titles of their fellow-creatures.
There are women who allow themselves to be called ladies,

afsken hja wête thåt thjuse nôme allêna to forsta wiva
hêreth. Ak lêtath hja hjara toghater fâmna hêta, vntankes
hja wête, thåt nêne mangêrt alsa hêta ne mêi, wâra hju
to êne burch hêrth. Jy alle wânath thåt jy thruch thåt
nôm râwa bêtre werthe, thach jy vrjettath thåt nyd thêr an
klywet ånd thåt elk kwâd sine tuchtrode sêjath. Kêrath
jy navt ne wither, så skil tid thêr waxdom an jêva, alsa
stêrik thåt mån et ende thêr of navt bisjâ ne mêi. Jow
åfterkvmanda skilun thêr mith fêterath wertha, hja ne
skilun navt ne bigripa hwânat thi slâga wêi kvme. Men
afskên jy tha fâmna nêne burch bvwe ånd an lot vrlête,
thach skilun thêr bilywa, hja skilun fon ut wald ånd holum
kvma, hja skilun jow åfterkvmande biwysa thåt jy thêr
willens skildech an send. Thån skil mån jo vrdema, jow
skina skilun vrfêth fon ut-a grêvum rysa, hja skilun
Wr.alda, hja skilun Frya ånd hjara fâmna anhropa, thâ
nimman skil-er åwet an bêtra ne müge, bifâre thåt Jol
in op en ore hlâphring trêth, men thåt skil êrist bêra as
thrê thûsand jêr vrhlâpen send åfter thisse êw.

ENDE FON RIKAS BRÊF.

* Hier eindigde het schrijven van Beeden. In het H. S. ontbreken twee
bladzijden volgens de paginatuur. Maar zonder twijfel ontbreekt er meer.
De afgebroken aanhef van het volgende wijst aan, dat de aanvang van het volgende geschrift verloren gegaan is en daarmede ook de aanduiding van den
naam des schrijvers, die een zoon of kleinzoon van Beeden kan geweest zijn.

although they know that that only belongs to the wives of princes. They also let their daughters be called maagden, although they know that no young girls are so called unless they belong to a citadel. You all fancy that you are the better for this name-stealing, but you forget that jealousy clings to it, and that every wrong sows the seed of its own rod. If you do not alter your course, in time it will grow so strong that you cannot see what will be the end. Your descendants will be flogged by it, and will not know whence the stripes come. But although you do not build citadels for the maidens and leave them to their fate, there will still remain some who will come out of woods and caves, and will prove to your descendants that you have by your disorderliness been the cause of it. Then you will be damned. Your ghosts will rise frightened out of their graves. They will call upon Wr-alda, Frya, and her maidens, but they shall receive no succour before the Juul shall enter upon a new circuit, and that will only be three thousand years after this century.

THE END OF RIKA'S LETTER.

---

* Here the writing of Beeden ends. In the manuscript two successive pages are missing according to the paging, but no doubt there are more wanting. The abrupt opening of what follows shows that the beginning of the following writing has been lost, and, in consequence, also the notification of the name of the writer, who may have been a son or a grandson of Beeden.

thêrvmbe wil ik thât forma vr swarte Adel skriva. Swarte
Adel wêre thene fjurde kening âfter Friso. Bi siu jüged
heth-er to Texland lêred, âfternêi heth-er to Stâveren
lêred, ånd forth heth-er thrvch ovir alle stâta fâren. Thâ
thât er fjuwer ånd tvintich jêr wêre, heth sin tât mâked
thât-er to Asega-âskar kêren is. Thâ-er ênmel âskar
wêre, âskte hi altid in-t fârdêl thêra ârma. Tha rika,
sêd-er, plêgath ênoch vnrjuchta thinga thrvch middel fon
hjara jeld, thêrvmbe âgon wi to njvdane thât tha ârma
nêi vs omme sjan. Thrvch thâ-s ånd ôra rêdne wêr-i
thene frjund thêra ârma ånd thêra rika skrik. Alsa ârg
is-t kvmen thât sin tât him nêi tha âgum sach. Thâ sin
tât fallen was, ånd hy vppa tham-his sêtel klywed, thâ
wild-er êvin god sin ambt bihalda, lik as tha keningar
fon-t âsta plêgath. Tha rika nildon thât navt ne dâja, men
nw hlip allet ôra folk to hâpe, ånd tha rika wêron blyde
that hja hêl-hûd-is fon thêre acht of kêmon. Fon to ne hêrade mån nimmar mâra ovir êlika rjucht petârja. Hi dumde
tha rika ånd hi strykte tha ârma, mith hwam his helpe
hi alle sêkum âskte, thêr-er bistek vp hêde. Kening
Askar lik-er immer hêten warth, wêre by sjugun irthfêt
lônge, så grât sin tôl wêr, wêron åk sina krefta. Hi
hêde-n hel forstân, så thât-er alles forstânde, hwêrwr that
sprêken warth, thach in sin dvan ne macht mån nêne
wisdom spêra. Bi-n skên ônhlite hêd-er êne glade tonge,
men jeta swarter as sin hêr is sine sêle fvnden. Thâ
that-er ên jêr kening wêre, nêdsêkte hi alle knâpa
fon sin stât, hja skoldon jerlikis vppet kåmp kvma ånd
thêr skin-orloch mâkja. In-t êrost hêde-r thêr spul mith,
men to tha lersta warth-et så menêrlik, that ald ånd jong
ut alle wrdum wêi kêmon to frêjande jef hja machte mith
dva. Thâ hi-t alsa fêre brocht hêde, lêt-er wêrskola
stifta. Tha rika kêmon to bârane ånd sêidon, that

therefore I will first write about black Adel.   Black Adel
was the fourth king after Friso.   In his youth he studied
first at Texland, and then at Staveren, and afterwards
travelled through all the states.   When he was twenty-
four years old his father had him elected Asega-Asker.
As soon as he became Asker he always took the part of
the poor.   The rich, he said, do enough of wrong by means
of their wealth, therefore we ought to take care that the
poor look up to us.   By arguments of this kind he became
the friend of the poor and the terror of the rich.   It was
carried so far that his father looked up to him.   When
his father died he succeeded, and then he wished to re-
tain his office as well, as the kings of the East used to do.
The rich would not suffer this, so all the people rose up,
and the rich were glad to get out of the assembly with
whole skins.   From that time there was no more talk of
equality.   He oppressed the rich and flattered the poor,
by whose assistance he succeeded in all his wishes.   King
Askar, as he was always called, was seven feet high, and
his strength was as remarkable as his height.   He had a
clear intellect, so that he understood all that was talked
about, but in his actions he did not display much wisdom.
He had a handsome countenance and a smooth tongue,
but his soul was blacker than his hair.   When he had
been king for a year, he obliged all the young men in the
state to come once a year to the camp to have a sham
fight.   At first he had some trouble with it, but at last
it became such a habit that old and young came from
all sides to ask if they might take part in it.
When he had brought it to this point, he established
military schools.   The rich complained that their

hjara bern nw nên lêsa nach skryva navt ne lêrade. Askar
ne melde-t navt, men as thêr kirt âfter wither skin-orloch
halden warth, gvng-er vppen vpstal stonda, ånd kêtha
blûd. Tha rika sind to my kvmen to bârana, thåt hjara
knåpa nên lêsa nach skryva noch lêra, ik n.åv thêr nawet
vp sêith, thach hir wil ik mine mênong sedsa, ånd an tha
mêna acht bithinga lêta. Thâ alrek nw nêisgyrich nêi
him vpsach, sêid-er forther, nêi min bigrip mot mån
hjud thåt lêsa ånd skriva tha fâmna ånd alda lichta vrlêta.
Ik n-il nên kwâd sprêka vr vsa êthla, ik wil allêna
sega, vndera tyda hwêrvp thrvch svme sâ herde hogath
warth, hâvon tha burchfâmna twyspalt inovir vsa lânda
brocht, ånd tha Modera für ånd nêi ne kvndôn twyspalt
navt wither to-t land ut ne dryva. Jeta ârger, thahwila
hja kâlta ånd petârade vr nâdelâsa plêga, send tha Gola
kvmen ånd hâvon al vsa skêna sûdarlanda râweth.
Hêmisdêga send hja mith vsa vrbrûda brotharum ånd
hjara salt-âthum al overa Skelda kvmen, vs rest thus to
kjasane twisk-et bêra fon juk jef swêrd. Willath wi fry
bilywâ, alsa âgon tha knåpa thåt lêsa ånd skryva fâr-
hôndis åfterwêi-n to lêtane ånd in stêde that hja invppa
mêide hwip ånd swik spêle, moton hja mith swêrd ånd
spêr spêla. Send wi in alle dêla ofned ånd tha knåpa
stor enoch vmb helmet ånd skild to bêrane ånd tha wêpne
to hôntêrane, then skil ik my mith jower helpa vppa
thene fjand werpa. Tha Gola mêieath then tha nither-
lêga fon hjara helpar ånd salt-âthum vppa vsa fjeldum
skryva mith-et blod, thåt ût hjara wndum drjupth.
Hâvon wi thene fyand ên mel far vs ût drêven, alsa
moton wi thêrmith forth gvnga, alhwenne thêr nên Gola
ner Slâvona nach Tartara mâra fon Fryas erv to vrdryvane
send. Tha-s rjucht, hrypon tha mâsta ånd tha rika ne
thvradon hjara mvla navt êpen ne dva. Thjus tosprêke hêd

children no longer learned to read and write. Askar
paid no attention to it; but shortly afterwards, when a
sham fight was held, he mounted a throne and spoke
aloud: The rich have come to complain to me that their
boys do not learn to read and write. I answered nothing;
but I will now declare my opinion, and let the general
assembly decide. While they all regarded him with
curiosity, he said further: According to my idea, we
ought to leave reading and writing at present to the
maagden and wise people. I do not wish to speak ill of
our forefathers; I will only say that in the times so vaunted
by some, the Burgtmaagden introduced disputes into our
country, which the mothers were unable, either first or
last, to put an end to. Worse still, while they talked and
chattered about useless customs the Gauls came and seized
all our beautiful southern country. Even at this very time
our degenerate brothers and their soldiers have already
come over the Scheldt. It therefore remains for us to
choose whether we will carry a yoke or a sword. If we
wish to be and to remain free, it behoves our young men
to leave reading and writing alone for a time; and instead
of playing games of swinging and wrestling, they must
learn to play with sword and spear. When we are com-
pletely prepared, and the boys are big enough to carry
helmet and shield and to use their weapons, then, with
your help, I will attack the enemy. The Gauls may then
record the defeat of their helpers and soldiers upon our
fields with the blood that flows from their wounds. When
we have once expelled the enemy, then we must follow it up
till there are no more Gauls, Slaves, or Tartars to be driven
out of Frya's inheritance. That is right, the majority
shouted, and the rich did not dare to open their mouths.

er sekur to fara forsonnen ånd vrskriva lêten, hwand s-
êwendis fon thêre selvare dêi wêron tha ofskriftum thêra
hwel in twintich hônda ånd thi alle wêron êuishlûdende.
Afternêi bifel-er tha skipmanna, hja skoldon dubbele
fårstêwene måkja lêta, hwêran mån êne stêlen krânboga
macht fåstigja. Thêra thêr åfterwêi bilêv warth bibot,
kvu imman swêra that-er nêne midle navt nêde, alsa moston tha rika fon sin gå-t bitalja. Hjud skil mån sjan
hwêr vppa al thåt bå hêi ûthlåpen is. An-t north-ende
fon Britanja thåt fvl mith håga bergum is, thêr sit en
Skots folk, vr-et måradêl ût Fryas blod sproten, vr-a êne
helte send hja ût Kåltana-folgar, vr-et ôra dêl ût Britne
ånd bannane, thêr by grådum mith tyd fon-ût-a tinlônum
thêr hinna fljuchte. Thêr ut-a tinlôna kêmon, håvath algadur vrlandiska wiva jeftha fon vrlandis tuk. Thi alle
send vnder-et weld thêra Golum, hjara wêpne send woden
boga ånd spryta mith pintum fon herthis-hornum åk fon
flintum. Hjara hûsa send fon sådum ånd strê ånd svme
hêmath inna hola thêra bergum. Skêpon thêr hja råwed
håve, is hjara ênge skåt. Mong tha åfter-kvmanda thêra
Kåltanafolgar håvath svme jeta ysera wêpne, thêr hja fon
hjara êthlum urven håve. Vmbe nw god forstån to werthande, môt ik min telling vr thåt Skotse folk resta lêta,
ånd êwet fon tha hêinda Krêkalanda skriva. Tha hêinda
Krêkalanda håvon vs to fara allêna to hêrath, men sunt
vnhüglika tidum håvon ra thêr åk åfterkvmanda fon Lyda
ånd fon Finda nitherset, fon tha lersta kêmon to tha lersta
en êle håpe fon Trôje. Trôje alsa heth êne stêde hêten,
thêr et folk fon tha fêre Krêkalanda innomth ånd vrho-
melt heth. Thå tha Trôjana to tha hêinda Krêkalandum
nestled wêron, tha håvon hja thêr mith tid ånd flit êue
sterke stêd mith wålla ånd burgum bvwed, Rome, that is

Representation of a Ship with forecastle and poop deck.
preserved on an old seal of Staveren.

He must certainly have thought over this address and
had it written out, for on the evening of the same day
there were copies in at least twenty different hands, and
they all sounded the same.   Afterwards he ordered the
ship people to make double prows, upon which steel crossbows could be fixed.   Those who were backward in doing
this were fined, and if they swore that they had no means,
the rich men of the village were obliged to pay.   Now
we shall see what resulted from all this bustle.   In the
north part of Britain there exists a Scotch people—the
most of them spring from Frya's blood—some of them
are descended from the followers of Keltana, and, for the
rest, from Britons and fugitives who gradually, in the
course of time, took refuge there from the tin mines.
Those who come from the tin mines have wives, either
altogether foreign or of foreign descent.   They are all
under the dominion of the Gauls.   Their arms are wooden
bows and arrows pointed with stag's-horn or flint.   Their
houses are of turf and straw, and some of them live in
caves in the mountains.   Sheep that they have stolen
form their only wealth.   Some of the descendants of Keltana's followers still have iron weapons, which they have
inherited from their forefathers.   In order to make myself well understood, I must let alone for a while my
account of the Scotch people, and write something about the
near Krekalanders (Italians).   The Krekalanders formerly
belonged to us only, but from time immemorial descendants of Lyda and Finda have established themselves
there.   Of these last there came in the end a whole troop
from Troy.   Troy is the name of a town that the far
Krekalanders (Greeks) had taken and destroyed.   When
the Trojans had nestled themselves among the near Krekalanders, with time and industry they built a strong
town with walls and citadels named Rome, that is,

Rum, hêten. Thâ thât dên was, heth thât folk him selva
thrvch lest ånd weld fon thât êle lånd måster måked.
Thåt folk thât anda sûdside thêre Middelsê hêmth, is får-
et måra dêl fon Fhonysja wêi kvmen. Tha Fhonysjar *
send en bastred folk, hja send fon Fryas blod ånd fon
Findas blod ånd fon Lyda his blod. Thåt folk fon Lyda
send thêr as slåvona, men thrvch tha vntucht thêr wyva
håvon thissa swarte månniska al-et ôra folk bastered ånd
brun vrfårvet. Thit folk ånd tham fon Rome kåmpath
ôlån vmb-et måsterskip fon tha Middelsê. Forth lêvath
tham fon Roma an fjandskip with tha Fonysjar, ånd hjara
prestera thêr-et rik allêna welda wille wr irtha, ne mügon
tha Gola navt ne sjan. Thåt forma håvon hja tha
Fphonysjar Mis-selja ofnomen, dånå alle landa, thêr sûdward, westward ånd northward lidsa, åk et sûdardêl fon
Britanja, ånd allerwêikes håvon hja tha Fonysjar prestera,
that hêth tha Gola vrjågeth, dånå sind thusanda Gola
nêi north Brittanja brit. Kirt vrlêden was thêr tha vreste
thêra Golum sêten vppa thêre burch, thêr is kêthen
Kêrenåk that is herne, hwanath hi sin bifêla jef an alle
ôra Gola. Ak was thêr al hjara gold togadur brocht.
Kêren herne jeftha Kêrenåk is êne stênen burch, thêr êr
an Kålta hêrde. Thêrvmbe wildon tha fåmna fon tha
åfterkvmande thêra Kåltana-folgar tha burch wither hå.
Alsa was thrvch tha fyanskip thêra fåmna ånd thêra Golum faithe ånd twist in ovir thåt Berchland kvmen mith
morth ånd brônd. Vsa stjûrar kêmon thêr fåken wol
hålja, thåt hja sellade fori tobirêde hûdum ånd linne.
Askar was often mith wêst, an stilnesse hêd-er mith tha
fåmna ånd mith svme forstum åtskip sloten, ånd him
selva forbonden vmbe tha Gola to vrjågane ût Kêrenåk.
As-er thêrnêi wither kêm jêf hi tha forsta ånd wig-
andliksta manna ysere helma ånd stêla boga. Orloch
was mith kvmen ånd kirt åfter flojadon ströma blod bÿ

---

* Fhonysiar, Carthagers.

Spacious. When this was done, the people by craft and force made themselves masters of the whole land. The people who live on the south side of the Mediterranean Sea, come for the most part from Phœnicia. The Phœnicians (Puniers or Carthaginians) are a bastard race of the blood of Frya, Finda, and Lyda. The Lyda people were there as slaves, but by the unchastity of the women these black people have degenerated the other people and dyed them brown. These people and the Romans are constantly struggling for the supremacy over the Mediterranean Sea. The Romans, moreover, live at enmity with the Phœnicians ; and their priests, who wish to assume the sole government of the world, cannot bear the sight of the Gauls. First they took from the Phœnicians Marseilles—then all the countries lying to the south, the west, and the north, as well as the southern part of Britain—and they have always driven away the Phœnician priests, that is the Gauls, of whom thousands have sought refuge in North Britain. A short time ago the chief of the Gauls was established in the citadel, which is called Kerenac (Karnac), that is the corner, whence he issued his commands to the Gauls. All their gold was likewise collected there. Keeren Herne (chosen corner), or Kerenac, is a stone citadel which did belong to Kalta. Therefore the maidens of the descendants of Kaltana's followers wished to have the citadel again. Thus through the enmity of the maidens and the Gaul's, hatred and quarrelling spread ever the mountain country with fire and sword. Our sea people often came there to get wool, which they paid for with prepared hides and linen. Askar had often gone with them, and had secretly made friendship with the maidens and some princes, and bound himself to drive the Gauls out of Kerenac. When he came back there again he gave to the princes and the fighting men iron helmets and steel bows. War had come with him, and soon blood was streaming down

---

* *Phonsiar* are Carthaginians.

tha hellinga thêra bergum del. Thâ Askar mênde that kans
him tolâkte, gvng-er mith fjuwertich skêpum hin ând nam
Kêrenâk ând thene vreste thêra Golum mith al sine gold.
Thât folk wêrmith hi with tha salt-âthum thêra Golum kâm-
ped hêde, hêd-er ût-a Saxanamarkum lvkt mith lofte fon
grâte hêra-râve ând but. Thus warth tha Gola nêwet
lêten. Afternêi nam-er twâ êlanda to berch far sinum
skêpum, ând hwânath hi lêter ûtgvng vmb alle Fonysjar
skêpa ând stêda to birâwane thêr hi bigâna kv. Tha
er tobek kêm brocht-i tomet sex hvndred thêra storeste
knâpum fon thât Skotse berchfolk mith. Hi sêide that
hja him to borgum jêven wêren, til thju hi sêkur wêsa
machte thât tha eldra him skolde trow bilywa, men-t was
jok, hi hild ra as lifwêre et sina hova, thêr hja allera
distik les krêjon in-t ryda ând in-t hôndtêra fon allerlêja
wêpne. Tha Denamarkar tham hjara selva sunt lông
boppa alle ôra stjûrar stoltlike sêkâmpar hête, hêdon sâ
ringe navt fou Askar sina glorrika dêdum navt ne hêred,
jef hja wrdon nydich thêr vr, thêrmête, that hja wilde
orloch brensa over-ne sê ând over sina landa. Sjan
hyr, ho hi orloch formitha machte. Twisk tha bvwfala
thêre vrhomelde burch Stavja was jeta êne snode burchfâm mith svme fâmna sêten. Hjra nôme was Rêintja
ând thêr gvng en grâte hrop fon hira wishêd ût. Thjus
fâm bâd an Askar hjra helpe vnder bithing, that Askar
skolde tha burch Stavja wither vpbvwa lête. As-er him
thêr to forbonden hêde, gvng Rêintja mith thrim fâmna
nêi Hals,* nachtis gvng hju rêisa ând thes dêis kêthe hju
vppa alle markum ând binna alle mêidum. Wralda sêide
hju hêde hja thrvch thongar tohropa lêta thât allet Fryas
folk moston frjunda wertha, lik sustar ând brothar tâmed,
owers skolde Findas folk kvma ând ra alle fon irtha
vrdilligja. Nêi thongar wêron Fryas sjvgun wâkfâmkes
hja anda drâme forskinnen, sjvgun nachta âfter ekkôrum.

---

* Hals, Holstein.

the slopes of the mountains. When Askar thought a favourable opportunity occurred, he went with forty ships and took Kerenac and the chief of the Gauls, with all his gold. The people with whom he fought against the soldiers of the Gauls, he had enticed out of the Saxenmarken by promises of much booty and plunder. Thus nothing was left to the Gauls. After that he took two islands for stations for his ships, from which he used later to sally forth and plunder all the Phœnician ships and towns that he could reach. When he returned he brought nearly six hundred of the finest youths of the Scotch mountaineers with him. He said that they had been given him as hostages, that he might be sure that the parents would remain faithful to him; but this was untrue. He kept them as a bodyguard at his court, where they had daily lessons in riding and in the use of all kinds of arms. The Denmarkers, who proudly considered themselves sea-warriors above all the other sea-people, no sooner heard of the glorious deeds of Askar, than they became jealous of him to such a degree, that they would bring war over the sea and over his lands. See here, then, how he was able to avoid a war. Among the ruins of the destroyed citadel of Stavia there was still established a clever Burgtmaagd, with a few maidens. Her name was Reintja, and she was famed for her wisdom. This maid offered her assistance to Askar, on condition that he should afterwards rebuild the citadel of Stavia. When he had bound himself to do this, Reintja went with three maidens to Hals (Holstein). She travelled by night, and by day she made speeches in all the markets and in all the assemblies. Wr-alda, she said, had told her by his thunder that all the Frya's people must become friends, and united as brothers and sisters, otherwise Finda's people would come and sweep them off the face of the earth. After the thunder Frya's seven watch-maidens appeared to her in a dream seven nights in succession. They had

---

* *Hals* is Holstein.

Hja hêde seith boppa Fryas landum swabbert ramp mith
juk ånd kêdne omme. Thêrvmbe moton alle folkar thêr ût
Frya sproten send hjara tonôma wêi werpa ånd hjara selva
allêna Fryas bern jeftha folk hêta. Forth moton alle vpstonda ånd et Findas folk fon Fryas erv dryva. Nillath
hja thåt navt ne dva, alsa skilun hja slåvona benda vmbe
hjara halsa krêja, alsa skilun tha vrlandaska hêra hjara
bern misbruka ånd frytra lêta, til thju thåt blod sygath
inna jowre grêva. Thån skilun tha skinna jowre êthla jo
kvma wekja ånd jo bikyvja vr jo lefhêd ånd vndigerhêd.
Thåt dvme folk, thåt thrvch todvan thêra Mågyara al
an sa fül dwêshêd wenth was, låvadon alles hwat hju
sêide ånd tha måmma klimdon hjara bern åjen hjara
brosta an. Thå Rêintja thene kening fon Hals ånd
alle ôthera manniska to êndracht vrwrocht hede, sand
hju bodon nêi Askar ånd tåg selva alingen thene Balda
sê. Dånå gvng hju by tha Hlith-håwar, althus hêten
vmbe that hja hjara fyanda immer nêi thet ônhlite
håwe. Tha Hlithhåwar send britne ånd bannene fon vs
åjn folk thåt inna tha Twisklanda sit ånd omme dwarelt.
Hjara wyva håvon hja mêst algadur fon tha Tartara
råwed. Tha Tartara sênd en dêl fon Findas slachte ånd
althus thrvch tha Twisklandar hêten vmbe thåt hja nimmerthe nên frêtho wille, men tha månniska alti ût tarta
to strydande. Forth gvng hju åftera Saxnamarka tweres
thrvch tha ôra Twisklanda hin, allerwêikes thåt selva
ûtkêtha. Nêi twam jêr om wêron, kêm hju allingen
thêre Rêne to honk. By tha Twisklandar hede hju hjara
selva as Moder ûtjån ånd sêid thåt hja mochton as fry
ånd franka månniska wither kvma, men thån mosten
hja ovir tha Rêne gvngga ånd tha Gola folgar ût Fryas
sûdarlandum jågja. As hja thåt dêde, sa skolde hjra
kêning Askar overa Skelda gvngga ånd thêr thåt land
ofwinna. By tha Twisklandar send fêlo tjoda plêga fon
tha Tartarum ånd Mågjara binna glupt, men åk fül send

said, Disaster hovers over Frya's land with yoke and chains; therefore all the people who have sprung from Frya's blood must do away with their surnames, and only call themselves Frya's children, or Frya's people. They must all rise up and drive Finda's people out of Frya's inheritance. If you will not do that, you will bring the slave-chains round your necks, and the foreign chiefs will ill-treat your children and flog them till the blood streams into your graves. Then shall the spirits of your fore-fathers appear to you, and reproach your cowardice and thoughtlessness. The stupid people who, by the acts of the Magyars, were already so much accustomed to folly, believed all that she said, and the mothers clasped their children to their bosoms. When Reintja had brought the king of Holstein and the others to an agreement, she sent messengers to Askar, and went herself along the Baltic Sea. From there she went to the Lithauers (Face-hewers), so called because they always strike at their enemy's face. The Lithauers are fugitives and banished people of our own race, who wander about in the Twisklanden. Their wives have been mostly stolen from the Tartars. The Tartars are a branch of Finda's race, and are thus named by the Twisklanders because they never will be at peace, but provoke people to fight. She proceeded on beyond the Saxsenmarken, crossing through the other Twisk-landers in order always to repeat the same thing. After two years had passed, she came along the Rhine home. Among the Twisklanders she gave herself out for a mother, and said that they might return as free and true people; but then they must go over the Rhine and drive the Gauls out of Frya's south lands. If they did that, then her King Askar would go over the Scheldt and win back the land. Among the Twisklanders many bad customs of the Tartars and Magyars have crept in, but likewise many of our thêr fon vsa sêdum bilêwen. Thêr thrvch håvath hja jeta fåmna thêr tha bern lêra ånd tha alda rêd jeva. Bit-an-fang wêron hja Reintja nydich, men to tha lesta wårth hju thrvch hjam folgath ånd thjanjath ånd allerwêikes bogath, hwêr-et nette ånd nêdlik wêre.

Alsa ringen Askar fon Rêintja hjra bodon fornom ho tha Juttar nygath wêron, sand hi bistonda bodon fon sin-ant wegum nêi tha kåning fon Hals. Thåt skip, wêrmith tha bodon gvngon, was fvl lêden mith fåmna syrhêdum ånd thêr by wêr en golden skild, hwêrvppa Askar his dånte kunstalik was utebyld. Thissa bodon mosten frêja jêf Askar thes kåning his toghter Frêthogunsta to sin wif håve machte. Frêthogunsta kêm en jêr lêter to Ståveren, bi hjara folgar wêre åk ênen Mågy, hwand tha Juttar wêron sunt lông vrbrud. Kirt åfter that Askar mith Frê-thogunsta bostigjath was, wårth thêr to Ståveren êne scherke bvwad, inna thju scherke wrdon tjoda drochten lykanda byldon stålth mith gold trvch wrochtne klåthar. Ak is er biwêrath that Askar thêr nachtis ånd vntydis mith Frêthogunsta får nitherbuwgade. Men så fül is sêkur, thju burch Stavia ne wårth navt wither vpebvwed. Rêintja was al to bek kvmen, ånd gvng nydich nêi Pront-lik thju Moder et Texland bårja. Prontlik gvng to ånd sand allerwêikes bodon thêr ûtkêthon, Askar is vrjêven an afgodie. Askar dêde as murk-i-t navt, men vnwar-lingen kêm thêr êne flåte ût Hals. Nachtis wrdon tha fåmna ût-êre burch drywen, ånd ogtins kvn mån fon thêre burch allêna êne glandere håpe sjau. Prontlik ånd Rêintja kêmon to my vmb skul. Thå ik thêr åfternêi vr nêi tochte, lêk it my to, that it kwådlik får min ståt bidêja kvste. Thêrvmbe håvon wi to sêmne êne lest forsonnen, thêr vs alle båta most. Sjan hyr ho wi to gvn-gen send. Middel in-t Krylwald biasten Ljvwerde lêith vsa fly jeftha wêra, thêr mån allêna thrvch dwarl-påda mêi nåka. In vppa thjus burch hêd ik sunt lônge laws have remained. Therefore they still have Maagden, who teach the children and advise the old. In the beginning they were opposed to Reintja, but at last she was followed, obeyed, and praised by them where it was useful or necessary.

As soon as Askar heard from Reintja's messengers how the Jutlanders were disposed, he immediately, on his side, sent messengers to the King of Hals. The ship in which the messengers went was laden with women's ornaments, and took also a golden shield on which Askar's portrait was artistically represented. These messengers were to ask the King's daughter, Frethogunsta, in marriage for Askar. Frethogunsta came a year after that to Staveren. Among her followers was a Magy, for the Jutlanders had been long ago corrupted. Soon after Askar had married Frethogunsta, a church was built at Staveren. In the church were placed monstrous images, bedecked with gold-woven dresses. It is also said that Askar, by night, and at unseasonable times, kneeled to them with Frethogunsta; but one thing is certain, the citadel of Stavia was never rebuilt. Reintja was already come back, and went angrily to Prontlik the mother, at Texland, to complain. Prontlik sent out messengers in all directions, who proclaimed that Askar is gone over to Idolatry. Askar took no notice of this, but unexpectedly a fleet arrived from Hals. In the night the maidens were driven out of the citadel, and in the morning there was nothing to be seen of the citadel but a glowing heap of rubbish. Prontlik and Reintja came to me for shelter. When I reflected upon it, I thought that it might prove bad for my state. Therefore, we hit upon a plan which might serve us all. This is the way we went to work. In the middle of the Krijlwood, to the east of Liudwerd, lies our place of refuge, which can only be reached by a concealed path. A long time ago I had

jonga wåkar stald, thêr alle êne grins an Askar hêde, ånd
alle ôra månniska dånath halden. Nv wast bi vs åk al
sa wyd kvmen, thåt fêlo wyva ånd åk manna al patêrade
vr spoka, witte wyva ånd uldermankes, lik tha Dêna-
markar. Askar hêde al thissa dwåshêde to sin båta an-
wenth ånd thåt wildon wi nv åk to vsa båta dva. Bi-ne
thjustre nacht brocht ik tha fåmna nêi thêre burch ånd
dånå gongen hia mith hjara fåmna in thrvch tha dwarl-
påda spokka in wttta klåthar huled, så that thêr afternêi
nên månnisk måra kvma ne thvrade. Tha Askar mênde
thåt-er thu hônda rum hêde, lêt-i tha Mågjara vnder allerlêja nôma thrvch ovir sina ståta fåra ånd bûta Grênegå
ånd bûta mina ståt ne wrdon hja nårne navt ne wêrath.
Nêi that Askar alsa mith tha Juttar ånd tha ôra Dêna-
markar forbonden was, gvngon hja alsêmina råwa; thach
that neth nêne gode früchda båred. Hja brochton allerlêja vrlandiska skåta to honk. Men just thêr thrvch nildon thåt jong folk nên ambacht lêra, nach vppa tha fjeldum navt ne werka, så that hi to tha lersta wel slåvona
nimma moste. Men thit was êl al åjen Wralda his wille
ånd åjen Fryas rêd. Thêrvmbe kv straf navt åfterwêga ne
bilywa. Sjan hyr ho straffe kvmen is. Ênis hêdon hja to
sêmine êne êle flåte wnnen, hju kêm fon ûta Middelsê.
Thjus flåte was to lêden mith purpera klåthar ånd ôra kos-
telikhêd, thêr alle fon of Phonisja kêmon. Thåt wraka
folk thêre flåte wårth bisûda thêre Sêjene an wal set, men
thåt stora folk wårth halden. Thåt most ra as slåvona
thianja. Tha skêneste wrdon halden vmbe vppet land to
bilywane ånd tha lêdliksta ånd swartste wrdon an bord
halden vmbe vppa tha benka to rojande. An-t Fly wårth
tha bodel dêlath, men svnder hjara wêta wårth åk hjara
straf dêlath. Fon tha månniska thêr vppa tha vrlandiska skepum stalt wêron, wêron sex thrvch bukpin felth.
Mån tochte thåt et eta ånd drinka vrjêven wêre,

established a garrison of young men who all hated Askar,
and kept away all other people. Now it was come to such
a pitch among us, that many women, and even men,
talked about ghosts, white women, and gnomes, just like
the Denmarkers. Askar had made use of all these follies
for his own advantage, and we wished to do the same.
One dark night I brought the Maagden to the citadel,
and afterwards they went with their serving-maids dressed
in white along the path, so that nobody dare go there any
more. When Askar thought he had his hands free, he
let the Magyars travel through his states under all kinds
of names, and, except in my state, they were not turned
away anywhere. After that Askar had become so connected with the Jutlanders and the Denmarkers, they all
went roving together; but it produced no real good to
them. They brought all sorts of foreign treasures home,
and just for that reason the young men would learn no
trades, nor work in the fields; so at last he was obliged
to take slaves; but that was altogether contrary to Wr-alda's wish and to Frya's counsel. Therefore the punishment was sure to follow it. This is the way in which
the punishment came. They had all together taken a
whole fleet that came out of the Mediterranean Sea.
This fleet was laden with purple cloths and other valuables
that came from Phœnicia. The weak people of the fleet
were put ashore south of the Seine, but the strong people
were kept to serve as slaves. The handsomest were retained ashore, and the ugly and black were kept on board
ship as rowers. In the Fly the plunder was divided, but,
without their knowing it, they divided the punishment
too. Of those who were placed in the foreign ships
six died of colic. It was thought that the food and

T

thêrvmbe wârth alles ovir bord jompth. Men bûkpin reste
ånd allerwêikes, hwêr slåvona jeftha god kêm, kêm åk
bûkpin binna. Tha Saxmanna brochten hjn ovir hjara
marka, mith tha Juttar for hju nêi Skênland ånd alingen
thêre kåd fon tha Balda-sê, mith Askar his stjûrar for
hjn nêi Britanja. Wi ånd tham fon Grênegå ne lêton
nên god ner minniska ovir vsa påla navt ne kvma, ånd
thêrvmbe bilêwon wi fon tha bûkpin fry. Ho fêlo månniska bûkpin wêiråpth heth, nêt ik navt to skrywane, men
Prontlik thêr et åfternêi fon tha ôra fåmna hêrde, heth
my meld, thåt Askar thûsandmel måra frya månniska ût
sinaståtum hulpen heth, as er vvla slåvona inbrochte. Thå
pest far god wyken was, tha kêmon tha fri wrden Twisklandar nêi thêre Rêne, men Askar nilde mith tha forstum
fon thåt vvla vr basterde folk navt an êne lyne navt ne·
stonda. Hi nilde navt ne dåja, that hja skoldon hjara
selva Fryas bern hêta, lik Rêintja biboden hêde, men hi
vrjet thêrbi that-i selva swarte hêra hêde. Emong tha
Twisklandar wêron thêr twå folkar, thêr hjara selva nêne
Twisklandar hêton. Thåt êne folk kêm êl fêr ût-et sûd-
åsten wêi, hja hêton hjara selva Allemanna. Thissa nôma
hêdon hja hjara selva jêven, thå hja jeta svnder wiva
inna tha walda as bannane ommedwarelde. Lêtar håvon
hja fon-et slåvona folk wiva råvath, êvin sa tha Hlit-
håwar, men hja håvon hjara nôme bihalden. Thåt ôra
folk, thåt måra hêinde ommedwarelde, hêton hjara
selva Franka, navt vmbe that hja fry wêron, men
Frank alsa hêde thene êroste kåning hêten, tham him
selva mith hulpe fon tha vrbrûda fåmna to ervlik kåning ovir sin folk måkad hêde. Tha folkar tham an him
påladon, hêton hjara selva Thjoth-his svna, that is folk-
his svna, hja wêron Frya månniska bilêwen, nêidam
hja nimmer ênen kåning ner forste nach måster bi-
kånnna nilde, as thene jenge tham by mêna willa was kêren vppa thêre mêna acht. Askar hêde

drink were poisoned, so it was all thrown overboard,
but the colic remained all the same. Wherever the
slaves or the goods came, there it came too. The Saxsen-
men took it over to their marches. The Jutlanders
brought it to Schoonland and along the coasts of the
Baltic Sea, and with Askar's mariners it was taken to
Britain. We and the people of Grênegâ did not allow
either the people or the goods to come over our boundaries,
and therefore we remained free from it. How many people
were carried off by this disease I cannot tell; but Prontlik, who heard it afterwards from the maidens, told me
that Askar had helped out of his states a thousand times
more free-men than he had brought dirty slaves in. When
the pest had ceased, the Twisklanders who had become
free came to the Rhine, but Askar would not put himself
on an equality with the princes of that vile degenerate race.
He would not suffer them to call themselves Frya's children,
as Reintja had offered them, but he forgot then that he
himself had black hair. Among the Twisklanders there
were two tribes who did not call themselves Twisklanders.
One came from the far south-east, and called themselves
Allemannen. They had given themselves this name when
they had no women among them, and were wandering as
exiles in the forests. Later on they stole women from
the slave people like the Lithauers, but they kept their
name. The other tribe, that wandered about in the
neighbourhood, called themselves Franks, not because
they were free, but the name of their first king was
Frank, who, by the help of the degenerate maidens, had
had himself made hereditary king over his people.
The people nearest to him called themselves Thioth-
his sons—that is, sons of the people. They had remained free, because they never would acknowledge
any king, or prince, or master except those chosen by
general consent in a general assembly. Askar had

al fon Rêintja fornommen, that tha Twisklandar forsta
mêst alti in fiandskip ånd faitha wêron. Nw stald-i hjam
to fåra, hjå skolde ênen hêrtoga fon sin folk kjasa vmbe
that-er ang wêre seid-er that bja skolde mit manlik
ôtherum skoldon twista ovir-et måsterskip. Ak sêid-er
kvndon sina forsta mith-a Golum sprêka. Thåt sêid-er
wêre åk Moder his mêne. Thå kêmon tha forsta thêra
Twislandar to ekkôrum ånd nêi thrija sjugun etmelde kêron
hja Alrik to-ra hertoga ut. Alrik wêre Askar his nêva,
hi jef him twên hvndred skotse ånda hvndred thêra storosta
Saxmanna mith to lifwêra. Tha forsta moston thrija
sjvgun fon hjara svnum nêi Stâveren senda to borg hjarar
trow. To nv was alles nêi winsk gvngen, men thå mån
ovire Rêne fara skolde, nildon thene kåning thêra Franka
navt vnder Alrikis bifêla navt ne stonda. Thêrthrvch lip
alles an tha tys. Askar thêr mênde thåt alles god gvng,
lande mith sina skêpa anna tha ôre syde thêre Skelda,
men thêr was was man long fon sin kvmste to ljucht ånd
vppa sin hod. Hja moston alsa ring fljuchta as hja kvmen
wêron, ånd Askar wrde selva fath. Tha Gola niston navt
hwa hja fensen hêde, ånd alsa warth hi åfternêi ûtwixlath
fori ênnen håge Gol, thêr Askar his folk mith forath hêde.
Thawila thåt-et alles bêrade, hlipon tha Mågjara jeta
dryster as to fåra ovir vsa bûra ra landa hinna. By
Egmvda hwêr to fåra tha burch Forâna stân hêde, lêton
hja êne cherka bvwa jeta grâter ånd rikar as Askar to
Stâveren dên hêde. Afternêi sêidon hja that Askar thju
kåse vrlêren hêde with tha Gola, thrvchdam et folk navt
låwa navt nilde, that Wodin hjam helpa kvste, ånd that
hja him thêrvmbe navt anbidda nilde. Forth gvngon hja
to ånd skåkton jonga bern tham hja by ra hildon ånd
vpbrochten in tha hemnissa fon hjara vrbruda lêre. Wêron
thêr månniska tham

[Het overige ontbreekt.]

already learned from Reintja that the Twisklander princes
were almost always at war with each other. He proposed
to them that they should choose a duke from his people,
because, as he said, he was afraid that they would quarrel
among themselves for the supremacy. He said also that
his princes could speak with the Gauls. This, he said,
was also the opinion of the mother. Then the princes of
the Twisklanders came together, and after twenty-one days
they chose Alrik as duke. Alrik was Askar's nephew.
He gave him two hundred Scotch and one hundred of the
greatest Saksmannen to go with him as a bodyguard.
The princes were to send twenty-one of their sons as
hostages for their fidelity. Thus far all had gone according to his wishes; but when they were to go over the
Rhine, the king of the Franks would not be under Alrik's
command. Thereupon all was confusion. Askar, who
thought that all was going on well, landed with his ships
on the other side of the Scheldt; but there they were
already aware of his coming, and were on their guard.
He had to flee as quickly as he had come, and was himself
taken prisoner. The Gauls did not know whom they had
taken, so he was afterwards exchanged for a noble Gaul
whom Askar's people had taken with them. While all
this was going on, the Magyars went about audaciously
over the lands of our neighbours. Near Egmuda, where
formerly the citadel Forana had stood, they built a church
larger and richer than that which Askar had built at
Staveren. They said afterwards that Askar had lost the
battle against the Gauls, because the people did not believe that Wodin could help them, and therefore they would
not pray to him. They went about stealing young children,
whom they kept and brought up in the mysteries of their
abominable doctrines. Were there people who

[Here the manuscript ends abruptly.]

Lightning Source UK Ltd.
Milton Keynes UK
UKHW010059030720
365925UK00003B/650

9 789353 866334